Collective Ratemaking in the Motor Carrier Industry

Implications to the American Public

COLLECTIVE RATEMAKING

IN THE

Edited by

GRANT M. DAVIS, PH.D.

Oren Harris Professor of Transportation
and
Director, Center for Transportation Research
University of Arkansas
Fayetteville

Motor Carrier Industry

Implications to the American Public

The Interstate
Printers & Publishers, Inc.
Danville, Illinois 61832

Collective Ratemaking in the Motor Carrier Industry: Implications to the American Public

Library of Congress Catalog Card No. 80-81105

ISBN 0-8134-2138-1

TABLE OF CONTENTS

PREFACE

Collective ratemaking in the regulated for-hire motor carrier industry is required under the provisions of Section 5a of the Interstate Commerce Act. Essentially, this statutory provision exempts joint rates and through routes from sections stipulated in the collective antitrust legislation enforced by the federal government. Because of the basic structure of common carriers by motor, carriers must of necessity meet to consider transportation prices and services provided by two or more carriers in providing a thorough transportation service. This institutional approach to arriving at joint rates and through routes is permissible if the collective agreements of the bureaus or conferences through which such prices are considered are approved by the Interstate Commerce Commission.

There are several societal benefits to be derived from collective ratemaking in the domestic for-hire and regulated motor carrier industry. Firstly, transportation joint rates, as well as through rates, are not as expensive as combination rates. Secondly, these arrangements lead to a reduction in the overall costs of production in our economy, which in turn can lead to an increased competitiveness, both domestically and internationally, in the area of commerce. Joint rates and through routes, moreover, tend to minimize resource consumption relative to a given transportation resource. Thirdly, transportation rates which must be published in freight tariffs thereby increase a firm's market knowledge regarding transportation cost in making a distribution decision. Fourthly, transportation rates published through the medium of a bureau or a conference must comply with certain specified standards of reasonableness, while simultaneously avoiding undue preference, prejudice, and discrimination. In this manner a published rate reveals the reasonableness of a given rate to the public, provided the rate has not been previously contested. Fifthly and lastly, rates published through rate conferences are influenced by supply and demand in that transportation prices result from the interaction of shippers and carriers in establishing a price for creating place utility. In short, society benefits from collective ratemaking in the motor carrier industry, and the Interstate Commerce Commission is materially assisted in its daily administration.

However, collective ratemaking is under serious attack.[1] The chief executive of the United States, presidential candidates, U.S. Senators, congressmen, economists, and the Department of Justice have not only attacked collective ratemaking in

---

[1]There is no question but that collective ratemaking is misunderstood by those who advocate substantial changes in this institutional method of pricing for the regulated segment of the intercity transportation industry. Specifically, refer to any recent issue of Traffic World for all of the proposed changes and modifications in collective ratemaking proposed by the executive branch of government advocating substantial changes in this form of pricing.

Congress but also in the courts and in the press, contending the methods result in higher transportation prices and violate antitrust laws. One commonality permeates these attacks on collective ratemaking in the for-hire common motor carrier industry, i.e., a basic lack of understanding regarding the functions of rate conferences.[2] Even the term "conference" contains ominous connotations to individuals and groups that have not directly worked with or been active in bureau activities.[3]

A continuing legal controversy regarding the provisions of the Act to Regulate Commerce and the antitrust laws of this country existed for almost seventy years. This polemic was resolved in 1948 with the passage of the Reed-Bulwinkle Act[4] which became Section 5a of the Interstate Commerce Act. The condition precedent for exemption from the antitrust laws was the right of each carrier to exercise independent action from collective conference action. This condition precedent was not violated, based on empirical evidence,[5] but in Ex Parte 297, Sub. 3, the U.S. Interstate Commerce Commission proscribed bureaus from protesting independently announced rates, even though almost 95 percent of conference protests of independently announced rates were subsequently sustained by the Interstate Commerce Commission. The reader should bear in mind that no carrier is compelled to join a rate conference.

My interest in collective ratemaking in the transportation industries dates back to 1963 when I was formally studying antitrust at Georgia State University. My professional interest was accentuated during my years of graduate study and reached its apex in Ex Parte 297, Sub. 3. Frankly, the entire system of collective ratemaking is permeated with misunderstandings by virtually everyone, except for those who directly participate in the process and several who function on the periphery of the industry.

In this regard, COLLECTIVE RATEMAKING is devoted to explaining how transportation can and does contribute to American society. To accomplish this objective, it examines the basic functions of motor carrier rate conferences, the fundamental economics associated with collective ratemaking, the antitrust laws and rate conferences, the U.S. Department of Transportation and motor carrier rate conferences, collective ratemaking and the deregulation movement and collective ratemaking and the shipper. To provide the individual reader with additional perspective regarding collective ratemaking in the regulated motor carrier industry, additional readings, selected from academically oriented journals, supplement some of the chapters.

Grant M. Davis

---

[2]Statement of the Antitrust Division of the Justice Department in Ex Parte 297, Sub. 3, 1978.

[3]*Northern Securities* v. *United States*, 132 U.S. 197; *United States* v. *Union Pacific Railroad Co.*, 226 U.S. 61; and *United States* v. *Southern Pacific Co.*, 259 U.S. 214, where railroad activities were involved.

[4]Enacted June 17, 1948, as Public Law 662, *62 Statutes at Large*, 472, 49 U.S.C. 5(b).

[5]Grant M. Davis and Charles S. Sherwood, *Rate Bureaus and Antitrust Conflicts in Transportation: Public Policy Issues* (New York: Praeger Publishers, Inc., 1975), Chapters 1-5. Also, consult Charles D. Drayton, *Transportation Under Two Masters* (Washington, D.C.: National Motor Freight Traffic Association), no publication date.

ABOUT DR. DAVIS

Grant M. Davis is currently the Oren Harris Professor of Transportation and the Director of the Center for Transportation Research in the College of Business Administration at the University of Arkansas, Fayetteville. He received his BBA in Economics from Georgia State University and his MA and PhD degrees in Transportation and Public Utility Economics from the University of Alabama. Prior to joining the University of Arkansas faculty, he had been on the faculties of Arizona State University, Auburn University, and the University of Alabama.

Dr. Davis is an active consultant to both government and business and currently is the Chairman of the Committee of Education to Practice for the Association of Interstate Commerce Commission Practitioners. Dr. Davis is the author of _The Department of Transportation_, published by D. C. Heath & Company, 1970, and the editor of _Transportation Regulation: A Pragmatic Assessment_, published by The Interstate Printers & Publishers, Inc., 1976. He is the co-author with Stephen W. Brown of _Logistics Management_, published by D. C. Heath & Company, 1974; the co-author with Martin T. Farris and Jack J. Holder, Jr., of _Management of Transportation Carriers_, published by Praeger Publishers, Inc., 1975; the co-author with Charles S. Sherwood of _Rate Bureaus and Antitrust Conflicts in Transportation: Public Policy Issues_, published by Praeger Publishers, Inc., 1975; the co-author with John E. Dillard, Jr., of _Improving Motor Carrier Productivity_, published by Praeger Publishers, Inc., 1977; and the co-author with Eugene H. Shepard, Jr., of _Motor Carrier Rate Structures: The Need for Basic Revision_, published by Praeger Publishers, 1979.

Dr. Davis has recently authored three additional books which will soon be published for the general textbook market. He has also contributed over 150 articles to academically oriented journals, such as the _Transportation Journal_, _Quarterly Review of Economics in Business_, _The Logistics and Transportation Review_, _Traffic Quarterly_, _Transactions_, _ICC Practitioner's Journal_, and many others.

LIST OF AUTHORS

Garland Chow, Assistant Professor of Business Administration, University of Maryland

Grant M. Davis, Oren Harris Professor of Transportation and Director of the Center for Transportation Research, University of Arkansas

Martin T. Farris, Professor of Transportation Economics, Arizona State University

John Fessenden, Attorney at Law, Arlington, Virginia

James C. Johnson, Associate Professor of Marketing and Transportation, St. Cloud State University

Richard F. Poist, Associate Professor of Business Administration, University of Maryland

Andrew F. Popper, Assistant Dean of the Law School, American University, Washington, D.C.

James P. Rakowski, Associate Professor of Transportation, Memphis State University

L. J. Rosenberg, Professor of Marketing, University of Arkansas

Charles S. Sherwood, Associate Professor of Transportation, Eastern Kentucky University

L. L. Waters, Professor of Transportation, Indiana University

Chapter 1

COLLECTIVE RATEMAKING IN THE MOTOR CARRIER INDUSTRY: IMPLICATIONS TO THE AMERICAN PUBLIC

Not only is the domestic American transportation system complex and sophisticated, but it is internationally unique in that it is the only system in which the means of transport are privately owned.[1] This private ownership has assisted materially in contributing to America's high standard of mobility and living. Although complex, the system has been responsive to changing consumer needs and societal goals.[2]

Unequivocally, the American system has evolved essentially through a mixture of competition and monopoly with government ground rules establishing the framework within which transportation services and corresponding prices were offered. Indeed, transportation prices, frequently referred to as rates, have played substantial roles in determining economic activity, location of communities, channels of distribution, and other notable facets.[3] But, transportation rates are a strange phenomena because the general public, as well as federal agencies responsible for transportation activities, do not appear to understand how these prices are established. These prices are permeated with socio-economic implications, i.e., establishing rates in the transportation industry is closely interrelated with the fundamental concept of common carriage, economic development, resource allocation, and even physical mobility.

---

[1]Roy J. Sampson and Martin T. Farris, Domestic Transportation: Practice, Theory and Policy (4th ed.; Boston: Houghton Mifflin Company, 1979), Chapter 1, and other basic texts discuss the American Transportation network.

[2]Grant M. Davis and Stephen W. Brown, Logistics Management (Lexington, Mass.: D. C. Heath and Company, 1974), Chapter 14.

[3]Grant M. Davis, Martin T. Farris, and Jack J. Holder, Jr., Management of Transportation Carriers (New York: Praeger Publishers, Inc., 1975), Chapters 8 and 9.

Numerous critics of our domestic transportation regulatory institutions have advocated abolishing the present system for pricing in the transport sector of the American economy, with free market forces substituting for the so-called forces of supply and demand presently employed. However, price-quantity service offerings in the industry are established by the forces of the market through the rate conferences. In this regard, conferences are misunderstood, misrepresented, misaligned, and miscalculated, even though they represent the key to market efficiency in transportation and orderly growth and development of our nation's infrastructure.

FUNCTION OF RATE BUREAUS

As previously indicated, rate bureaus, particularly in the motor carrier industry, are frequently misunderstood by members of Congress, certain members of the Interstate Commerce Commission, the Antitrust Division of the Justice Department, various economists, and, of course, the general public. In short, considerable confusion exists with respect to just exactly what functions bureaus perform, much less their significant role in providing a forum for establishing price and service in an industry that affects 45 percent of the gross national product.[4] Also, within this environment, the industrial shipper (buyer) has as much impact in establishing price in the transportation industries as the carrier member (seller). In this case shippers represent transportation demand, and carriers constitute the supply side of the equation.

Transportation regulation,[5] particularly collective ratemaking, plays an important economic and administrative role in state transportation matters. For the most part, the respective states have adopted the federal codification of economic regulatory laws dealing with common carriage such as reasonable rates, service, and proscriptions against undue preference, prejudice, and discrimination. Rates must meet certain legal standards and must be published in tariffs with advance modification dates for the public to consider.[6] In short, the bureaus ease the daily administration of the respective state commissions through their rate publishing activities. Appearing before Senator Cannon's subcommittee on commerce in Chicago on November 17, 1979, the Honorable Robert S. Moore, Jr., Chairman of the Arkansas Transportation Commission testified:

> ". . . collective ratemaking and bureaus play an important role in regulating transportation because they assist my commission in the daily administration of its duties. . . ."[7]

Transportation rate conferences represent legitimate enterprises which are sanctioned under Title 49 of the U.S. Code.[8] They are non-profit organizations

---

[4]For an excellent discussion of rate bureau activities, refer to Charles A. Taff, *Commercial Motor Transportation* (4th ed.; Homewood, Ill.: R. D. Irwin, Inc., 1967), and other editions.

[5]Most states have adopted the ICC form of regulation in terms of rate control and entry control. For an examination of actual state practices, refer to Charles F. Phillips, Jr., *Economics of Regulation* (Homewood, Ill.: R. D. Irwin, Inc., 1970).

[6]Also, consult Kenneth Flood, *Industrial Traffic Management* (2d ed.; Dubuque, Iowa: Wm. C. Brown Publishing Co., 1974).

[7]Statement of the Honorable Robert S. Moore, Jr., Chairman of the Arkansas Transportation Commission, before a subcommittee of the U.S. Committee on Commerce, Chicago, Illinois, November 17, 1979, and subsequent reporting in *Traffic World*.

[8]*Supra*, note 1.

comprised of carrier members for the singular purpose of establishing rates and services through collective decision-making. Why is there a need for collective decision-making? The answer is simple—it is required by existing federal law. Unfortunately, transportation rate bureaus are perceived by numerous individuals as being cartels, which they are. But, these critics fail to note the difference between cartels that contribute to society[9] and those which abuse society.[10]

The domestic transportation industry is highly fragmented by modes, routes, markets, and spatial geography.[11] That is, there are almost 500 railroads, 16,000 motor carriers regulated by the U.S. Interstate Commerce Commission (ICC), 100 air carriers, 42 pipelines, 200 water carriers, and numerous freight forwarders. In this regard, Figure 1 depicts the 1977 distribution between the modes for intercity freight and Figure 2 forecasts intercity freight growth. Table 1, moreover, illustrates the anticipated growth by mode through the year 2000. As indicated, this economically significant market is anticipated to expand considerably.[12] These modes transverse thousands of miles of track, highways, waterways, and airways. It is amazing to note the efficiency of this system when compared to other indices of production and price.[13] Indeed, transportation prices are efficient when compared to other sections of our domestic economy. Transportation prices, expressed as an index, are compiled and published by the Air Transportation Association of America (ATA) located in Washington, D.C. Any casual review of these indices will reveal the "bargain" aspects of regulated rates to the consumer and their contribution to diminishing inflation from a cost-push dimension.

In the regulated for-hire motor carrier industry, the industry is subdivided on the basis of common carriers, contract carriers, agricultural carriers, and private carriers. Of the more than 100,000 motor carriers in this country, only 16,000

---

[9]A review of the existing literature concerning cartel pricing focuses upon consumer exploitation rather than the positive aspects and benefits that might accrue from positive cartels. For example, in the Alcoa case, a monopoly that could be subjected to public control and could benefit society was broken up by the Antitrust Division of the Justice Department into an oligopoly with all of the attendant wastes and economic inefficiencies. Attempts to measure $p > MC$ in the industry as an entity are meaningless because of inadequate traffic lane data.

[10]The Nadar Report concerning collective ratemaking provides an example of so-called "societal abuses" in that, in this particular report, the Commission was accused of ignoring independent action on the part of collective bureaus. The Report stated in effect that independent action was not being exercised, even though the available evidence as indicated in Grant M. Davis and Charles S. Sherwood, Rate Bureaus and Antitrust Conflicts in Transportation: Public Policy Issues (New York: Praeger Publishers, Inc., 1975), Chapter 1, proved otherwise. Other academic and law journals attacked the validity of the Nadar Report. The Nadar Report is cited in Robert Fellmeth, The Interstate Commerce Commission (New York: Grassman Publishers, 1970), p. 423.

[11]For an excellent discussion of the domestic transportation industry, consult D. Philip Locklin, Economics of Transportation (8th ed.; Homewood, Ill.: R. D. Irwin, Inc., 1978), Chapters 1 thru 3.

[12]Consult U.S. National Transportation Policy Study Commission's forecast for future transportation demand.

[13]Compare the consumer price index with the ATA index found in their annual report to substantiate this observation.

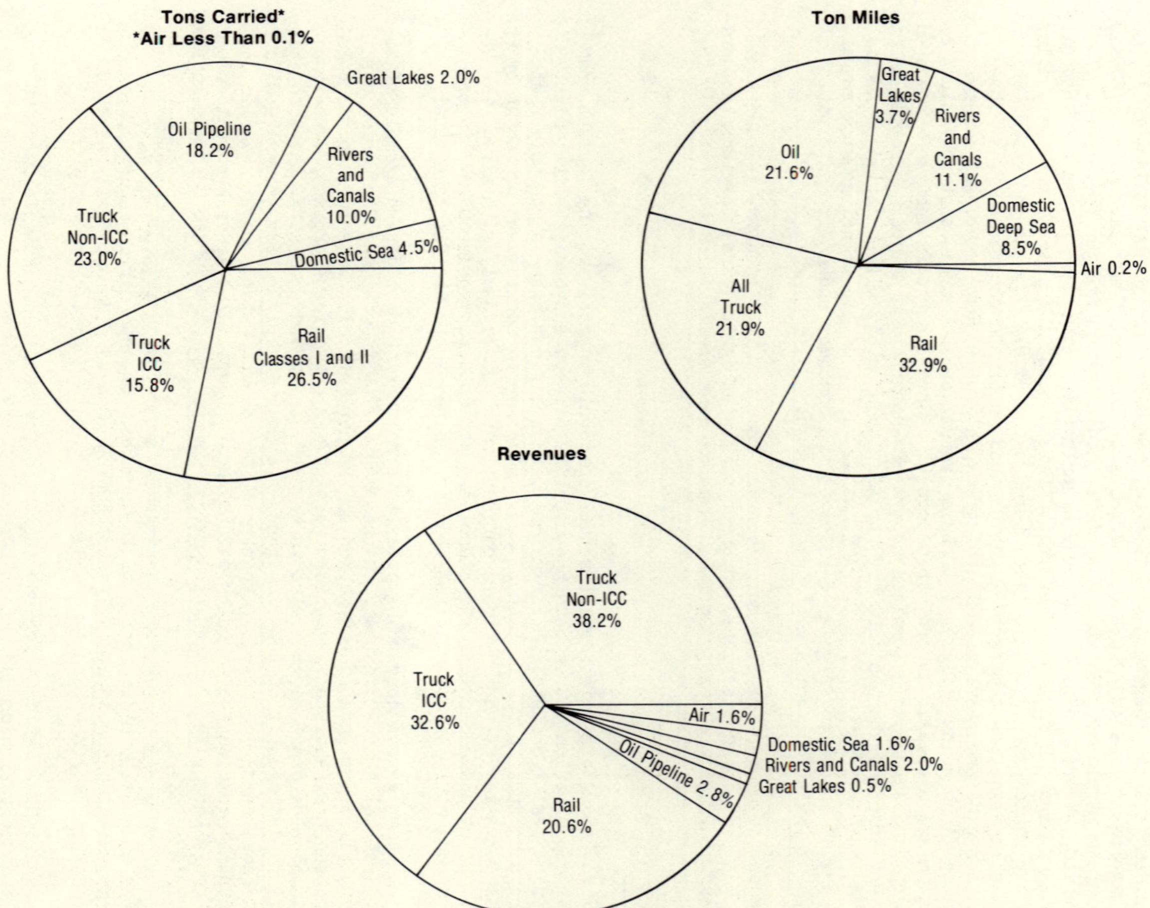

FIGURE 1. Distribution of Freight by Mode, 1977. (Source: Transportation Association of America, <u>Transportation Facts and Trends</u>, Washington, D.C., 1979.)

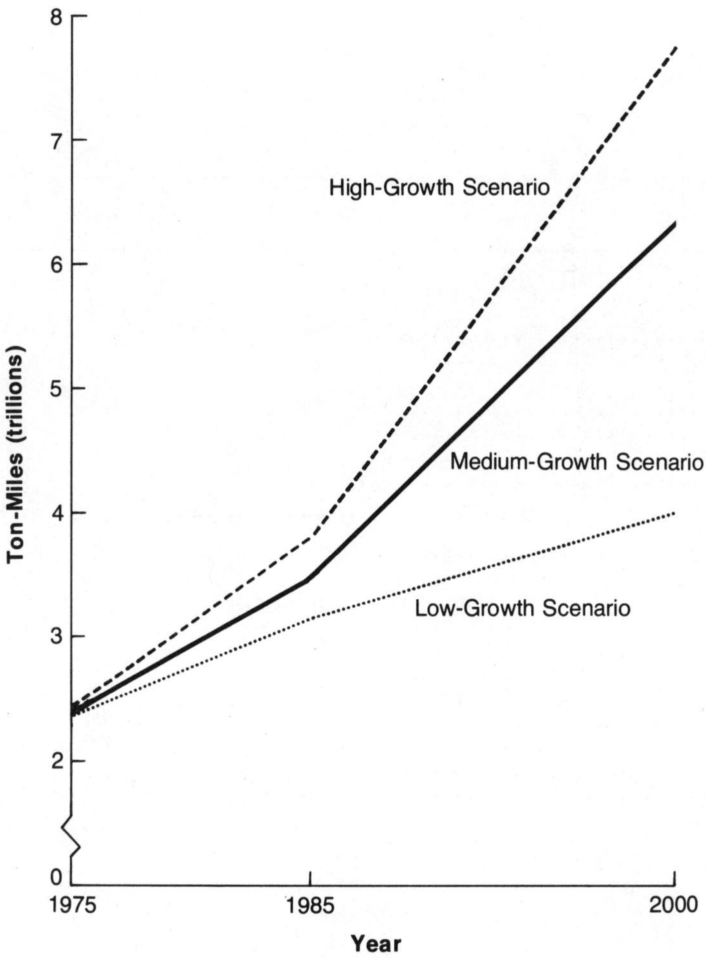

FIGURE 2. Forecast Intercity Freight Ton-Miles,[a] by Scenario, 1975 to 2000. (Source: See Appendix Table 37, NTPSC forecasts, National Transportation Policy Study Commission.)

[a]Goods movement includes the 19 commodity classes covered in the 1972 data base of the Transportation System Center of DOT. Intercity flows are those of sufficient length to cross Bureau of Economic Analysis region boundaries. Except for coal movement, which is covered in Chapter 8, shorter truck movements are covered in this chapter in the urban freight and rural freight sections. Shorter movements by pipeline, rail and water are not included. In 1975, these shorter movements which were not included accounted for about 12 percent of total ton-miles. See Appendix Tables 34 and 40.

TABLE 1

Forecast Movements of Intercity Goods by Mode,[a] 1975 to 2000

(billions of ton-miles)[b]

	1975	1985	2000
Low-Growth Scenario			
Rail	673	973	1,153
Motor Carrier	293	454	542
Private Truck	195	281	332
Water	428	678	967
Oil Pipeline	437	459	679
Gas Pipeline	312	252	300
Air Freight	4	5	62
Total	2,342	3,102	3,978
Medium-Growth Scenario			
Rail	673	1,146	1,983
Motor Carrier	293	516	841
Private Truck	195	316	525
Water	428	764	1,433
Oil Pipeline	437	497	1,062
Gas Pipeline	312	235	356
Air Freight	4	6	10
Total	2,342	3,480	6,209
High-Growth Scenario			
Rail	673	1,312	2,651
Motor Carrier	293	524	1,020
Private Truck	195	341	638
Water	428	810	1,629
Oil Pipeline	437	566	1,264
Gas Pipeline	312	242	402
Air Freight	4	7	13
Total	2,342	3,801	7,616

[a] See footnote 6, Chapter 9.

[b] Figures may not add due to rounding.

Source: National Transportation Policy Study Commission.

are for-hire carriers and regulated by the ICC.[14] These firms are designated as common carriers, and, prior to commencing service to the public, most receive certificates of public convenience and necessity, in exchange for providing adequate service and charging reasonable rates, as well as avoiding undue preference, prejudice, and discrimination in terms of customer class, commodities, and geographical sites. By charging reasonable prices that are just and compensatory and by avoiding undue preference, prejudice, and discrimination, motor carriers rates conferences contribute beneficially to society.[15]

Title 49 of the U.S. Code requires that all rates must be published in freight tariffs that cannot be changed without a thirty day notice. In this regard, conference rates and services are published in freight tariffs that have to comply with tariff circular rules. These tariffs (class, exemption, commodity) represent various competitive forces present in the intercity freight transportation market because of commercial trade relationships. All rates, moreover, must be just and reasonable and comply with known administrative standards regarding standards of reasonableness, because the National Transportation Policy enacted by Congress stipulates that, when administering the Act, the ICC must regulate in such a fashion as to preserve the inherent advantage of each of the modes that falls within its jurisdictional review; and to insure an economically sound common carrier system that meets the needs of commerce, national defense, and the postal service.[16] Although this policy has been described as nebulous and lacking definitive precision,[17] the Commission is directed to preserve inherent advantages and to provide an economically sound common carrier system.[18] This policy statement is an integral part of the Interstate Commerce Act that demands reasonable rates and avoidance of undue discrimination and that applies to all the modes regulated by the Commission.

The fundamental economic contributions to society from collective ratemaking are three-fold. Firstly, motor carrier rate bureaus represent an integral part of the common carrier system by providing a forum for considering service-offerings in the marketplace.[19] Secondly, conferences provide the avenue for reflecting the inherent advantages of the several hundred carriers that comprise various conferences by reflecting _service_ vs. _cost_ considerations proffered to industrial shippers. Thirdly, conferences provide the instrumentality for considering what constitutes undue discrimination, preference, and prejudice. In short, collective ratemaking ensures an orderly process in developing and maintaining our common carrier system.[20]

---

[14]U.S. Interstate Commerce Commission, Annual Report (Washington, D.C.: U.S. Government Printing Office, 1978).

[15]Title 49 U.S.C.

[16]Consult Grant M. Davis and Jack J. Holder, Jr., "Does the U.S. Have a Cohesive National U.S. Transportation Policy?—An Analysis" _ICC Practitioners' Journal_, Vol. 41, No. 3 (March/April 1974), pp. 332-349.

[17]Martin T. Farris, "Transportation Regulation and Economic Efficiency," _American Economic Review_, Vol. 59 (May 1969), pp. 244-250.

[18]Grant M. Davis, "The Basic Behavior of Regulatory Commissions—A Comment," _Transportation Journal_, Vol. 12 (Fall 1972), pp. 36-39.

[19]Grant M. Davis, "The Important Role of Rate Bureaus," _Traffic World_ (August 18 and September 4, 1975), pp. 16-26.

[20]Grant M. Davis and Eugene H. Shepard, Jr., _Motor Carrier Rate Structures_ (New York: Praeger Publishers, Inc., 1979), Chapters 1 and 2; and Davis and Sherwood, _loc. cit._

A brief perusal of any basic principles of transportation textbook reveals that rate conferences disseminate information to members, provide a forum for rate discussion, furnish weighing and inspection services to members and non-members, and supply a host of other useful functions necessary for the orderly operation of the domestic transportation industry.[21]

What is not generally known is that carrier rate conferences represent a significant appendage to the Interstate Commerce Commission in that the agency would not be able to administer or fulfill its mission of administering Title 49 without the direct assistance of bureaus. One of the most common fallacies affiliated with transportation regulation is "the ICC sets the rates" in the industry. This is simply not true. In the area of rate jurisdiction, which affects resource allocation, usage, and economic activity, the Commission has the following prerogatives regarding a rate dispute: (1) establish a maximum rate; (2) set a minimum rate; (3) establish a range of rates; or (4) set an exact rate.[22] Given the trillions of rates currently published governing the movement of goods in this country, it would be a virtual impossibility for the Commission to administer its legal change without the mechanism of collective ratemaking. These rates, moreover, must be reasonable and must avoid undue preference, prejudice, and discrimination.[23]

A quintessent facet of common carriage is the existence of joint rates and through routes. A joint rate merely is one rate for the through movement of a consignment from the point of origin to destination by two or more carriers.[24] Because of the large number of carriers certified in the United States, with their frequently limited geographical market coverage, joint rates are prerequisites for orderly commerce, because of the need for a price for a given transportation movement, which in turn determines the activities of commerce. But, moreover, a joint rate is cheaper than a combination rate because two or more carriers participate in one rate rather than two or more.[25] Even though motor carriers are not required by the ICC to publish joint rates, rates apply via given routes and under the terms and conditions of the bill of lading (contract of carriage). This is a practical requirement and business practice.

Motor carriers participate in through routes wherein two or more carriers provide a through service at rates lower than combination rates. Because of this factor, industrial shippers are able to provide a through service to virtually every part of the United States. In the absence of a routing concurrence, achieved through the medium of conferences, combination rates would be required, thereby increasing overall shipping cost and hence cost of production to society as a whole in

---

[21] Supra, note 19; and Martin L. Fair and John Guandolo, Transportation Regulation (7th ed.; Dubuque, Iowa: Wm. C. Brown Co., 1972), Section II.

[22] Compiled from existing ICC statutory requirements covering rates. For an extended discussion of rates, consult John Guandolo, Transportation Law (2nd ed.; Dubuque, Iowa: Wm. C. Brown Co., 1973).

[23] For an excellent discussion of reasonable freight rates, see Shenn, Reasonable Freight Rates (Washington, D.C.: Traffic Service Corporation).

[24] This legal principle is substantiated in numerous cases adjudicated by the U.S. Interstate Commerce Commission.

[25] This observation and economic fact is expanded upon by Melvin L. Greenhut and his economic theory of location because of the "tapering principle." Also, see J. Richard Jones and Martin T. Farris, Transportation Costs and the Location of Distribution Centers in the Pacific Southwest (Tempe, Ariz.: Arizona State University, Bureau of Business and Economic Research, 1971).

our economy, which, in turn, could increase inflation and aggrevate the existing balance of trade equilibrium problem that this country is presently experiencing. These two factors alone—joint rates and through routes—are necessary for commerce and for the efficiency of America's distribution efforts.[26]

Various publications and studies portray collective ratemaking as an ominous threat to the American public. The more prolific critics of the conference method of ratemaking correctly contend that conferences are cartels and can be explained by the oligopolistic model employed by economists attempting to explain industrial behavior.[27] But, this is not the case. As will be demonstrated in Chapter 2, rate conferences are best described as representing a highly differentiated monopolistic competitive industry.

What are the basic mechanisms used by rate conferences? They are quite simple in nature and follow a subsequent procedure:

1. A new rate may be proposed by a shipper, a carrier, or an interested party.

2. A proposed rate or service is published in the conference _Weekly Docket Bulletin_ and distributed to carriers and shippers in the bureau's geographical coverage area.

3. A hearing date is normally established at the bureau headquarters for participation by all interested parties.

4. An informal hearing is conducted by the conference's Standing Rate Committee which is an employee board of the conference.

5. The Standing Rate Committee publishes its decision in the _Weekly Docket Bulletin_.

6. Any party not satisfied with the Standing Rate Committee's decision as published in the bulletin may appeal to the general rate committee which is composed of carrier members.

7. The general rate committee's decision is published in the bulletin.[28]

Throughout the process is the right of appeal by the customer of freight service—the industrial shipper. In the event that any party in a conference proceeding is not satisfied with the ruling at any stage of the hearing or described process, he may request the proposed rate to be published for his own account, independent of the conference action. It is this right of independent action that constitutes the "condition precedent" for exemption from our antitrust laws that regulate joint rates and through routes.

There are seven rate bureau territories by motor carriers. These include: (1) New England; (2) Middle-Atlantic; (3) Southern; (4) Central; (5) Middle-West;

---

[26] Grant M. Davis and Charles S. Sherwood, "The Case for Single-Line Immunity," _ICC Practitioners' Journal_, Vol. 43 (September/October 1976), pp. 740-747.

[27] This argument is also tied in closely with an attempt to measure the "dead weight" cost of regulation. See Paul W. MacAvoy, editor, _The Crisis of the Regulatory Commissions_ (New York: W. W. Norton & Co., 1970).

[28] For an indepth analysis of conference functions, consult G. E. Lowe, _Practice and Procedure Before Rate-Making Associations_ (Washington, D.C.: Traffic Service Corporation, 1967), pp. 1-61.

(6) Southwest; and (7) Pacific. Conferences, of course, are further subdivided within these comprehensive geographical regions. Also, membership in a conference is not mandatory for any carrier who may elect to publish his own tariff, but conference membership is normally less expensive than single-line publication. Bureaus, moreover, employ the same reasonable standards as the ICC, and, hence, most of their tariff publications are sustained in the event that litigation develops.

In summary, rate bureaus or conferences are merely the mechanism by which rates are published in the for-hire segment of the intercity freight motor carrier industry. The bureaus provide the procedural framework wherein the industrial shipper and the seller of freight services establish rates and services. Society benefits from this institutional framework because appelate rights are insured and because joint rates and through routes which benefit commerce through lower costs are facilitated.[29]

---

[29] See Roger E. Jerman, Ronald D. Anderson, and James A. Constantion, "Physical Distribution Management Views on Regulation Issues," *The Logistics and Transportation Review*, Vol. 13, No. 2, pp. 123-132, where managerial personnel who work daily with collective ratemaking in industrial traffic favor this form of pricing. This survey substantiates the findings reported by Grant M. Davis, Charles S. Sherwood, and L. J. Rosenberg, "A Dichotomous Perception of Transportation Regulation-Deregulation—An Analysis," *The Logistics and Transportation Review*, 1977.

The Important Role of Rate Bureaus in Transportation*

GRANT M. DAVIS

[Editor's Note: Prior to Ex Parte 297, a rate conference could petition the Interstate Commerce Commission to suspend and investigate a rate independently announced by a carrier member of the conference. Although this practice was not widespread, a Nader group contended the condition precedent for exemption from antitrust was being violated. The following article provides the reader with insight into the fallacy of the Nader Report, in addition to presenting a historical perspective regarding collective ratemaking.]

Legislative attempts to eliminate or modify rate bureaus can be categorized by various decades with individual years serving as benchmarks. The genesis of the present movement was in 1962 with President John F. Kennedy's highly touted transportation message. This message primarily called for increased reliance on competition and less regulation.

Additional measures were introduced in 1971, 1972, 1973, and 1974--all unsuccessful. Congress, in fact, very recently held hearings on H.R. 6351, H.R. 7681, and a companion bill, S. 1876. H.R. 7681 and S. 1876 are the Administration bills and were introduced on June 5 by Senator Vance Hartke (D-Ind.).

The primary provisions relating to H.R. 7681 and S. 1876 are:

Title I—Financial Assistance to Railroads.

Title II—Provisions Relating to Discriminatory State Taxation.

Title III—Provisions Relating to Economic Regulation of Railroads.

Title IV—Agreements Between Railroad Carriers.

Title V—Establishment of Uniform Cost Accounting.

---

*Reprinted by permission of _Traffic World_.

Title VI--Interstate Commerce Commission Report.

Title VII--Miscellaneous.

Although Title III contains provisions regarding bureau activities in the area of rate publications, Title IV contains two provisions that will be detrimental to regulated segments of the transportation industry.

Section 403 proposes to amend section 5a by adding the following sentence at the end of the present wording:

> In addition to the records required by the first sentence of this paragraph, each conference, bureau, or other organization established or continued pursuant to an agreement among common carriers by railroad and approved by the Commission under the provisions of this section shall maintain records of the votes of its members on each matter voted on.

If enacted, this amendment would constitute an initial step toward disclosing individual carrier votes on matters before bureau committees. Certain shippers, of course, would attempt to employ information derived from committee votes to reward or punish carriers. Available evidence certainly supports this observation. Most carriers have no objection to an aggregate vote report such as 10 for 5 against on a given proposal. As a result of an ICC order, bureaus now provide reasons for approving or rejecting a given proposal. Justification for disposing of a docket is more meaningful to an industrial shipper than who or whom voted for a given rule of rate change.

A second detrimental feature of Title IV of H.R. 7681 and S. 1876 proposes to amend paragraph (6) of section 5a in the following manner:

> The Commission shall not approve under this section any agreement which established a procedure for the determination of any matter through joint consideration unless it finds that under the agreement that is accorded to each party the free and unrestrained right to take independent action . . . and in no event shall any bureau, conference, committee, or other organization . . . participate in discussions, make agreements, or conduct votes on single line rates established by any railroad carrier, regulated under part 1 of this Act, nor appear in any proceeding before the Commission regarding said single line rate. . . .

Excluded from this prohibition of single-line rates are general increases and decreases. This proposed amendment certainly ignores existing realities in the transportation industry regarding undue preference and discrimination. Rates on transcontinental traffic from the ports of Los Angeles, San Francisco and Seattle to New York, for instance, on identical commodities, cannot be considered in a vacuum. Should a change occur from Seattle to New York, traffic from the other cities would in all probability change.

What other adverse features would occur if single-line immunity was eliminated? There are four: (1) Common carrier services would deteriorate because of rate wars brought about by major value shippers receiving cut-rates; (2) joint rate service would deteriorate; (3) certain tariff publication costs would increase; and (4) consumer prices would increase. Congressional approval of this section would indeed by costly.

Section 405 of the proposed bill directs the ICC to investigate rate bureaus to ascertain if "conferences are preventing an efficient utilization of transportation resources or have established practices which are inconsistent with efficient, flexible, and economic operation." The Commission would, of course, be compelled to consult with the Justice Department and the Department of Transportation. But, the ICC has already completed its investigation of rate bureaus, a study which will subsequently be examined. Needless to say, DOT would doubtlessly establish standards for whatever "an efficient utilization of transportation resources" means. Rate bureaus are mere instrumentalities for establishing rules and rates for their membership. Member carriers determine efficient utilization of transportation resources not rate bureaus.

EX PARTE 297

Having concluded a two-year study, the ICC served its report and order in Ex Parte No. 297 concerning rate bureaus on June 16, 1975. Independent action, according to the agency's report, had not been abused, although some activities were condemned, such as bureau mergers and consolidations. In short, the Commission found:

1. Rate bureaus assist the making of appropriate rates.

2. Procedural changes would foster actions favorable to the general public, shippers, and to bureau members.

3. The right of independent action does not adversely affect the rate structure.

4. A system need not be established by the Commission to monitor public hearings before rate bureaus, but formal minutes, and not verbatim transcripts, are required of rate committee proceedings.

5. Commission representatives may attend all rate bureau meetings; but copies of correspondence and documents concerning all rate bureau meetings need not be filed with the Commission.

6. A uniform system of accounts for rate bureaus will be promulgated.

7. Rate bureaus are not prohibited from furnishing technical and professional services to other bureaus or non-members provided that the limitations expressed in the report are observed.

8. Rate bureaus may not invest in another commercial business, whether related or unrelated to their primary function of processing and publishing rates and related matters for member carriers.

9. Rate bureaus are prohibited from acquiring other rate bureaus without prior Commission approval.

10. Rate bureaus may not be profit-making enterprises.

11. A carrier member of a bureau, which carrier is affiliated in any way with a shipper, may not serve on a bureau's board of directors, general rate committee, or any other committee which has an effect, either directly or indirectly, on the ratemaking function of the bureau without specific prior Commission approval.

12. A maximum period of 120 days is prescribed for the processing of proposals to final disposition.

13. Public notice of proposals need not identify the proponent.

14. Rate bureaus are prohibited from broadening the territorial or commodity scope of an individual rate proposal without prior adequate notice.

15. Adoption of shortened special procedures involving proposals covering special docket applications is not warranted in this proceeding.

16. Section 22 quotations require special bureau procedures limiting notification to members and the governmental agency.

17. Docketing of rate bureau proceedings with respect to general rate increase proposals need not be mandatory.

18. The Commission need not obtain and publish reports of the deliberations within the industry concerning the matter of general increases.

19. The various rate bureaus need not join in seeking general rate increases.

20. The various rail rate bureaus are not required to substantiate general increases on a regional basis only, but regional costs should be presented in a more explicit manner.

21. Rate bureaus are prohibited entirely from protesting proposals of carrier members, and not merely limited to instances in which the proposed rate is less than the long-term variable cost or any other specific instance.

22. Rate bureaus are prohibited from discouraging independent action proposals of member carriers in any way, including the protesting of the filing of any rates pursuant to such action.

23. Rate bureaus should be prohibited from discouraging members from publishing individual tariffs.

24. Immunity from antitrust laws shall be continued.

25. Immunity from antitrust laws shall continue to be extended to agreements with respect to proposals of single-line movements.

26. Additional legislation is not necessary, and need not be sought, to better effect the goals for which section 5a was enacted.

Commissioner Hardin concurred in the report's results, and Commissioners Gresham, O'Neal, Brown, and Corber dissented in part.

The author vigorously disagrees with points 6 and 22 of the order in Ex Parte number 297. Regarding uniform accounts for rate bureaus, the Commission report stated: ". . . although the field investigators did not reveal any significant irregularities, we are of the opinion that a uniform system of account should be prescribed by the Commission . . ." (p. 821)

By requiring conferences to maintain a uniform system of accounts, a costly new set of accounts must be maintained at carrier expense. No public need exists for requiring bureaus as well as carriers to maintain uniform accounts for periodic audits by the ICC. This cost will merely be shifted to the ultimate consumer and the burden will be uneven.

Relative to point 22, prohibiting rate bureaus from protesting independent movements, several observations are warranted. First, empirical evidence indicates that only a paucity of independently announced rates are protested by bureaus.

Secondly, as corporate entities, bureaus should be entitled to protest any rate they believe will be detrimental to their aggregate membership. By eliminating the right to protest a rate, a conference will become a nonentity. Third, and lastly, a carrier pays for membership in the rate bureaus. By instructing the bureau to protest a given rate, a member carrier, particularly small carriers, can avoid attorney fees.

EMPIRICAL STUDIES

In 1970 Ralph Nader's Center for Responsive Law contended that rate bureaus were fundamentally cartels and the right of individual carriers to exercise independent action was primarily a hoax. During that same year, moreover, the Department of Transportation introduced legislation designed to substantially modify conference activities. The organization's philosophy regarding an efficient transportation network and their patent opposition to rate bureaus was succinctly stated by former Secretary of Transportation John Volpe:

> It appears . . . that the rate bureaus and associates have a retarding effect on carrier pricing and service. Consequently, the retention of section 5a in the carrier agreements established under it, in their present forms would be inconsistent with our policy objective of placing increased reliance on their own particular markets. Furthermore, this departure from our national policy of free and open competition expressed in the antitrust laws, as authorized in section 5a has been justified by the existence of extensive regulatory authority over carrier rates and practices. Since we are attempting to lessen regulatory supervision over rates, this principal justification for collective carrier pricing is of less reliance now.

This statement reflects a myopic belief that undue preference and discrimination no longer constitute problems in the regulated segment of the domestic transportation industry. The key to understanding the need for the procedural dimension of rate bureaus is the need for collective act via different route configuration.

The basic economic characteristics of the transportation industry, together with common carrier obligations, explain the essential functions of rate bureaus. Because of the existence of economies of scale, external economies, joint cost, unused capacity, and other combinations of these factors, together with supplementary cost and an inability to accurately allocate these costs, rate stability appears to be an obvious socio-economic goal. Indeed, ICC Chairman George Stafford contends that this country cannot perform its present transportation <u>procedural operations</u> without rate conferences. Interestingly, the objections pertaining to rate uniformity, stability, and joint rates and through rates are the same as those originally stated by the ICC during the early years of its development.

Also, because of common carrier obligations and the necessity for avoiding undue preference and discrimination, rate conferences create an institutional environment in which debate occurs regarding pricing transportation services. As previously indicated, it is only through this institutional arrangement that the buyer of transportation—the shipper—has as much impact on the ultimate price as the seller of the transportation unit—the carrier.

Critics of conferences accuse the organizations of a plethora of undesirable activities, but have failed to investigate the condition precedent for exemption from the contemporary antitrust laws—the right to exercise free and unrestrained independent action. In 1970, the Nader group merely counted the number of independent actions protested by rate bureaus and concluded that this right was being abused!

During 1972 and 1973, Professor Charles S. Sherwood and I started an indepth evaluation of rate bureaus and their activities. The results were published in 1975 in a book entitled Rate Bureaus and Antitrust Conflicts in Transportation: Public Policy Issues, New York: Praeger Press. Although we were concerned with aggregate conference activities, we focused our primary effort toward identifying whether or not rate bureaus interfered with the right of carriers to exercise independent action.

During the course of our initial attempt to gather data, we contacted carriers proper but discovered that little detailed rate information was maintained concerning specific commodity movements on independently announced rates. Collectively, some bureaus were reluctant to cooperate in the study because of the dual investigations being simultaneously conducted by the ICC and the Justice Department. In this regard, we turned to the consumer of transportation--the industrial shipper--for data concerning the right of independent action.

Shipper questionnaires were mailed to 200 traffic executives selected randomly from the 1973 edition of The Official Directory of Industrial and Commercial Traffic Executives. A total of 64 shippers responded, with traffic expenses exceeding $151.2 billion for 1972. During 1972, 29 per cent of all rate proposals before rail and motor carrier bureaus were independently announced. Shippers experienced 93.1 per cent success in 1972 for independently filed independent announcements, and bureaus, 95.4 per cent success. Traffic expenses under independently announced rates, moreover, were $150,568,000 during 1972. Lastly, of 10,249 independent announcements filed in 1972, the bureaus protested only 193, or 1.88 per cent.

Although there were several limitations to the study conducted by us, we believe that the condition precedent for exemption from antitrust--the right to exercise independent action--has not been abused. Additional research conducted by myself and Professors Sherwood and L. J. Rosenberg discloses that most transportation managers prefer to operate within rate bureaus because of the procedural safeguards available to all parties in setting price.

A recent study conducted by the Motor Common Carrier Association involving nine major motor carrier rate bureaus revealed that over 81 per cent of all proposals submitted during 1974 were recommended. Only 12 per cent were not recommended. During this same time frame, 59 per cent of the proposals involved reductions with the balance representing increases. Eight bureaus reported 7,472 independent actions exercised in 1974. Of these, 6,170 were taken prior to any action by the Standing Rate Committee and 84 per cent constituted reductions. Bureaus protested only 81 of the 7,472 independent actions, just over 1 per cent, and the 81 protests resulted in 34 suspensions, one suspension in part, two rejections, five adjustments, and 39 of the protests were dismissed. This same study, moreover, reveals that the number of rate proposals, particularly independent actions, is considerably lower during the first two quarters of 1975 relative to 1974.

RECOMMENDATIONS

Based upon the empirical research conducted by Professor Sherwood and myself, we advocate five major recommendations for changing rate bureaus.

First, rate bureaus should be allowed to retain the right to protest independent actions. Available evidence indicates that bureau protests are not automatic and are filed only when specific economic criteria are involved, and bureau criteria are closely rated to ICC standards regarding suspension and proposed changes. In the event that the right to protest independent actions is changed, some substitute form of screening in all probability would develop. In this regard, the present system is superior.

Secondly, rate bureaus should be allowed to retain antitrust immunity collectively for discussing single-line rates. Removing single-line immunity would create a situation of uncertainty and increase the burden of individual shippers by decimating the uniformity of our present rate structures. And, considering the increase of tariff publication costs, together with the additional traffic personnel that would be required, available evidence does not support the contention that freight rates would fall if carriers autonomously established single-line rates. Additional research is being conducted in this area and will be published soon.

Thirdly, a maximum time period should be prescribed for processing rate proposals by bureaus. During the course of our investigation of rate conferences, delay was cited as the primary shipper complaint against bureaus. Although dockets should ideally be processed as rapidly as possible, due process should not be abused for the sake of speeding up a bureau decision.

Fourth, rate bureau agreements presently on file with the Commission should be modified to include specific procedural requirements to provide for how committees vote. In this regard, the final vote of rate committees should be available to the shipping public, i.e., the aggregate vote for and against a given proposal. Some large grain shippers contend individual carrier voting records should be publicized, but this recommendation would destroy the beneficial procedural dimension of bureau pricing. Besides, the condition precedent for exemption from the antitrust statutes is the right to freely exercise independent action—not how a carrier votes during the course of participating in a conference committee.

Fifth, and lastly, bureaus and shippers should confer and discuss important controversial issues before filing any significant proposed rate or rule change. Available shipper evidence collected by Professor Sherwood and myself indicates some delays could have been averted if interested parties had fully discussed some proposals prior to filing. This recommendation, of course, would permit the conference to more adequately react to changing economic conditions.

Transportation rate bureaus are cartels, but the procedural features of these conferences appear to give the purchaser of transportation services as much input into pricing decisions as the carrier seller. Even though considerable attention has been focused upon bureau activities during the past three years, the essential conditional precedent for exemption from antitrust laws—the right of each carrier to freely exercise independent action—does not appear to have been abused. Insofar as contemporary law requires carriers to perform collective action to better serve society, rate conferences will continue to play an important function in the regulated segment of the domestic transportation industry.

Collective Ratemaking: An Indivisible System*

JOHN FESSENDEN

[Editor's Note: Frequently rate structures and practices of railroads are confused with those of the regulated motor carrier industry. However, even though both are common carriers and are charged by law to avoid undue preference, prejudice, and discrimination and to publish joint rates and through routes, the fundamental characteristics, economies, and route structures and configurations are different. The 4-R Act, moreover, precludes bureau consideration of single-line rates, even though competitive market structures may be adversely affected.

In a pamphlet entitled "Collective Ratemaking: An Indivisible System," John Fessenden cogently points out: (1) limitations on joint rates ignore existing business conditions; (2) a strong commercial relationship exists between joint- and single-line rates; (3) considerable confusion prevails regarding the 4-R Act as it relates to railroads; (4) without collective ratemaking, undue preference, prejudice, and discrimination would result; (5) collective ratemaking contributes substantially to implementing and achieving the goals of the National Transportation Policy; and (6) without collective ratemaking, carrier services would deteriorate materially because of rate and route structures.]

Over the past eight or nine years, increasing attention has been focused on federal regulation of interstate transportation service and a variety of proposals

*Reprinted by permission of the author.

to partially or wholly deregulate transportation have been put forward. Most of these proposals have included a repeal of the antitrust immunity for collective ratemaking in surface transportation conferred by the Reed-Bulwinkle Act (Section 5a of the Interstate Commerce Act, now designated 49 U.S.C. Section 10706). In recognition of the public need for coordination between carriers in order to provide a network of service involving joint-line transportation, both between points not served by a single carrier and as competition for service offered by single-line carriers, the proponents of deregulation have attempted to make their proposals palatable by limiting the repeal of antitrust immunity to collective consideration, discussion or agreement on single-line rates. Thus, the debate which has taken place over the past eight or nine years has tended to focus upon individual carrier service rather than upon rates for transportation. This has had the effect of producing extensive and sometimes heated discussions about collective ratemaking in a context which not only has no basis in reality but which leads to conclusions or recommendations that would be destructive.

The so-called "National Transportation Modernization Act of 1971" sponsored by the Department of Transportation was one of the first major proposals for substantial deregulation of surface transportation. It included a partial repeal of antitrust immunity to the extent of collective ratemaking of single-line rates. Testifying before the Subcommittee on Transportation and Aeronautics of the Committee on Interstate and Foreign Commerce, House of Representatives, on April 27, 1972, T. B. Alfriend, speaking on behalf of the motor carrier rate bureaus made the following statement:

> The importance of . . . coordinated service is evidenced by the fact that over 30 percent of all of the shipments of the motor common carriers of general freight moves from origin to destination in joint service by two or more carriers. The maintenance of joint service and the maintenance of reasonable levels of rates for that service require that rates be made by the carriers and regulated by the Interstate Commerce Commission in the light of the average circumstances and conditions under which transportation is performed and the average cost of all of the carriers performing it. The making and regulation of rates in this fashion can be accomplished only if the carriers are permitted to act collectively and the I.C.C. is permitted to regulate them collectively.
>
> Of course not all of the transportation performed by motor common carriers is performed in joint service. Most of it, particularly that between major cities, is performed in single-line service. Nevertheless, the maintenance of basic rate structures, in which rates for the same quantity and quality of service are the same throughout each ratemaking territory, requires that the levels of rates reflect average circumstances and conditions and average costs. To require each individual carrier to establish its own rates on the basis of its own costs, in other words to forbid collective ratemaking on the basis of average costs, would destroy the rate structures.

It should be noted, that even the representatives of carriers in the early stages of the development of the issue failed to recognize the misplaced emphasis of the proposal in attempting to deal with ratemaking in terms of carrier service rather than in terms of carrier rates. Thus there grew the notion that collective ratemaking involved two separate and distinct functions, i.e., (1) consideration, discussion and agreement on single-line rates and (2) consideration, discussion and agreement on joint-line rates. With this utterly mistaken premise, it is no wonder that people relatively familiar with the realities of the transportation business simply assumed that the two ratemaking functions could be considered separately and that antitrust immunity for one could be withdrawn without materially impairing the other.

The confusion described is apparent in the antecedents of the 4R Act of 1976 as well as in the Act itself. In 1975, the Senate Committee on Commerce, in reporting S. 2718, referred to the Interstate Commerce Commission's investigation of rate bureaus in Ex Parte No. 297, and noted the Commission's findings that the railroad rate bureaus had not abused their immunity and that the bureaus serve a useful function by performing the important task of providing a forum for the orderly formulation of rates and rules for the transportation of almost every conceivable type of commodity moving in commerce. After stating that it agreed with the Interstate Commerce Commission's conclusions, the Committee nonetheless recommended legislation which would prohibit railroad rate bureaus from acting upon single-line rates. The Committee's explanation follows:*

> Section 5b would introduce a number of changes in the Commission's regulation of railroad rate bureaus. The primary purpose of section 5b is to restrict rate bureau processing of two types of rate adjustments to fosture [sic] greater competition among the railroads. The first restriction in paragraph 5 would prohibit railroads which are members of a rate bureau from discussing, agreeing or voting on a rate when applied from only one point on a railroad to another point on the same railroad. Railroads would thus be encouraged to put into effect rates which applied solely to their own lines without first obtaining the views of other railroads through rate bureau procedures. The Committee recognizes that a carrier having a single-line route between two points may find it in its best interest and the best interest of its shipper to participate also in joint-line routes. In many instances, carriers are required by Commission orders or by the dictates of the carriers' direct economic self-interest to interchange traffic at intermediate gateways with competing lines. The new section 5b is intended to allow a single carrier between two points to discuss, agree and vote on joint-line rates between the two points.

One cannot help but wonder just how the Senate Committee believed that a rail carrier providing single-line service between two points could make its individual rates for that service independent of any participation in joint rates for the same service without the one influencing or affecting the other, or without the one totally defeating the other. In any event, the unrealistic dichotomy was perpetuated throughout Congressional consideration of S. 2718 and the bill was ultimately enacted as the 4R Act of 1976. As passed, the legislation applied only to railroads, and ratemaking organizations were prohibited from permitting "a rail carrier to participate in agreements related to, or to vote on single-line rates proposed by another rail carrier." A "single-line rate" means "a rate or allowance proposed by a single rail carrier that is applicable only over its line and for which the transportation can be provided by that carrier."**

The regulatory changes made in the 4R Act, including treatment of railroad rate bureaus, constituted an almost incidental part of the legislation, the principal part and purpose of the legislation being the structuring of financial relief to meet the problems of the bankruptcy of the Penn Central, and to try to avoid further major rail failures. As a consequence, many of the regulatory changes were worked out as compromises with the railroads themselves in terms of provisions which the carriers believed they could accept. In view of the fact that the vast preponderance of rail traffic moves at commodity rates over tariff designated routes, the railroads apparently believed that the tightly-worded definition of a "single-line

---

*Senate Report No. 94-499, 94th Cong. 1st Sess., pages 54-55.

**49 U.S.C. 10706(a).

rate" would make the prohibition on collective consideration of single-line rates workable.

Only with this kind of understanding is the Congressional action on the subject fully comprehensible in view of the conclusions reached by the Interstate Commerce Commission in Ex Parte No. 297 on June 3, 1975. In that report, 349 I.C.C. 811, 847-851, the Commission set forth the following penetrating analysis of the inseparable relationship between rates for single-line transportation service and rates for joint-line transportation service, implicitly recognizing the important distinction between rates covering transportation service and individual carrier operations performing that service:

> The antitrust immunity of section 5a is statutory, and our power is to grant or deny carrier applications for section 5a relief.[4] With the notable exception of the United States Department of Justice, no party of this proceeding advocates that the Commission's authority to grant antitrust immunity be withdrawn or curtailed. At this point, this proceeding has mandated several procedural and organizational changes in approved section 5a agreements which the evidence indicates will better effectuate the goals of the national transportation policy and effective regulation.
>
> We are convinced from the evidence of record that the Commission's administration of section 5a has contributed significantly to the creation of an effective and dependable national transportation system. The changes mandated herein, and the investigative approach utilized, are a more effective method of ensuring such a system than the denial of antitrust immunity. Such denial would be a giant step backwards in effective regulation of stable rate structures and reduce this Nation's transportation system to a state of uncertainty with respect to reasonable and lawful levels of rates. We conclude that immunity from antitrust laws should be continued.
>
> We now return to the question of whether such antitrust immunity should be restricted so as not to apply with respect to proposals for single-line movements. This proposition was soundly rejected by virtually all carriers as well as shipper parties on the grounds that collective consideration of single-line and joint-line rates cannot practically be separated. That is, what may be a single-line rate for one carrier can be part of a through joint rate for another, and the elimination of antitrust immunity for single-line discussion will destroy [sic] the very essence of collective ratemaking. While this argument may seem simplistic at first glance, further scrutiny reveals that it has merit.

The record is particularly persuasive in showing the need for rate bureau member carriers to consider and discuss single-line rates in conjunction with their

---

"[4]An excellent discussion of the anticompetitive aspects of conference ratemaking appears in Rate Bureaus and Antitrust Conflicts in Transportation—Public Policy Issues, by Grant M. Davis and Charles S. Sherwood (Praeger Publishers, 1975). The report contains a resumé of rate bureau development and an analysis of the economic and procedural framework for conference ratemaking. The authors conducted a study evaluating the effects of rate bureau activity on competition. One conclusion they reached was that antitrust immunity for single-line rates should be retained."

joint-rate activities. We are cited to numerous examples of the symbiosis of single-line and joint-line rates. Without attempting a complete restatement of these examples some of the more significant categories of situations described in the record are as follows:

1. REMOVAL OF PREFERENTIAL TREATMENT OF SHIPPERS. In WASHINGTON POTATO & ONION SHIPPERS ASSN., INC., v. U.P.R. CO., 300 I.C.C. 537 (1957), we found single-line and joint-line rail rates on potatoes prejudiced shippers in the State of Washington and preferred shippers in the States of Idaho and Oregon. Elimination of the preferences was ordered. Joint action of the involved railroads accomplished the required adjustment. This would not have been possible without consideration of single-line as well as joint-line rates.

2. DUAL CAPACITY RATES SERVING AS SINGLE-LINE AND JOINT-LINE RATES. Two situations are described. In one the single-line functions as both a single-line and a joint-line rate, illustrated by wheat gathering rates in producing territory which are single-line to such milling points as Minneapolis-St. Paul but joint-lines for movements to beyond milling points such as Chicago. In the other described situation conference joint-line tariffs expressly adopt single-line rates of carriers serving both origin and destination points for competitive joint-line routings between such points.

3. PORT EQUALIZATION. Import-export traffic moves to and from interior points through numerous ports along the various coasts. The routings can be competitive from different ports (for example, Seattle to Chicago and Los Angeles to Chicago) involving both single- and joint-line movements. Discussions by rate bureau members aid in eliminating inequalities in port relationships over both the single- and joint-line routings.

4. EQUALIZED OPPORTUNITIES FOR COMPETING PRODUCING POINTS. There are numerous situations in which discrete producing points compete in the same market but are served by different transportation companies. One producing point may have single-line service to market while a competitor has joint-line service to the same market.[5] Inequalities in market opportunities would arise in the absence of consideration of the single-line rates along with the joint-line rates.

These situations could be multiplied many times on the basis of the record of this proceeding. Together they embrace service by all the different surface modes—rail, truck, motor passenger and water. They demonstrate a symbiotic relationship between single-line and joint-line rates which must be considered in order to maintain competitive equality for carriers as well as shippers, remove distortions in port relationships, effect compliance with statutory restraints against discriminations and preferences, and simply observe the realities of diverse rates in a coordinated transportation network.

"[5]Each point may have single-line service from separate carriers to the primary market. One example cited to us in the record is Sterling, Nebr., served by Burlington Northern to Chicago and Goodland, Kans., served by the Chicago, Rock Island & Pacific to the same market. Without rate equality one of these competing producing points would be economically disadvantaged. Joint consideration of their respective rates by rate bureaus avoids that result."

If rate bureau members were denied antitrust immunity to consider single-line rates in these situations, they could not function. Such a result would make virtually impossible joint-line service essential to a national transportation system.

As one party stated in this proceeding, single-line traffic is the business that is most important to any carrier, and joint-line traffic is only an adjunct to performance of a full transportation service for customers. While we are not prepared to accept this statement as a general rule, we do recognize the importance of single-line traffic. In practice, a single-line rate published by a rate bureau generally has application to all carrier members holding authority to perform the involved transportation. In the case of motor carriers, the number of competitive carriers is often quite large. It is rare to find only one motor common carrier serving any two given points in single-line service. Accordingly, any change in the single-line rate of one affects the rate of at least one or more competing carriers. This is so regardless of whether the rate is published in bureau tariffs or individual tariffs, and regardless of mode.

Similarly, other carriers not holding single-line authority between the given points may wish to compete for the traffic in joint-line service with one or more connecting carriers. The result is a joint-rate determined through rate bureau discussion and procedure. In such a situation, single-line and joint-line rates for ratemaking purposes become so intertwined as to be inseparable in a cause and effect relationship. Herein lies the heart of the problem, which is also the heart of the collective ratemaking process between and among two or more carriers. If collective discussion of single-line rates is not allowed, each carrier will attempt to adjust its individual rates in an effort to expand or retain its share of available traffic. As each single-line rate is adjusted, every joint-line rate would be required to be readjusted in order to offer a competitive service. The result would be something less than a stable rate structure between any two or more points. When this reasoning is applied to the entire territory encompassed by most rate bureaus, it becomes obvious that rate stability will be a difficult goal. When considering the range of territory encompassed by some rail rate bureaus, the problem looms even larger.

The solution is just as obvious. Present practice must be retained. To prohibit collective discussion of single-line rates would force many carrier members with extensive single-line operating authority to file such proposals as independent actions, or to withdraw from participation in the bureau in favor of individual tariff publication. Experience teaches, and the evidence confirms, that carriers often need the technical assistance of the bureaus' staff when formulating rates on given commodities. Therefore, so long as carrier members have the right of independent action conferred by paragraph (6) of section 5a, and the bureau is prohibited from protesting member carrier rates, we are of the opinion that it is not advisable to impose any restriction which would have the effect of driving carrier members from participating in their respective bureaus. Such action would not foster the national transportation policy, but would seriously disrupt collective ratemaking which serves that policy. Accordingly, we conclude that immunity should continue to be extended to agreements which permit collective discussions with respect to single-line movements. Of course, in no way does our continued extension of immunity to agreements which permit collective discussions with respect to single-line movements interfere in any manner with a proponent's right of independent action.

Following the passage of the 4R Act, the rail carriers filed new ratemaking agreements in compliance with the new section 5b adopted as part of the Act. The Department of Justice participated in the proceedings before the Interstate Commerce Commission opposing those agreements and arguing for a very liberal interpretation of the provision prohibiting collective consideration of single-line rates so that any rate proposal which could have single-line application would be excluded from collective action, even though it might apply over the lines of several carriers and might also apply for joint-line service. The Administrative Law Judge rejected the contention in favor of the plain meaning of the statutory language, but the Interstate Commerce Commission, inexplicably ignoring its own decision in Ex Parte No. 297, substantially adopted the Department of Justice position. The Commission's decision is undergoing administrative review and the final conclusion of the Commission is not known. In any event, and despite the fact that Congress deliberately excluded motor carriers from its revision of collective ratemaking for railroads, the Commission has proposed in Ex Parte No. 297, Sub 3 to impose upon motor carriers the Congressional prohibitions on collective ratemaking by railroads as interpreted by the Commission in the rail 5b cases. The Commission went so far as to announce a preliminary vote to prohibit single-line ratemaking by motor carrier rate bureaus some six months ago, but has never issued an implementing decision.

The time has come when the confusion over the subject must be eliminated. There are some 3,000 motor common carriers of general commodities which participate in the tariffs of the major motor carrier rate bureaus. Those bureau tariffs establish a uniform rate structure in which rates for the transportation of articles of commerce between all points are established without regard to whether the physical carrier service utilized is single-line or joint-line in nature. Proposals for changes in those rates under the rate bureau procedures, whether made by carriers or by shippers, almost never specify whether they are limited to single-line application, or to joint-line application. They are made simply as proposals to change transportation rates and they apply for the accounts of all carriers authorized to provide the physical service without regard to whether the actual service is single-line or joint-line. Thus, as shippers and carriers so well know, and as the Interstate Commerce Commission ought to know, there are not two separate motor carrier rate structures, one for single-line service and one for joint-line service, nor could there be for obvious competitive reasons.

In fundamental terms, if it is desirable public policy for the motor common carriers to provide a transportation network under which freight can be tendered to a carrier at any point, with a carrier obligation to accomplish the movement to destination at reasonable rates known to the shipper in advance, whether the service can be performed by the carrier alone or whether it requires a connecting carrier or carriers, the motor carriers must be permitted to participate in collective ratemaking involving joint consideration, discussion and agreement upon the rates to be submitted to the Interstate Commerce Commission for final approval. Any attempt to differentiate between single-line service performed under those rates and joint-line service performed under those rates will effectively prohibit collective ratemaking in its entirety, and this inexorable fact must be recognized before grave damage is done, albeit innocently, to the nation's transportation system.

As is well known, carriers which participate on a voluntary basis in collective ratemaking have an absolute, inalienable right to take independent action in the establishment of rates at any time. Under that right, a carrier desiring to establish a particular rate for application over its own line, without consideration or discussion with other carriers is absolutely free to do so. Experience over many years demonstrates that carriers do exercise that right and this conclusion was the thrust of the study published in 1975 by Grant M. Davis and Charles S. Sherwood entitled *Rate Bureaus and Antitrust Conflicts in Transportation—Public Policy Issues*. One frequently hears, however, the argument that rate bureaus effectively interfere with the right of independent action by protesting such actions before the Interstate Commerce Commission and somehow persuading the Commission to suspend them. While the motor carrier rate bureaus do not concede that the charge was ever valid, it is now totally academic, because the bureaus lost the right to protest independent actions in the Interstate Commerce Commission's final decision in Ex Parte No. 297 in 1976, 351 I.C.C. 437.

It should be clear that proposals to do away with collective making of single-line rates are the equivalent of proposals to do away with collective ratemaking itself. Therefore, if the goals and purposes long recognized as requiring collective ratemaking in transportation, i.e., a uniform, stable, nondiscriminatory, non-preferential structure of rates available to all, remain legitimate public purposes, then proposals ostensibly limited to curbing single-line ratemaking must be defeated just as if they were openly made as proposals to prohibit all collective ratemaking. . . . . . .

<u>Collective ratemaking cannot function without single-line immunity</u>.

Chapter 2

The Economics of Rate Conferences

To insure and facilitate orderly commerce, and, hence, economic growth in the U.S. infrastructure, rate bureaus have evolved.[1] The need for through service and joint rates first arose in the railroad industry because of the economic structure of the industry—a natural monopoly in some respects and a tendency to ruinous competition in others.[2] Collective ratemaking developed in this industry both to stabilize rates and to meet the legal and economic requirements for joint rates and through routes: both required by the Interstate Commerce Act.[3] The subsequent history of collective ratemaking and its conflicts with the U.S. Department of Justice are well known and have received extensive historical documentation.[4] In other words, the rail industry was and is a natural monopoly with inordinate amounts of fixed costs, economies of scale, and a corresponding tendency to discriminate, as evidenced by the short- and long-haul proscriptions.[5]

Conversely, there are over 16,000 motor carriers regulated by the Interstate Commerce Commission that possess a highly fragmentized operating authority and dis-

---

[1]U.S. Congress, Transportation Routes to the Seaboard, 43rd Cong., 1st Sess., Senate Report No. 307, Part 1. Also because of the structure of corporative activities in the railroad industry, consult D. Philip Locklin, Economics of Transportation (7th ed.; Homewood, Ill.: R. D. Irwin, Inc., 1966), p. 195 and Chapter 15.

[2]Ernest W. Williams, Jr., "Railroad Traffic and Costs," American Economic Review, Vol. 33 (June 1943), pp. 360-362; and Daniel Marks, "Group or Conference Ratemaking and National Transportation Policy in the United States," Law and Contemporary Problems (Autumn 1959), p. 591.

[3]Grant M. Davis and Charles S. Sherwood, Rate Bureaus and Antitrust Conflicts in Transportation: Public Policy Issues (New York: Praeger Publishers, Inc., 1975), Chapter 3.

[4]Consult any principles of transportation textbook, especially those sections pertaining to the Reed-Bulwinkle Act of 1948.

[5]Kent T. Healy, The Effects of Scale in the Railroad Industry Committee on Transportation (New Haven: Yale University, 1961), Chapter 1. Also see Merton H. Miller, "Decreasing Average Costs in the Theory of Railroad Rates," Southern Economics Journal, Vol. 21 (April 1955).

play differing economic characteristics, when viewed on an aggregate basis, from the rail industry. That is, a majority of motor costs are variable, and their ability to engage in discriminatory pricing practices appears somewhat limited. Also, the industry is not legally required to publish joint rates and through routes, but for all practical purposes it does so.[6] However, available evidence suggests that economies of scale are present in the industry,[7] particularly through the medium of route intensification,[8] and through practices ranging from procurement to other managerial techniques.[9] But, ruinous competition can exist in the industry as evidenced by Professor D. Philip Locklin[10] and the Interstate Commerce Commission.[11] To view the industry in the aggregate is misleading for several reasons. Firstly, the industry does not conform to the economist's purely competitive model because of market entry limitations and the fundamental fact that the unit of production, in this instance, a freight ton-mile, is not a homogeneous unit of production.[12] Secondly, the intercity trucking industry does not neatly "fit" into the purely competitive model.[13] Thirdly, and more importantly, the industry must of necessity be perceived and examined on a market basis, recognizing that carrier markets are not homogeneous and that levels of price and services competition vary.[14]

The solution to understanding the socio-economic significance of rate bureaus in the motor carrier industry is quite simple. The industry is charged by law to publish rates that are just and reasonable. While confronted with known and established standards of reasonableness, such as recognition of value-of-service, the industry is prohibited from engaging in undue discrimination, preference, or prejudice. This legal proscription is extremely important as it relates to the shipment of commodities and to geographical locations because of existing and potential trade

---

[6] Robert W. Harbeson, "Transportation Regulation: A Centennial Evaluation," *ICC Practitioners' Journal*, Vol. 34 (July/August 1972), pp. 628-637.

[7] Grant M. Davis and L. J. Combs, "A Statistical Analysis of Economies of Scale in the Class I Regulated Motor Carrier Industry," a paper presented before *Southern Economics Association*, Atlanta, Georgia, November 14, 1974, and Garland Chow's subsequent work.

[8] Paul W. Emery, "An Empirical Approach to Motor Carrier Scale Economies Controversy," *Land Economics* (August 1965).

[9] Statement of J. B. Speed, President, Arkansas Best Freight, *Annual Transportation Forum*, Little Rock, Arkansas, May 1977.

[10] Locklin, *loc. cit.*

[11] There are several cases involving motor carrier rate levels that indicate that ruinous competition does exist in this particular industry. These are reported in Donald V. Harper, *Transportation in America* (Englewood Cliffs, N.J.: Prentice-Hall, Inc., 1978).

[12] George W. Wilson, *Essays on Some Unsettled Questions: The Economics of Transportation* (Bloomington, Ind.: Graduate School of Business, Indiana University).

[13] Statement of Grant M. Davis before the U.S. Interstate Commerce Commission in Ex Parte 297, Sub. 4. Also, consult John C. Spychalski, "On Transportation Regulation," *ICC Practitioners' Journal*, Vol. 39 (November/December 1971), pp. 37-52.

[14] That is to say, conceptualizing a market is considerably more meaningful than conceptualizing the industry in an aggregate sense.

relationships. For example, if a steel rate is established between Atlanta and Birmingham and similar transportation characteristics and other economic factors are present, this conceivably could be detrimental to shippers of the same commodity, by the same carrier, say for example, between Chicago and Cleveland.[15] This is not to suggest that trade patterns are maintained, but instead there must be evidence that neither commodities nor communities are unduly discriminated against, and one does not receive undue preference to the prejudice of the other.[16] Through the deliberation process which takes place within the bureau environment, these factors are considered in arriving at a rate or a service decision.

Another important economic aspect of bureaus is the form of service offered to the public. Rates are published in class tariffs, which have the same effect as federal statutes, and involve shipper input.[17] Bureaus employ rate standards similar or identical to those utilized by the Interstate Commerce Commission when establishing rates. That is to say, rates must be just and reasonable and compensatory to comply with statutory tests. Failure to comply with these standards, of course, can result in reparation awards to damaged shippers.[18] In fact, the bureau process subjects all rates to expert analysis for compliance with legal standards before they are filed with the Commission for review.

In all transportation firms there is an unavoidable proportion of joint or common costs that can't be specifically or precisely allocated to a given unit of transportation production. Due to the legal charge to recognize commodity value in setting rates via reasonable classifications, the transportation industry solves the joint cost problem or dilemma by utilizing a varient of the cost accountant's approach to joint cost product pricing, designated as "relative market value." In the transportation industry this is termed "value of service pricing," which is simply "charging what the traffic will bear" or "demand related pricing." This particular form of pricing evolved from a polemic involving Professors Toussig and Pique.[19] Value of service pricing merely allocates joint costs on the basis of commodity value, or, in other words, it is third degree price discrimination which is analogous to the progressive income tax. These rates are published principally in class tariffs which are predicated on value and are progressive with distance.[20] Segregating the various freight submarkets is necessary to implement this form of pricing, together with three other conditions,[21] but the Interstate Commerce Act requires the establishment and publication of reasonable classifications. Rates in

---

[15]This actual situation exists not only between Chicago and Cleveland but also between Cleveland and Dallas with respect to freight moving by common motor carrier.

[16]Statement of Grant M. Davis in the Santa Fe Trail application before the U.S. Interstate Commerce Commission, Houston, Texas, 1978; Fair and Guandolo, loc. cit.

[17]See Kenneth J. Flood, Industrial Traffic Management (Dubuque, Iowa: Wm. C. Brown Co., 1978).

[18]Fair and Guandolo, loc. cit.

[19]Davis and Combs, loc. cit.

[20]For an interesting discussion and revelation concerning the confusion that exists with this type of pricing, consult the 1979 issue of Transportation Research Forum, Papers and Proceedings, containing one paper dealing with value and another with distance.

[21]C. E. Ferguson and S. Charles Maurice, Economic Analysis (Homewood, Ill.: R. D. Irwin, Inc., 1970), pp. 237-238.

the other two types of tariffs, commodities, and exceptions reflect market and product competition and come primarily from "cost of service" considerations.[22]

The basic economic consideration involving freight rates is the method by which they are established. Not only do rate conferences have to conform and comply with known and discernible procedures, but the industrial purchaser also has an active role in the rate determination process. Moreover, through the process of shipper-carrier interaction, the appropriate type of rate increase, when an increase is necessary, is determined, e.g., specific, general, percentage, flat, or actual.[23]

The conference method of ratemaking has successfully demonstrated its ability to allocate resources in the intercity freight market efficiently. Conferences also have proven more efficient, *certis paribus*, in terms of publishing freight tariffs than many individual publications.[24] Given the positive attributes of the economic factors permeating the conference method of ratemaking, these agencies would in all likelihood have to be instituted in order to publish through service rates, in addition to avoiding undue preference, prejudice, and discrimination relative to classes of customers, commodities, and communities.[25] Conferences, because they maintain a known, stable, and predictable rate structure, permit important inputs to the various decisional criteria employed by a business seeking to locate a new economic activity—facilities, modal offerings, labor force, and other important factors.[26]

---

[22]A. L. Morton, "Intermodal Competition for the Intercity Transport of Manufacturers," *Land Economics*, Vol. 48 (November 1972), pp. 357-366; and J. Slass, "The Demand for Intercity Motor Freight Transport: A Macroeconomic Analysis," *Journal of Business*, Vol. 44 (January 1971), pp. 62-68.

[23]In practice, these types of increases can be a mixture of both. Also, consult Grant M. Davis and Alvin Swimmer, "A Methodological Approach for Evaluating Transportation Rate Increases," *ICC Practitioners' Journal*, Vol. 40 (March/April 1973), pp. 308-325.

[24]Grant M. Davis and Charles S. Sherwood, "The Case for Single-Line Immunity," *ICC Practitioners' Journal*, Vol. 43 (September/October 1976), pp. 740-746.

[25]On a practical basis, federal rate regulation cannot be effectively administered without rate bureaus.

[26]Jones and Farris, *loc. cit.*

The Operational Reality
of Independent Rate Making:
Some Empirical Findings*

CHARLES S. SHERWOOD

[Editor's Note: Before Ex Parte 297, Sub. 3, rate bureaus were exempt from antitrust persecution because each member could exercise the right of independent action from any bureau activity. Occasionally some bureaus were requested by carrier members to petition the ICC to suspend an independently announced rate. Although this practice was legal and was not widespread, it was terminated in Ex Parte 297. Was this action incorrect? Charles S. Sherwood in "The Operational Reality of Independent Rate Making: Some Empirical Findings" suggests that the answer to the forementioned question is no, in that the same reasonable standards employed by the ICC are used by the respective conferences.]

The United States' antitrust laws explicitly prohibit cooperation among competitors for the purpose of establishing prices for their goods and services. Despite numerous specifications contained in the Sherman Act and definitive opinions rendered by the U.S. Supreme Court, legislative and judicial framers of public policy have recognized that under certain controlled circumstances justification exists for permitting and facilitating cooperation among competitors. One notable example of such a situation exists in the regulated segment of the transportation industry where common carriers determine their rates, classifications, and other sundry charges and service through group discussion. These rate bureaus, granted legal antitrust immunity by the Reed-Bulwinkle Act, have periodically represented a source of polemics and conflict between antitrust laws and public policy (and regulatory directives) for the past eighty-five years.

Bureau immunity from antitrust prosecution, however, is not complete. Formal institutional procedures require that each carrier be afforded the free and unre-

*Reprinted by permission of the Transportation Journal.

strained right to engage in independent action as a condition precedent for operational approval. Throughout their history the quintessential element providing justification for rate bureau operations has been this allowance for carriers at their discretion to establish rates independently. This provision was designed to provide a safeguard against many of the disagreeable effects normally associated with a cartel type of organization. But, whereas it is possible to legislate safeguards which provide for autonomous behavior it is not possible to legislate the propensity with which such opportunities are exercised. As a result, the future of conference rate making is dependent upon the operational reality of independent action.

The purpose of this study is dichotomous. First, the source and substance of current criticisms of rate bureau activities as they relate to independent action will be examined. Secondly, the current status of independent activity will be presented based on an empirical survey of shippers and rate bureaus. Past studies have concentrated on incidence and bureau protests of independent actions but limited data exist with respect to the degree of success or importance to the shipper of this crucial competitive safeguard. Consequently, an attempt is made to evaluate four dimensions of independent rate making from both the shipper's and bureau's standpoint: (1) Incidence; (2) Success (3) Importance and (4) Bureau protests.

CRITICISMS OF RATE BUREAUS

Historically, rate bureaus evolved as a direct result of a desire by railroads to avoid the vagaries of destructive competition.[1] Subsequent federal regulatory legislation stimulated their growth in an attempt to achieve a system of uniform and stable rates. Cooperative behavior, moreover, was encouraged further by directives of the original Act to Regulate Commerce which required through routes and joint rates. However, their corporate existence was considered an anathema to the politicoeconomic system of free competition and they were eventually deemed to be in violation of the country's antitrust regulations.[2] Despite these adverse judicial opinions as awareness of the necessity for some degree of cooperation among carriers in order to achieve a coordinated and efficient transportation system endured.

Renewed Justice Department prosecutions during the 1940's rejuvenated industry and congressional attempts to attain legal status for rate bureaus and despite strong opposition and a presidential veto, immunity to discuss rates and related matters was conferred upon these organizations in 1948.[3] A review of congressional hearings and legislative debates surrounding this significant legal exemption indicates that the key provision justifying antitrust immunity was the right of bureau members to independently establish rates free from bureau constraints. Indeed, subsequent Interstate Commerce Commission interpretations of section 5a carefully protected this important safeguard against any possible deleterious effects of cooperative rate making.[4]

Although the Reed-Bulwinkle Act resolved a perennial conflict between federal antitrust statutes and Interstate Commerce Act directives, it did not stifle academic and industrial criticism. In addition, new public policy statements, exemplified by President Kennedy's 1962 "Transportation Message" revealed that there was a growing desire for simultaneously increasing competition and reducing transportation regulation.[5] Even though rate bureaus were not specifically enumerated, the message's implication was simply that independent action had failed to provide the desired degree of competition. One writer characterized this observation by stating: ". . . in practice, this right is little more than a sterile gesture. To the rate bureaus, it represents a minor annoyance which cannot break down the self-imposed restraints 'born of history, habit, and strong mutual self-interest.'"[6]

The lack of independent activity was further attacked in a widely publicized Nader report in 1970 which contended "the right to independent action as a safeguard against excessive charges and monopoly pricing is a myth."[7] The report concluded that "rate bureaus negate whatever elements of intramodal rate competition that might remain from the increased concentration levels and regulatory impingements of recent decades."[8] In an attempt to support these comprehensive and nebulous allegations rate bureau statistics were cited indicating that in 1968 less than 15 percent of the rates of 17 motor carrier rate bureaus were established independently from bureau procedure. Five reports, moreover, showed between 25 percent and 35 percent independent rates and only two with more than 35 percent. Based solely on these limited statistics, a myopic conclusion was inferred that these percentages demonstrated a lack of the free and unrestrained right of carriers to initiate independent action.[9]

A second often criticized bureau activity concerns their ability to protest independent action.[10] This right, which until recently had been carefully safeguarded by Interstate Commerce Commission interpretations of section 5a, was frequently cited by critics as an avenue to discourage independent activity.[11] The Nader report also refers to the "now prevalent automatic practice of challenging a deviant or new rate as a matter of course."[12] This conclusion was reached without any empirical evidence with respect to the percentage of proposals or rates protested by rate associations.

On November 11, 1971, the Department of Transportation submitted a bill to Congress entitled "Transportation Regulatory Modernization Act of 1971" that contained provisions for reducing the scope of rate bureau operations. Emphasizing conflicts with present national transportation policy, the Department recommended removing a bureau's right to protest independently established rates and collectively discuss single line rates.[13] Both provisions were aimed at attaining an increase in the amount of independent carrier activity. Legislative hearings revealed conflicting testimony with respect to the reality of independent action and the use of bureau protests as an automatic weapon against recalcitrant members. While this bill was never reported out of committee, it generated considerable interest in the question of conference rate making.[14] In response to questions surrounding the Regulatory Modernization Bill, the Commission ordered a sweeping probe of all carrier rate making organizations.[15]

In January of 1974 the Department of Transportation renewed its efforts to reduce the influence of rate bureaus. A new bill, entitled "Transportation Improvement Act of 1974," would have prohibited railroads from discussing single line rates and protesting independent actions and prohibited motor carrier bureaus from protest demonstrated that the rate appeared to be less than variable cost of service.[16]

These attempts to reduce conference rate making activities culminated in June 1975 when the I.C.C., citing a potential stifling effect on price competition, issued an order prohibiting rate bureaus from opposing independent filings of its member carriers.[17] This move represented a reversal of Commission policy which historically has supported bureau protests of independent action as being sanctioned by sections 216 (e) and (g) of the Interstate Commerce Act.[18]

While the move by the I.C.C. has settled the question for the moment, it does not appear that the controversy has ceased. For example, late in August 1975, six motor carrier bureaus asked the I.C.C. to reconsider its order, claiming it acted beyond its statutory authority. They strongly objected to the prohibition of protesting independent actions. Regardless of the outcome of this challenge, one factor remains clear and that is the singular importance of independent action as the controlling element justifying the antitrust immunity enjoyed by these associations. The following empirical survey provides some insight into rate bureau activity and the reality of independent rate making.

CURRENT STATUS OF INDEPENDENT ACTION

In an attempt to determine the operational reality of independent action and the extent of bureau protests of independent action an empirical survey covering the calendar year 1972 was conducted.[19] Data was obtained from sixty-four shippers representing twenty different industries. Aggregate traffic expenses for the use of regulated railroad and motor carriers by these shippers during 1972 was in excess of $1.2 billion. Also, bureau statistics were obtained from the Interstate Commerce Commission and additional information was secured from two major railroad bureaus and sixteen major motor carrier bureaus. Four dimensions of independent activity were established; incidence, success, importance of independent action, and incidence of bureau protests of independent actions were selected for analysis.

Incidence

The absolute number of independent actions was obtained directly from rate bureau annual report forms filed with the Commission. This form provided the number of independent proposals filed before and during (or after) regular bureau consideration. A percentage incidence of independent filings was derived as follows:

Percentage Incidence of IA's = Total IA's/
(Regular + Emergency Proposals + IA's taken before Regular Procedure)

This figure provides some indication of the frequency with which the option of independent action is utilized. Data depicted in Table 1 shows the percentage incidence of independent actions for the 34 most active motor carrier bureaus and 16 most active railroad bureaus during 1972 where activity was based on the total number of proposals filed with the bureaus.

This data reveals that almost three out of every ten proposals filed with these bureaus represented independent action. While it is inconceivable to maintain that this figure represents a "significant" degree of autonomous behavior, it does provide evidence that such action is a reality and not a myth. Relative frequencies of independent action experienced by individual bureaus are presented in Table 2. These figures indicate that 58 percent of the bureaus reported that more than 20 percent of their proposals were filed independently. Even more significant is the fact that 28 percent of these bureaus experienced a percentage incidence exceeding 50 percent.

Evaluating the incidence of independent action based on proposals can possibly be misleading in that the number of rates contained within these proposals are not reflected. Three motor carrier bureaus with an aggregate of 15,768 regular and emergency proposals and 3,135 independent proposals reported that these proposals represented an estimated 441,043 and 121,629 rates respectively. Therefore, while independent proposals for these bureaus accounted for 16.6 percent of the total proposals, independent rates represented 21.6 percent of the rates involved in these proposals. The implication is that the number of independently filed rates as a percentage of all rates may be higher than the number of independent proposals as a percentage of total proposals. If this observation is correct, the incidence of independent action may be even higher than the 29 percent originally indicated.

TABLE 1

Incidence of Independent Action—1972

Source	Total Regular and Emergency Proposals	IA's Filed Before Regular Procedure	IA's Filed After Regular Procedure	Total IA's	Percentage Incidence of IA's
Motor Carrier Bureaus	32,922	10,592	1,870	12,462	28.6%
Railroad Bureaus	21,824	3,984	3,702	7,686	29.8%
Total	54,746	14,576	5,572	20,148	29.1%

Source: Rate Bureaus and Organizations, _Annual Report to the Interstate Commerce Commission, 1973_, Annual Report Form ROB.

TABLE 2

Percentage of Proposals Filed During 1972
Represented by Independent Action

Source	Less Than 20%	20%–50%	More Than 50%	Total
Motor Carrier Bureaus	11 (32.4)[a]	11 (32.4)	12 (35.2)	34
Railroad Bureaus	10 (62.5)	4 (25.0)	2 (12.5)	16
Total	21 (42.0)	15 (30.0)	14 (28.0)	50

[a]Represents percentage of total.

Source: Rate Bureaus and Organizations, _Annual Report to the Interstate Commerce Commission_, 1973, Annual Report Form ROB.

Success

Although the absolute or percentage incidence of independent action provides some insight regarding the reality of this form of rate making, it fails to furnish evidence regarding the relative success of autonomous action. An inordinately high incidence of independent filings is inane unless a significant number of these proposals subsequently become effective. That is, if very few of the independently announced rates ever become effective due to bureau pressure or protests the impact of independent rate making would be minimal.

In order to establish the degree of success of independent rate making, shippers were requested to indicate the number of independent actions filed on their behalf during 1972 by carriers and how many of these proposals were published in tariffs. Likewise, bureaus were requested to provide the number of independently filed proposals which became effective during that same time span. Results aggregated from sixty-one shippers and eleven motor carrier bureaus indicated that shippers experienced success in 93.1 percent of the cases and bureaus reported an even higher success rate of 95.4 percent. Such high success rates tend to refute the widespread contention that independent actions are subject to bureau harassment and protest. Even in the event that such tactics are prevalent, existing empirical data implies that such actions are ineffective.

Additional evidence of the high success rate for independent action was obtained by using the actual number of independently announced <u>rates</u> which were published. Five motor carrier bureaus, representing a total of 3,377 independent proposals, reported that 101,174 or 82.1 percent of the rates contained in these proposals had become effective. These high success rates, combined with the percentage incidence of independent rate making, imply that this activity is a viable force in the regulated segment of the transportation industry and not a meaningless safeguard against possible abuses of antitrust immunity.

<u>Importance</u>

Another crucial dimension of independent action is the relative importance of independently established rates. A large number of rates originally set via independent action does not necessarily indicate the extent to which freight moves under these rates or the volume of traffic they generate. In this regard, the importance of a rate or a rate change may be defined from the shipper's viewpoint as the yearly traffic expense incurred for freight moving under that particular rate.

Two measures of importance were developed based on traffic expenses. The first reflects the average importance of an independently announced rate change compared to the average importance of all rate changes. Shippers were requested to report how many rate changes occurred during 1972 which affected their firm and to estimate the yearly traffic expense that would be incurred under these new rates. Sixty-one firms reported that a total of 1,437 rate changes occurred with the average traffic expense affected being $69,251, but the average traffic expense affected by new independently established rates was $85,390 or 23 percent higher. Therefore, from the standpoint of the responding firms, independent actions were more important than rate changes which occurred following regular bureau procedure.

A second measure employed reflects the overall importance of independently established rates to the individual shipper. Traffic executives were asked to disclose their firm's total traffic expenses for the use of regulated carriers during 1972. They were requested, moreover, to estimate what percentage of this total was incurred under rates which were <u>originally</u> established through independent action. Aggregate data for forty-four responding firms indicated that only 12.4 percent of their expenses were traceable to independent rates. While the majority of estimates were less than 15 percent, several firms indicated that the percentage was as high as 95 percent.

<u>Bureau Protests of IA's</u>

Ex Parte 297 has eliminated the bureau's right to protest independent actions. Critics opposed to this right contended that an agency should not have the power to oppose actions of its members who it purportedly represents. Such activity, it was alleged, constituted undue harassment and acted to stifle innovative or independent action. The incidence and high success rate for independent action previously described does not tend to support these contentions. Additional evidence regarding the incidence of bureau protests of independent action, however, is necessary before deriving any conclusions regarding the removal of this activity.

Using the number of independent actions obtained from their annual report, rate bureaus were asked to indicate how many of these actions were protested to the Interstate Commerce Commission. Eighteen bureaus representing 29,209 regular and emergency proposals and 10,249 independent actions reported that 193 protests were filed yielding a protest rate of less than two percent. It is significant to note that eleven of these eighteen bureaus indicated that no protests of independent action were filed during 1972.

Further perception into the incidence of bureau protests was obtained by examining the number of rates actually protested. Viewing only protested proposals may be misleading in that in most cases every rate contained within an independent proposal was not necessarily contested. Data obtained from five major motor carrier bureaus showed that of 103,210 rates contained in independent proposals 855 were protested or less than one percent of all the independent rates. Using either proposals or rates as a base, it is difficult to conclude that rate bureaus were abusing protest procedures or that such action was automatic to any degree.

CONCLUSIONS

The purpose of this article has been to review the origins and basis for current polemics surrounding the independent action dimensions of conference rate making. An attempt was made, moreover, to determine the operational reality of autonomous behavior based on incidence, success, and importance of independent rate making. Finally, in light of recent commission decisions, the propensity with which bureaus protested independent actions was examined.

The results of an empirical study indicated that for the calendar year 1972 the incidence, success rate, and importance of new independently established rates when measured by the amount of shipper's traffic expense affected were all high. Concurrently, bureau protests of independent proposals and rates were extremely low. This data tends to support the contention that independent rate making is a reality and not just a meaningless safeguard against possible rate bureau abuses of power. However, the overall importance of independent rates to shippers indicated that a limited amount of traffic expense is incurred under rates that were originally established outside of rate bureau procedures.

This contradiction is not atypical when examining bureau activities and emphasizes the necessity for careful congressional evaluation before any regulatory changes are instituted. These evaluations should consider <u>all</u> dimensions of independent rate making not merely the incidence with which it occurs but also its degree of success and importance to shippers and carriers. In addition, all parties involved in the rate making process must carefully evaluate the effects of alternative procedures before advocating the elimination of existing institutional mechanisms. Finally, it appears that a reassessment of a bureau's right to protest independent actions may be in order. In light of the alternative means of screening rates, the I.C.C. may find the cure more painful than the problem.

Footnotes

[1]For an extensive review of early rate bureaus activities, consult Grant M. Davis and Charles S. Sherwood, _Rate Bureaus and Antitrust Conflicts in Transportation: Public Policy Issues_ (New York: Praeger Press, 1975), Chapter 2.

[2]United States v. Trans-Missouri Freight Association, 166 U.S. 290 (1897) and United States v. Joint Traffic Association, 171 U.S. 505 (1898).

[3]_Reed-Bulwinkle Act_, 62 Stat. L. 472, 49 U.S.C. 5b.

[4]For a discussion of some of these interpretations see John Guandolo, _Transportation Law_, (Dubuque, Iowa: Wm. C. Brown Company Publishers, 1973), pp. 685-691 and George W. Hilton, "Experience Under the Reed-Bulwinkle Act," _I.C.C. Practitioners' Journal_, (September 1961), XXVIII, pp. 1214-1215.

[5]See U.S. Congress, House, House Document No. 384, 87th Cong., 2nd Sess., 1962.

[6]Walter Adams, "The Role of Competition in the Regulated Industries," _American Economic Review_, (May 1958) 48, p. 533.

[7]Robert C. Fellmeth, _The Interstate Commerce Omission_, (New York: Grossman Publishers, Inc., 1970), p. 137.

[8]_Ibid_., p. 141.

[9]_Ibid_., p. 140. For an opposite view of Fellmeth's report, reference Charles A. Webb, "Mr. Nader: Meet the Consumers of Transportation," _I.C.C. Practitioners' Journal_, (May-June 1970), pp. 554-566.

[10]See for example the position of the Department of Justice given in 298 I.C.C. 411 (1956).

[11]For examples of Commission rulings regarding a bureau's right to protest independent action see 283 I.C.C. 682 (1951), 287 I.C.C. 9 (1958), 288 I.C.C. 578 (1959), 297 I.C.C. 603 (1956), and 321 I.C.C. 460 (1964).

[12]Fellmeth, _op. cit_., p. 139.

[13]See Grant M. Davis, _The Department of Transportation_, (Lexington, Mass.: D. C. Heath & Co., 1970), Chapter 5 where the agency's goals favoring deregulation of transportation are explained.

[14]An in-depth evaluation of this and other bills introduced during the second session of the 92nd Congress can be found in Grant M. Davis, "The Transportation Acts of 1972--An Evaluation," _The Arkansas Business and Economics Review_. (August 1972), Vol. 5, pp. 26-30.

[15]Ex Parte 297—Rate Bureau Investigation was ordered on June 25, 1973.

[16]U.S. Congress, House, "Transportation Improvement Act," HR 12891, 93rd Cong., 2nd Sess., 1974.

[17]Ex Parte 297, Rate Bureau Investigation (Washington: U.S. Interstate Commerce Commission, June 3, 1975, pp. 811-61).

[18]Section 216(e) provides that any organization may make a complaint regarding rates, fares, etc. Section 216(g) empowers the commission to investigate "Upon complaint of any interested party."

[19]Because of the extensive amount of time required on the part of responding firms in order to collect the required data the time span covered by this study had to be limited to one year. It should also be noted that the study was conducted prior to the issuing of Ex Parte 297.

Chapter 3

COLLECTIVE RATEMAKING AND ANTITRUST LAWS

The United States is unique in many ways that range from private ownership of transportation entities[1] to the existence of antitrust statutes. The latter phenomena are predicated on the philosophy that competition results in lower prices, improved quality of products, technological innovations, improved capital base, and a higher standard of living. Competition in the marketplace is optimally supposed to efficiently clear markets and produce desired output. Indeed, the only way that a firm in a purely competitive industry structure can earn an economic profit[2] during the short-run period is through efficiency, and this efficiency is reflected in lower product prices. Since the market mechanism is the principal allocation of resources in our capitalist economy, profits function to attract resources to industries that should expand.[3]

As previously indicated, the purely competitive model does not accurately describe or fit the regulated segment of the intercity trucking industry.[4] Competition exists in the industry, but because of proscriptions against undue preference, prejudice, and discrimination, this competition is primarily in the form of service levels. Nevertheless, due to operating authority, competition in the industry can be and is substantial between carriers serving a city market pair. This competition

---

[1]With the exception of Conrail and Amtrak, the modes of transportation in this country are privately owned. For a contrast of this system, consult the U.S. National Transportation Policies in the year 2000 published by the National Transportation Policy Study Commission, i.e., the sections dealing with comparative transportation systems in other countries.

[2]Donald S. Watson, Price Theory and Its Uses (3rd ed.; Boston: Houghton Mifflin Company, 1972), Chapter 17.

[3]Frank H. Knight, Theory, Uncertainty, and Profit (New York: Harper & Row, 1921), Chapters 1 and 2.

[4]Statement of Grant M. Davis before the U.S. Interstate Commerce Commission in Ex Parte 297. Also, Grant M. Davis and Stephen W. Brown, "Physical Distribution Strategies," The Logistics and Transportation Review, Vol. 1, No. 1 (Summer 1972), pp. 89-98.

has accelerated with Commission adoption of superhighway deviation rules,[5] alternate route authority,[6] and gateway elimination.[7]

However, an individual motor carrier is rarely, if ever, authorized to provide service to all points within the United States, hence, the need for rates covering service by one or more than one carrier. For many years, the railroad industry was confronted with the perplexing dilemma of joint rates and through route mandates from Congress and the antitrust statutes forbidding price setting and market sharing. The dilemma of conflicting federal statutes--the antitrust laws enforced through the courts by the Antitrust Division of the Justice Department in terms of prohibitions against mutual considerations of pricing and the Interstate Commerce Act compelling joint rates and through routes--was ultimately resolved by Congress in 1948 by the Reed-Bulwinkle Act. That statute specifically authorized carriers to form groups for joint or collective consideration of rates, provided certain condition precedents were met. These included: (1) the right of each carrier member of a rate conference to exercise independent action at any time in connection with bureau rate matters; and (2) the bureau agreement to be approved by the Interstate Commerce Commission.[8] The agency has not approved any bureau agreements that have failed to meet statutory requirements. Motor carrier rate agreements are, of course, covered by Reed-Bulwinkle, which became Section 5a of the Interstate Commerce Act.[9]

The Interstate Commerce Commission has periodically responded to pressure from the Antitrust Division regarding collective ratemaking, even though Section 5a provided explicit immunity from the antitrust laws. The challenge continues despite carriers exercising their rights to use independently announced rates in securing their marketing objectives. An inordinate amount of publicity developed from the Nader Report[10] dealing with the ICC, and recent legislation has removed some of the single-line immunity from rail carriers not participating in traffic.[11]

Because of pressure, the ICC instituted Ex Parte 297 and ordered bureaus not to petition the Commission for suspension of an independently announced rate. In the past, acting on instructions from carrier members, bureaus could protest an independently announced rate. The majority of such protests were sustained by the

---

[5] V. Ray Alderson, "Adaption of the Motor Carrier Industry to Present and Perspective Supplies of Fuel," _Transportation Journal_, Vol. 13, No. 3 (Spring 1974), pp. 20-22.

[6] D. Philip Locklin, _Economics of Transportation_ (8th ed.; Homewood, Ill.: R. D. Irwin, Inc., 1978).

[7] U.S. National Transportation Policy Study Commission, Chapter 5.

[8] Grant M. Davis and Charles S. Sherwood, _Rate Bureaus and Antitrust Conflicts in Transportation: Public Policy Issues_ (New York: Praeger Publishers, Inc., 1975), Chapter 3.

[9] Now 49 U.S.C. 10706.

[10] For a reaction to this report, see David E. Wells, "Mr. Nader: Meet the Consumers of Transportation," _ICC Practitioners' Journal_, Vol. 37 (July/August 1970), pp. 768-781.

[11] 4-R Act, 1976.

ICC[12] because the bureaus employed the same standards and tests regarding lawfulness as the Commission. Indeed, in one study it was reported that the ICC upheld rate bureau protests of independently announced rates in 93 percent of all I & S dockets.[13] This certainly indicates that the condition precedent for exempting collective ratemaking from the antitrust laws was not violated by the conferences. Nevertheless, in Ex Parte 297, the Commission prohibited protests against member carrier's independent actions. Still not satisfied, some politicians and executive agencies have launched new drives to eliminate collective ratemaking in its entirety. Bureaus would become merely tariff publishing agencies, functioning purely on a fee basis.[14]

What is the shipper's role in antitrust immunity? Presently, transportation shippers are immune from antitrust prosecution for activities occurring during collective ratemaking. But, as Andrew F. Popper cogently indicates, this immunity will terminate if collective ratemaking is eliminated from the Interstate Commerce Act, thereby exposing shippers and consignees to the vagaries of antitrust enforcement.[15] Not only would shippers and consignees be confronted with the threat of antitrust proceedings in transportation pricing, but the present economic benefits derived from through service rates would also be lost.

Another interesting dilemma that shippers face in the event that collective ratemaking is repealed involves trade associations. On matters of mutual concern, shippers have traditionally banded together in organizations such as the National Industrial Traffic League and the Southern Traffic League for the purpose of supporting or opposing a given carrier proposal involving rates or service. Frequently, these trade associations will intervene in litigation being heard by the ICC, other independent regulatory agencies, and the courts. The impact of eliminating collective ratemaking, with its attendant benefits, could be disastrous to this group.

Any historical review of antitrust laws and their enforcement reveals that the U.S. Department of Transportation (DOT) has been involved in numerous cases that have been inordinately time consuming and expensive to the litigants involved.[16] Also, the 1980 fiscal year budget reveals a substantial increase in appropriation requests and personnel, but a substantial decline in DOT activities.[17] These data, of course, suggest the Department's resources are concentrated on a limited number of firms and activities. Given the history of DOT activities in the area of collective ratemaking, DOT interest in the field will undoubtedly accelerate.[18]

---

[12]Educators' meeting sponsored by the American Trucking Association, Columbia, Maryland, 1977.

[13]Grant M. Davis, "The Important Role of Rate Bureaus in Transportation," Traffic World (1975).

[14]Activities of the Justice Department, Senator Kennedy's Committee on the Judiciary proposals, and the Carter Administration proposals.

[15]Andrew F. Popper, "Shipper Antitrust Liability in a Rate-Deregulated Market: Fundamental Inquiries and Analysis," independent research paper, Washington, D.C., 1979.

[16]U.S. Department of Transportation, annual reports for the years 1972-1979.

[17]Administrative budget of the United States. Also, consult U.S. Department of Transportation, annual report for the year ending 1979.

[18]Considering the active role of the U.S. Department of Transportation in pursuing its policy goal entitled "Achieving Economic Efficiency in Transportation," there is no question in this author's mind but that the DOT efforts will accelerate in this particular activity.

Another interesting aspect of the present antitrust laws that apparently has been overlooked by the Antitrust Division of the Department of Justice involves the domestic airline industry. This industry is not exempt from antitrust in pricing decisions and does not engage in collective ratemaking. But, when airline rate decreases are announced, other carriers promptly meet the new rate level, reemphasizing the observation that the industry is a classic example of a differentiated oligopoly. Yet, general increases have occurred in this segment of the intercity passenger market.[19]

In summary, the antitrust laws are presently excluded from regulating collective ratemaking, where shippers and carriers establish prices that must be reasonable and compensatory. Shippers, carriers, and the public in general benefit from known administrative procedures and appellate rights in this area and, more importantly, from the economic advantages of the stable structure of through service rates which collective ratemaking makes possible.

---

[19] Air Transportation Association of America, Transportation Facts (Washington, D.C.: ATA, 1979).

Shipper Antitrust Liability
in a Rate-Deregulated Market:
Fundamental Inquiries and Analysis*

ANDREW F. POPPER

[*Editor's Note*: When certain conditions are present, Section 5(a) of the Interstate Commerce Act exempts both carriers and shippers from the nebulous antitrust statutes. For a number of years empirical evidence suggested that shippers favored collective ratemaking, but the principal defenders of the pricing method were the ICC and the carrier industry per se. However, only recently, shippers have commenced speaking out in support of collective ratemaking because of the possible alternatives of conducting commerce without the vagueness of the antitrust laws. Andrew F. Popper in "Shipper Antitrust Liability in a Rate-Deregulated Market: Fundamental Inquiries and Analysis" lucidly demonstrates how shippers and trade associations would be precluded in transportation matters. This article also contains inordinate antitrust implications because of positions assumed by associations of shippers such as the National Industrial Traffic League and other groups on rate matters.]

Since the passage of the Reed-Bulwinkle Act[1] in 1948, the process of collective rate making has allowed motor common carriers to participate in establishing rates for transportation services by collective or concerted action without being subjected to antitrust liability. This process of rate establishment has involved both the carrier and the shipper community. Price negotiations are carried out between horizontally and vertically aligned competitors resulting in rates that reflect "negotiated" profit margins, and "negotiated" methodologies for joint

*Reprinted by permission of the author.

transportation services. This negotiation is at once two things: a process critical to the formulation of the remarkably complex rates required in the very sophisticated domestic transportation market, and a collective agreement or understanding resulting in the fixing, stabilizing, or adjusting of prices. Stripped of antitrust immunity, this process would be a direct and probably per se violation of the antitrust laws, depending on the size and power of the parties involved. Per se violations such as price fixing are particularly problematic because of the lack of opportunity to raise justifications for a specific price stabilizing process.[2] Indeed, liability would flow to both carriers and shippers (viewing the shippers and their associations as "purchasers" of a service) who engage in conduct which has the understood and predictable effect of price setting.

For the purposes of this analysis, several assumptions have been made regarding shippers. First, it is assumed that "collective action" is in fact a substantial part of the present practice of shippers, through various shipper associations or, in a less formal manner, by agreement between shippers who have mutually consonant transportation needs. This action involves a process of general agreement between shippers which range from commodity classification questions to projected pricing of direct transportation needs, as well as other common collectively resolved matters.

Second, it is presumed that the collective shipper activity is done with the intention of expediting and simplifying the transportation of goods, and not with the express intent of "fixing a price" or creating "monopoly power" by shipper groups. While stabilizing prices or rendering prices uniform is the apparent effect of such collective action, it in no way reflects the kind of intent commonly referred to as predatory intent. Instances of predation in rate negotiation are relatively few and are not discussed in this analysis.

Third, it is presumed that concepts such as "collective conduct," "concerted action" and "conspiracy" are used to describe action where a group of shippers act in concert to achieve a desired end, either in communicating price demands to carriers or rate bureaus, or in communicating other service variables to the carriers or their representatives. Such terminology is not used to suggest overt unlawful activity, and indeed, at the present time, most such activity is fully shielded from antitrust scrutiny, as is suggested in section one of this analysis.

The question of whether the immunity should be retained pursuant to the Reed-Bulwinkle Act has received considerable attention recently as a matter of legal and economic theory. The White House,[3] the Congress,[4] and various administrative agencies[5] have directed considerable energy toward resolving the question of the immunity granted to carriers who participate in collective rate establishment. The analysis that follows is not aimed at carrier immunity, but rather at the shipper community and the consequences of eliminating the immunity that surrounds collective rate establishment.

I. The first question that must be asked is whether shippers are in fact immune from antitrust liability vis-a-vis their participation in collective rate making. Does the explicit immunity which results after a 5(a) agreement has been approved for a bureau or carrier group implicitly or derivatively immunize shippers?

Clearly, if a statute expressly immunizes conduct, detailing who is to be immunized, there is little problem. The problem faced by the shippers involves instead non-explicit immunity. The Supreme Court has suggested that there is no "implicit immunity" in the antitrust area as those laws are applied to various regulated industries. In United States v. Philadelphia National Bank[6] the court found the banking industry which is regulated by the Federal Reserve, Department of Treasury, and rigorous state laws, not immunized by implication. Simply stated, the antitrust laws "will not be displaced unless it appears that the antitrust and regulatory provisions are plainly repugnant" and at that point an efficient and precise regulatory system must supplement those laws.[7]

The traditional approach of the Supreme Court relating to implied immunity has focused on two "non-explicit" immunities, both based on constitutional compulsion. The first is the so-called Noerr[8] doctrine which is directly applicable to the motor carrier industry.[9] Noerr and later cases establish an immunity for collective action by apparent competitors where the sole purpose is influencing a legislative determination. Because such lobbying is vital to the legislative process and because the proscription of such activity based on the antitrust laws might be a constitutionally impermissible intrusion of First Amendment rights[10] the courts have carved out a very narrow exception for such behavior. The exception for Noerr lobbying is limited by at least two factors. The first is related to "sham" activity, i.e., First Amendment activity designed to injure competitors rather than advocate a point of view effecting legislation. The second is a "purpose" limitation, relating to the absolute necessity that the otherwise impermissible collective activity not be directed to matters such as price establishment, territorial allocation, or similar prohibited acts. Shipper associations may have difficulty with these tests.

The second traditional immunity is embodied in Parker v. Brown,[11] as modified in Lafayette[12] involving the state action doctrine. Under that doctrine, activity which has been the subject of state regulation may be immunized, but again only in the most narrow context. Neither of these exceptions, however, supports the derivative immunity presently enjoyed by shippers as it emanates from the Reed-Bulwinkle Act. Interestingly, the case of United States v. Southern Motor Carriers Rate Conference[13] suggests that there may be a need for Parker compulsory state regulation and Noerr factors before immunity attaches to collective rate making effecting intrastate rates.

What is the basis then for the immunity of the shippers? Is there a derivative immunity outside of the specific legislative mandate? Relating to regulated industries, Professor Sullivan has stated:

> If any generalization is warranted, it is that there is an increasing tendency to assume that competition, and hence antitrust norms, ought to apply, except to the extent that these are inconsistent with clear, discernible regulatory objectives expressed or implied in the regulatory statute.[14]

It is safe to say that under the Reed-Bulwinkle Act,[15] it is anticipated that shippers will have input into the rate establishment process to a significant degree to optimize the flow of information vital to the establishment of collectively produced rates. To have this input become a critical part of a statutory scheme and then to impose liability on shippers for such activity would be inconsistent with Congressional intent.

There are two basic requirements, outside of those mentioned, that must be met before collective shipper conduct can be clearly said to fall in the penumbra of the Reed-Bulwinkle immunity; initial consideration of general competitive consequences and some form of continuing regulatory supervision.[16] For the shippers, there was consideration in the legislative debate surrounding the passage of the act in 1948.[17] This consideration appears to have manifested itself in integrating the shippers into the rate establishment process in numerous ways. On April 28, 1978, Chairman Daniel O'Neal of the Interstate Commerce Commission testified as follows:

> The rates to be published by the carriers may be agreed upon jointly through the carrier's rate bureau activities or by independent action of the carrier. A protest challenging the lawfulness of the proposed rate may be filed by any person, except that a rate bureau may not protest their carriers' independent actions. Many shippers subscribe to tariff watching services or join associations such as the National Small Shipments Traffic Conference in order to more effectively monitor or protest rate actions which affect them.
>
> * * *
>
> After a rate has been allowed to become effective (i.e., not suspended) and not investigated, shippers can challenge its lawfulness by filing a complaint. Such proceedings may result in a finding that the rate is shown to be unlawful and an order requiring its cancellation.[18]

Furthermore, the ICC has recently adopted rules on rate bureau activity to open the process, fully eliminate bureau protests on independent action, and, in general, increase the degree of regulatory oversight, thus completing the second tier of the immunity analysis.[19]

Taken at its most basic level, consideration of competitive consequences of immunity must occur at the legislative inception of the grant and, to a degree, thereafter. Further, in the "subsequent review" function of the government, the overall process must be assessed from time to time, to insure its proper functioning. A perfect example of such ongoing review is Ex Parte 297, Sub-No. 4[20] where the Interstate Commerce Commission, having jurisdiction over an immunized process (carrier collective rate making) is reviewing the process in detail. This review obviously does not include a "congressional level" inquiry as to whether the immunity is justifiable from a policy standpoint.

Indeed the ICC has been reviewing the collective rate making process almost constantly for the last seven years:

> The Commission's reassessment of collective ratemaking began in 1972. In July 1973, on our own motion, we instituted a major investigation which resulted in a number of new requirements for approval of ratemaking agreements.
>
> * * *
>
> In June 1977 we instituted another proceeding at the request of the Department of Justice. . . . We directed that the rate bureaus must notify carriers and shippers of proposals to change such rates, provide an opportunity for reply, and obtain the carriers' written consent before making the changes.
>
> * * *
>
> In December 1977 we instituted a rulemaking on our own motion to determine whether the restrictions imposed by the 4-R Act on railroad ratemaking agreements should also govern the collective ratemaking agreements of other modes.
>
> * * *
>
> In December 1977 we started an ambitious project of reevaluating

every existing rate bureau agreement to determine whether it still conforms with the statute. Many of these agreements were approved over 15 years ago. Most of the parties to the agreements have subsequently filed the additional evidence we requested.

Our staff has also been conducting random inspections of rate bureau proceedings. We have promised to give priority attention to any specific complaints or irregularities. Thus far, the monitoring reports have shown the bureaus to be in substantial compliance with their agreements and with the Commission's requirements.[21]

Thus there seems little question that there is administrative oversight regarding the ongoing immunity grant. There is also judicial review of administrative action. In deciding if state regulation provided a bar to activity outside of a direct Noerr exception,[22] a federal district court joined the entourage of those involved in review of collective rate making.[23] That court found "price fixing" not within Noerr as a state immunity phenomenon and not a compulsory part of the state regulated collective ratemaking process.[24] The court also found as follows relating to the type of immunity which might be enjoyed by shippers:

> The case may arise in which a regulatory or legislative scheme, while not explicitly requiring a particular act, is structured so as to render the act indispensable to compliance with the scheme. In this sense an anticompetitive activity may be protected because it is impliedly or constructively compelled by the state.[25]

It should be noted that this form of derivative immunity is generally problematic in the antitrust world. Its existence is predicated on a legislative enactment directed to carriers, for carrier activity. Yet to disclaim its force is to ignore Congressional intent in the initial balancing of public interests that led to the passage of the act, and to ignore thirty years of non-prosecution of shippers for collective activity by various shipper associations.

The immunity the shipper enjoys can also be said to emanate from the statute itself. The Reed-Bulwinkle Act immunizes those specifically included in an agreement and, by reference, those "other persons" critical to such an approved collective rate making agreement.

> If the Commission approves the agreement, it may be made and carried out under its terms and under the conditions required by the Commission, and the Sherman Act (15 U.S.C. 1, et seq.), the Clayton Act (15 U.S.C. 12, et seq.), the Federal Trade Commission Act (15 U.S.C. 41, et seq.), sections 73 and 74 of the Wilson Tariff Act (15 U.S.C. 8 and 9), and the Act of June 19, 1936, as amended (15 U.S.C. 13, 13a, 13b, 21a), do not apply to parties and other persons with respect to making or carrying out the agreement.[26] (emphasis added)

The "other persons" critical to the efficient functioning of the collective rate establishment process include shippers, since shippers are designated entities for challenge and protest of rates.[27] That shippers' collective activity enjoys this immunity was quite clear to the Congress when the Reed-Bulwinkle Act was passed. The minority report to the bill states the immunity in broadest terms:

> This bill would not only allow antitrust exemption of the private

rate-making conferences and bureaus maintained by the carriers, as did the legislation proposed in 1943, but would allow exemption of every operation of the regulated transportation industry from antitrust prosecution.[28]

The majority report provided a slightly different focus, looking to the function of the bureau as "media through which (carriers) . . . confer with their shippers and consult their wishes and needs before reaching their determination with respect to rates; . . . as a result . . . the volume of rate litigation . . . is greatly reduced." Shipper support for the initial bill was apparently based on facilitating the process of rate making[30] not on the immunity which has flowed to the shipper groups which collectively impact the rate process. It is noteworthy, however, that the support came from a joint association, the National Industrial Traffic League,[31] a group which would have a difficult time functioning today as a collective rate negotiator in the absence of Reed-Bulwinkle protection.[32]

The period prior to the passage of the Reed-Bulwinkle Act was characterized by a frontal assault on the collective rate making process. This is also set out in the legislative history:

> Efforts at Chicago in 1942 to indict certain railroads, motor carriers, and others under the antitrust laws for participating in those activities were stopped because it was believed that such prosecution would seriously interfere with the war effort. Early in 1943 an indictment under the antitrust laws of certain motor carriers and motor carrier rate associations was returned at Denver and, after trial, all of the defendants were acquitted by the verdict of a Federal court jury. In 1943 a certificate was issued by the Chairman of the War Production Board declaring rate bureaus and similar carrier organizations to be requisite to the prosecution of the war. In 1944 an injunction suit under the antitrust laws was brought by the Department of Justice in the United States District Court for the District of Nebraska against the western railroads and the Association of American Railroads and others to enjoin them from carrying on various cooperative activities, and that suit is still pending. In the same year a further injunction suit under the antitrust laws was brought in the United States Supreme Court by the State of Georgia against the eastern and southern railroads to enjoin them from various cooperative activities. The Court took jurisdiction of that suit, and has appointed a special master to take evidence as to the allegations involved therein and to make appropriate findings and conclusions. Evidence has been offered before the master, but the Court has not yet decided the case on its merits. The Georgia suit involves activity only in the field of rate making while the Nebraska suit involves activity with reference to both rates and matters of transportation service.[33]

There is little reason to think that repeal of the Reed-Bulwinkle Act would lead to a situation different from that set out by the committee report. The immunity is truly a bar to otherwise commonplace antitrust prosecution against carriers and shippers who participate in collective negotiation of rates.

II. Assuming there is presently immunity pursuant to section 10706,[34] a repeal of Reed-Bulwinkle would mean the loss of that immunity and application of the antitrust laws. Which antitrust laws are in fact in question?

The system of antitrust enforcement is vast and complex. Sections four and five of this analysis address who can be sued and by whom. This question is more basic. The Sherman Act[35] states in relevant part:

> §1.
> Every contract, combination in the form of trust or otherwise, or conspiracy, in restraint of trade or commerce among the several States, or with foreign nations, is declared to be illegal. Every person who shall make any contract or engage in any combination or conspiracy hereby declared to be illegal shall be deemed guilty of a felony, and, on conviction thereof, shall be punished by fine not exceeding one million dollars if a corporation, or, if any other person, one hundred thousand dollars or by imprisonment not exceeding three years, or by both said punishments, in the discretion of the court.[36]
>
> §2.
> Every person who shall monopolize, or attempt to monopolize, or combine or conspire with any other person or persons, to monopolize any part of the trade or commerce among the several States, or with foreign nations, shall be deemed guilty of a felony, and, on conviction thereof, shall be punished by fine not exceeding one million dollars if a corporation, or, if any other person, one hundred thousand dollars or by imprisonment not exceeding three years, or by both said punishments, in the discretion of the court.[37]

While the act does not preempt or supersede state law[38] it stands as the "magna carta" of free enterprise and is one of the singularly most powerful pieces of legislation within the enforcement capabilities of the federal government. It is directed at competition and not necessarily at competitors[39] though it is available to redress aggrieved competitors with treble damages. It is a law that operates with almost regulatory power in terms of "reasonable prices" after the exchange of price related data:

> (In certain markets) . . . (t)he exchange of price data tends toward price uniformity. For a lower price does not mean a larger share of the available business but a sharing of the existing business at a lower return. Stabilizing prices as well as raising them is within the ban of §1 of the Sherman Act. As we said in United States v. Socony-Vacuum Oil Co., "in terms of market operation stabilization is but one form of manipulation." The inferences are irresistible that the exchange of price information has had an anticompetitive effect in the industry, chilling the vigor of price competition.[40] (footnote omitted)

The Sherman Act can be applied with equal vigor to intracorporate conspiracy,[41] highly localized or "mini-market" monopolization,[42] maximum pricing schemes designed to keep prices below a set level,[43] cases where horizontal agreements facilitate competition,[44] condemning such agreements despite their positive effect. Indeed, the act can be used where price influencing agreements artificially control or impact otherwise free market forces.[45] In certain circumstances this powerful legislation can be brought to bear on a particular practice despite the absence of any effect on price, quantity of goods effected or other typical marketing indicia, simply because the kind and subject matter of an agreement (e.g. a group boycott) or the participants in an agreement (horizontally aligned competitors) are deemed, in themselves, dangerous to competition.[46]

Investigation and pre-complaint inquiry is greatly facilitated by the power of the Department to issue civil investigation demands[47] under the Antitrust Civil Process Act which provides as follows:

(a) Whenever the Attorney General, or the Assistant Attorney General in charge of the Antitrust Division of the Department of Justice, has reason to believe that any person under investigation may be in possession, custody, or control of any documentary material relevant to a civil antitrust investigation, he may, prior to the institution of a civil or criminal proceeding thereon, issue in writing, and cause to be served upon such person, a civil investigative demand requiring such a person to produce such material for examination.[48] (emphasis added)

Virtually identical power exists at the Federal Trade Commission, which also has the following subpoena power:

(a) The Commission or any member thereof may issue a subpoena, directing the person named therein to appear before a designated representative at a designated time and place to testify or to produce documentary evidence, or both, relating to any matter under investigation by the Commission. The Directors, Deputy Directors, and Assistant Directors of the Bureaus of the Commission's regional offices, pursuant to delegation of authority by the Commission, without power of redelegation, also may issue investigational subpoenas, and, for good cause shown, may extend the time prescribed for compliance with subpoenas issued during the investigation of any matter. The Director, Deputy Director, Assistant Director, Regional Director, or Assistant Regional Director, who issues any subpoena under this section is authorized to negotiate and approve the terms of satisfactory compliance therewith. Specifically, the subpoena power conferred by section 329 of the Energy Policy and Conservation Act (42 U.S.C. 6299) is included within this delegation. The General Counsel, pursuant to delegation of authority by the Commission, without power of redelegation, may issue investigational subpoenas for matters arising under Section 4.1(e) of these Rules. The General Counsel also may take all other action with regard to subpoenas as are described and delegated in this subsection.[49]

The Federal Trade Commission, like the Department of Justice, is empowered to enforce the Sherman Act, the Clayton Act, and the Federal Trade Commission Act. The Federal Trade Act is extremely broad: "(a) (1) Unfair methods of competition in or affecting commerce and unfair or deceptive acts or practices in or affecting commerce, are declared unlawful."[50]

It presently exempts "common carriers subject to the Acts to regulate commerce"[51] though it is unclear as to how this exemption would be impacted by repeal of Reed-Bulwinkle.[52] The Federal Trade Commission has vast power and the capacity to not only prosecute "violators" of its "unfair practices" mandate, but also issue rules and regulations which form guidelines for behavior within a specific industry.

Trade regulation rule proceedings may be commenced by the Commission upon its own initiative or pursuant to written petition filed with the Secretary by any interested person stating reasonable grounds therefor.[53]

With the power to prosecute or issue rules if there is "any interested person" of the reasonable view that a practice is unfair, the F.T.C. stands as a massive antitrust enforcement agency. It has broad discretionary power to impose remedies so long as there is some reasonable relationship between the remedy and the violation.[54] With such power, dissolution and industrial restructuring are not unlikely remedies for shipper associations which participate in collective price fixing.

Beyond the Sherman Act and the Federal Trade Commission Act, there are two other statutes commonly thought of when the term "antitrust laws" is mentioned.[55] They are the Clayton Act[56] and the Robinson Patman Act.[57] Both laws condemn various price related restraints which would be relevant to collective rate negotiation but for the fact that both acts require that a commodity transaction be contemplated, and not a service transaction. Transportation services by common carriage are not a commodity transaction, giving the term its "natural meaning."[58] Should Reed-Bulwinkle be repealed and concomitantly the commodity clauses be excised so as to include shipper-carrier collective rate establishment, the effect would be dramatic. For example, the Clayton Act provides:

> It shall be unlawful for any person engaged in commerce, in the course of such commerce, to lease or make a sale or contract for sale of goods, wares, merchandise, machinery, supplies, or other commodities, whether patented or unpatented, for use, consumption, or resale within the United States or any Territory thereof or the District of Columbia or any insular possession or other place under the jurisdiction of the United States, or fix a price charged therefor, or discount from, or rebate upon, such price, on the condition, agreement, or understanding that the lessee or purchaser thereof shall not use or deal in the goods, wares, merchandise, machinery, supplies, or other commodities of a competitor or competitors of the lessor or seller, where the effect of such lease, sale, or contract for sale or such condition, agreement, or understanding may be to substantially lessen competition or tend to create a monopoly in any line of commerce.[59] (emphasis added)

The phrases "may be to substantially lessen competition" and "tend to create a monopoly" are expressly designed to allow for terminating competitive infraction in its incipiency, *i.e.* at the first plausible sign of concentration. This provides for extremely broad latitude and prosecutorial discretion.

III. The next logical inquiry relates the application of the antitrust laws on activities that are intrastate (i.e., local shipper group associations) and of only limited market effect. Do these two factors foreclose federal antitrust scrutiny?

The direct answer is that the absence of patent interstate effect on a market that has national dimensions has rarely been a stumbling block to the application of the antitrust laws.[60] In the context of interstate shipping, it is hard to see how a jurisdictional bar to the antitrust laws based exclusively on intrastate impact would be found.

As to market effect itself, the courts vary from requiring an appreciable effect on a clearly defined market to the notion that price fixing has a *per se* unlawful effect, regardless of the market shares and discernible impact of the parties' behavior in the market place. Two fairly recent Supreme Court decisions deal with this phenomenon.

In *U.S. v. American Bldg. Maintenance Industries*[61] the Court found: ". . . the Sherman Act has been applied to local activities which, although not themselves within the flow of interstate commerce, substantially affect interstate commerce."

This appears to suggest a need for market effect beyond that of the predictable impact of smaller association collective price establishment depending on how the market is drawn. However, in the same term the Court handed down the decision in *Hospital Building Company v. Trustees of Rex Hospital*[62] which seems to suggest a rather different interpretation of the law.

This case involved an alleged conspiracy between a small private hospital, two corporate officers, and a health planner to block the relocation of a competitor private hospital which was in the midst of a development program. The hospitals involved were extremely small[63] and the percentage of commerce affected was not substantial, viewing the national, statewide or even local region health care delivery systems. The Court treated the issue of substantial effect as follows:

> An effect can be "substantial" under the Sherman Act even if its impact on interstate commerce falls far short of causing enterprises to fold or effecting market price. It was sufficient . . . that the allegations in the complaint, if proved, could show that the conspiracy resulted in "unreasonable burdens on the free and uninterrupted flow . . . (of a given entity in commerce)." We did not demand allegations, either express or implied, that the conspiracy threaten the demise of out-of-state business or that the conspiracy affect market prices.[64]

The consequences of this opinion on the shipping community are dramatic. Any notion of safety that a small shipper association has vis-a-vis antitrust enforcement based on size is an illusion. Where a group (two or more) of horizontally aligned entities uses its collective power directly or through a negotiator or agent, the Sherman Act prohibition against "combinations in restraint of trade" is activated.

Another part of the same inquiry addressed further in question seven involves whether the antitrust laws were intended for smaller manufacturers who are purchasers of transportation services. That is, is it clear that small shippers or small shipper associations will actually be sued? Is not the Sherman Act directed to sellers, not buyers?

Regarding the scope of the Sherman Act, the Court held that the act encompassed all non-exempt commerce: "language more comprehensive is difficult to conceive. On its face it shows a carefully studied attempt to bring within the Act every person engaged in business whose activities might restrain or monopolize commercial intercourse among the states."[65] (emphasis added)

There seems therefore to be little question of the vulnerability of the small shipper association and no question of vulnerability of a group of shippers who have any substantial degree of market power and who act collectively.[66] These larger entities tempt both the application of section one of the Sherman Act, relating to contract and combinations in restraint of trade, and also section two, particularly where there is monopsony.

Where the market place for collective interaction becomes the forum for price fixing, the size of the market will be of little significance.[67] Collective activity which facilitates competition is questionable but collective activity designed to fix a price is unreasonable and condemned.[69]

IV. On the other side of the prior question comes the issue of who can avail himself of these antitrust laws in attacking a shipper group which participates in collective price establishment.

Section 4 of the Clayton Act provides that:

> Any person who shall be injured in his business or property by reason of anything forbidden in the antitrust laws may sue therefor in any district court of the United States in which the defendant resides . . . without

> respect to amount in controversy, and shall recover threefold the damages by him sustained, and the cost of suit, including a reasonable attorney's fee.[70]

This language clearly opens the door for treble damage actions by shippers of like commodities excluded from the association, carriers claiming price effecting consequences, and probably consumers as well. The consumer actions could be initiated by the various state attorneys general pursuant to the Antitrust Improvement Act of 1976[71] or in a consumer class action pursuant to <u>Reiter v. Sonotone</u>.[72] In any event, protected are "all who are made victims of the forbidden practices by whomever they may be perpetrated."[73]

There are also three other groups who will have an active and apparent stake in antitrust prosecution should deregulation occur: the United States Federal Trade Commission, the United States Department of Justice, and the forty or so state attorneys general charged with the responsibility of antitrust enforcement. On June 29, 1979, Elliot Seiden, Chief of the Transportation Section of the U.S. Department of Justice, Antitrust Division, presented a paper to the ICC Practitioners' Association, in which he advised that group that the consequence of deregulation for the carriers would be the possibility of criminal sanctions should collective rate establishment continue. He stated "if antitrust immunity for agreements between motor carriers is withdrawn . . . collective ratemaking activities will expose . . . corporate officers as well as the companies to the penalties of the Sherman Act."[74] While Mr. Seiden is referring to carriers, it seems safe to assert that shippers would likely be subjected to similar liability if they collectively establish rates. Indeed, Mr. Seiden goes on to note that these penalties are civil and criminal sanctions, involving fines up to $1,000,000 and incarceration up to three years.[75] To avoid these onerous consequences, the Department urges that impacted entities "begin considering, even today, the preparation and dissemination to your clients of antitrust compliance programs."[76] This is good advice, should deregulation occur, for there is no question that absent the cooperative shaping of price programs <u>with the government</u>, antitrust liability will occur.

At the Federal Trade Commission (FTC), a similar interest is evident. In recent years the FTC has undertaken to exercise its jurisdiction over many practices which are far less direct in their effect on pricing. In a consent order of July 1979, the FTC has barred interference by the Inland Empire Roofing Contractors Association in the pricing practices of the Association's membership. This group of roofers had used the Association as a vehicle for price compilation and establishment, a process not dissimilar with that of literally hundreds of shipper associations. Also in July 1979, the FTC entered into a consent agreement with the Appliance Dealers Cooperative of New Jersey to cease interfering with price decisions of members, a process the FTC believes should be impacted only by normal market forces. The Appliance Dealers Cooperative is a buyers' association; i.e., it acts on behalf of its membership to purchase appliances. Again, the parallel with shipper associations is apparent.

One final note on the FTC interest. As mentioned in part two of this analysis, section five of the Federal Trade Commission Act condemns "unfair methods of competition in commerce, and unfair or deceptive acts or practices . . ."[77] It is an extremely broad provision which can be used as a jurisdictional base over acts as varied as deceptive practices in advertising or for relatively straight-forward antitrust price fixing problems. For price formula problems, the FTC standards are vague and do not give an absolutely clear picture as to how the Commission might react to shippers involved in collective rate establishment. Last year the FTC articulated this standard:

> We must note that our conclusion that Section Five prohibits such conduct depends importantly upon the extreme <u>artificiality of the formula pricing</u>

involved . . . The artificiality of pricing system is what at once suggests that its results are likely to depart from competitive norms and on the other hand that its use has little redeeming commercial justification, assumptions that are borne out by the record before us.[78] (emphasis added)

This standard raises the issue of "commercial justification" of collective shipper and carrier price establishment. Whether such justification exists is an open question discussed in section seven, part five of this study. Viewing the Supreme Court's analysis of association price establishment and the notion of a justification, it appears that the defense would be unavailable. In *United States v. Container Corporation of America*,[79] the defendants participated in a voluntary noncoercive price exchange program that involved the exchange of price data of consummated, not current, transactions. The Court held this price exchange to be *per se* unlawful on the basis that "(p)rice is too critical, too sensitive a control to allow it to be used even in an informal manner to restrain competition."[80] However, the Court recognized earlier in the opinion that there may, from time to time, exist certain "controlling circumstances" which might justify a price exchange, e.g., the prevention of fraud or the elimination of certain forms of double dealing. Since this is not the kind of justification extant in collective rate establishment, it seems no such defense would succeed.

V. On the question of collective rate making being "justifiable" or explained by business circumstances, the significance of such justification is unclear. Certainly, the regulatory system allows for a public convenience and necessity balancing—but will the antitrust system do likewise?

In *United States v. Socony Vacuum Oil*[81] the court held that "the elimination of so-called competitive evils is no legal justification for such buying programs," nor a defense to other forms of price fixing. Indeed, *Socony* deflates any "social benefit" defense where the entities act in combination and tamper with a given price structure. This price fixing prohibition is true "(e)ven though the members of the price fixing group were in no position to control the market, to the extent that they raised, lowered, or stabilized prices they would be directly interfering with the free play of market forces."[82]

The justifications relating to convenience and economies have not fared well after *Socony*, due in large part to *Socony's* overt and unequivocal language.

> Congress has not left (the Supreme Court) the determination of whether or not particular price fixing schemes are wise or unwise, healthy or destructive. It has not permitted the age-old cry of ruinous competition and competitive evils to be a defense to price fixing conspiracies. It has no more allowed genuine or fancied competitive abuses as a legal justification for such schemes than it has the good intentions of the members of the combination.[83]

It is also true that in recent years, the Supreme Court has become more lenient in the business justification area.[84] However, they have not relaxed the stance on direct competitor price fixing to any significant degree. In April, 1979, the court did take a slightly less animated look at an agreement that focused on a negotiation process (blanket licensing) impacting price without applying the *per se* illegality formulation of *Socony*. The case, *Broadcast Music Inc. v. Columbia Broadcasting*,[85] states: "Not all arrangements among actual or potential competitors that have an impact on price are *per se* violations of the Sherman Act, or even unreasonable restraints." In that case, however, the fee set was standard, open to all purchasers, and was a fee for the use of any compositions, factors not easily equated with the complex motor carrier rate setting process.

VI. Perhaps a not so obvious question plaguing the notion of shipper liability relates to the fact that shippers are consumers of the service, not sellers, and as purchasers, do not set prices, but rather pay those that are set. Can a shipper of goods in commerce be a "price fixer" for the rates ultimately charged by a carrier or carriers?

This question is answered based on which shipper is involved, how the price is established, how much commerce in a given line is affected and the like. A leading scholar, Professor Lawrence Sullivan, has stated, "if dealers (purchasers) negotiated concertedly with manufacturer (seller) over the price charged by the manufacturer on sales to dealers, the dealers would be violating the *per se* rule against concerted action by competitors affecting price."[86] Sullivan goes on to note that as to purchaser price fixing, "the case law gives little aid about how far joint negotiation may go; indeed, even despite the clarity of the *per se* analysis, the case law may invite a *vague* hope that dealers can concertedly negotiate with the manufacturer about price,—or . . . through an association, could gather and present data the thrust of which was that the manufacturer's prices were too high . . ."[87]

In the final analysis Sullivan seems to follow the *Socony* line of reasoning on purchaser price fixing. "But when the activity we are being asked to approve is joint negotiating over price, we are too close to the central nervous system of the market to affirm the joint activity without a profound and convincing showing of benefits which offset the risks."[88]

Again, if there is a doubt that a private entity or Justice would be successful in an action against shipper (purchaser) associations, there is little question that the F.T.C. would prevail. In *Virginia Excelsior Mills, Inc. v. Federal Trade Commission*[89] the court addressed the question of whether smaller collective action cases were within the ambit of Section 5 of the Federal Trade Commission Act.[90] The court took as a given that these cases were within Section five, addressing thereafter the issue of whether the conduct was *per se* unlawful, as opposed to subject to a rule of reason analysis. As to collective conduct, the court held:

> Evidently, and appropriately, the Commission wishes to make it clear that, however the concerted action of the producers was characterized, it should not continue. However, in some businesses, it is common practice for several producers to utilize the services of one sales agency, and there is nothing unlawful in such an arrangement when each producer reserves, and exercises, independence in pricing, acceptance of orders, production and other material matters. That there may be no misunderstanding of the scope of the order, in this respect, it is appropriate that we limit the prohibition against the maintenance of a common selling agent to its utilization in aid of a purpose which could not be lawfully accomplished under the order by a direct agreement among the participating producers.[91]

Following the *Excelsior* standard, a shipper association would have to prove the patent impracticability of individual negotiation, an insurmountable burden.

VII. Shipper associations are designed to facilitate the free flow of information between manufacturers and expedite the exchange of ideas and the development of just and appropriate standards for the shipment of the goods produced. Could this activity really be characterized as an unreasonable restraint of trade?

This question is predicated on the assumption that collective rate establishment by shipper and carrier associations will be evaluated, at least in the first instance, by "rule of reason" as opposed to *per se* analytical norms.[92] This is a very legitimate question that is not easily answered, for the resolution depends on eight factors:

1. The veracity of the claim that the shippers' association is primarily interested in data dissemination, not price setting;

2. The size and market power of the association's membership;

3. The extent to which the association implicitly or explicitly binds or compels its membership to adhere to prices or price establishment programs;

4. The membership policy of the association;

5. The extent to which the dissemination of data which is price sensitive can be justified under the "controlling circumstance" exception established in *United States v. Container Corporation of America*,[93] as modified by *United States v. United States Gypsum*;[94]

6. Whether the specific type of data exchanged relates to prior or future transactions;

7. Market comparisons between the exchange of data in a collective rate setting economy versus a setting in which rates are individually negotiated.

8. The market structure of the shipper and carrier groups in the relevant geographic area.

1. *Veracity of Claim of Non Price-Fixing*

As to factor one, an association need not have an avowed purpose to educate the public or its members. However, if the data exchange is price sensitive (as are most data exchanges that a shipper association undertakes) there must be some element of justification resembling a regulatory "public interest test." In *Maple Flooring Mfgrs. Assn. v. United States*[95] the court found that the exchange of data relating to standardization and certification was of sufficient public merit as to offset the anticompetitive consequences of the exchange of price sensitive information. This finding was based on the clear absence of concerted price fixing and the presence of full disclosure of all collective activity to the Department of Commerce. Typical public interests might include an assertion that rates will be unfair, impossible to fairly allocate, incomprehensible, or inconsistent with a price that resembles cost plus a reasonable rate of return if the collective association exchanges and negotiations are not permitted.

> Trade associations must strive to serve the public if the associations' practices are to survive antitrust scrutiny . . . (T)rade association activities which smack of price fixing, group boycott or other *per se* violations, under the guise of standards or ethical (considerations) . . . , will be struck down by the courts without difficulty.[96]

2. and 8. *Power of Participants and Structure of Marketplace*

As to factors two and eight, size and market power, few generalizations seem safe. The greater the market power of the trade association members, the more likely that antitrust consequences will attach to exchange of price-related data. Likewise, the more concentrated the marketplace inhabited by the association members, the more likely that careful scrutiny will be given to the association's practices.[97] The converse of these propositions, however, cannot be said to be uniformly upheld. In a nonconcentrated market where members have only minor market shares, the exchange of price information may very well give rise to liability if there is discernible market impact.

> There is, of course, a theoretical possibility that defendants could engage in a practice of exchanging current price information that was sufficiently prevalent to have had a market-wide impact that they did not know about, but as a practical matter that possibility is surely remote.[98]

However, while not dispositive, market structure is critical. "A number of factors including most prominently the structure of the industry involved and the nature of the information exchanged are generally considered in divining the procompetitive or anticompetitive effects of this type of interseller communication."[99]

In a marketplace where a relatively small number of shippers control a substantial portion of the market (oligopsony, or a concentrated purchaser market) the consequences of data exchange or joint negotiation may be presumptively unlawful. This has been federal dogma for half a century, expressed frequently in the courts and in Congress in final and assertive terms:

> The increased concentration of economic power is dooming free enterprise. The present trend of great corporations to increase their economic power is the antithesis of meritorious competitive development.[100]

The validity of these assertions is open to challenge, and in recent years the notion that size and concentration are anathema to the national policy favoring competition has been openly attacked.[101] The attacks, however, have not been readily translated into judicial determinations that evidence similar treatments to concentrated or nonconcentrated markets.[102]

3. and 4. <u>Association Membership Policy and Practices</u>

Factors three and four relate to elements approaching intent to restrain trade, i.e., coercive compliance and boycott elements. Either factor could tend to make the anticipated practice <u>per se</u> unlawful under the Sherman Act or under the Clayton Act. The statutory language of section 3 of the Clayton Act is significant in that it prohibits the acts of boycott, coercion, or intimidation.[103] It should be noted that "intent" is not just direct motive, as is commonly construed, but can include any behavioral manifestation that has as its logical consequence an overt effect on pricing.

Should a dominant shipper association, by collective action, refuse to deal with a carrier, a host of Supreme Court cases would be reliable guideposts for <u>per se</u> condemnation.[104] Further, if the motivation for collective action by shippers is that individually they would not be able to get the particular term or arrangement desired, the association is in very real danger.

> If an individual competitor lacks the bargaining power to get a particular contract term, the courts apparently will not let him join with other competitors and use their collective bargaining power to compel the insertion of such a term in the contract, no matter how desirable.[105]

Further, such agreements or plans construed as boycotts, may be *per se* unlawful regardless of the absence of proof of intent or competitive effect.[106] Should a boycott be found, the vulnerability of an association becomes manifest.

A logical response to this line of reasoning might be to assert that the group boycott cases generally involve a single line of commerce, i.e., the boycotters are boycotting a competitor, removing the necessity of proving effect within that single line. Should the fact that shippers and carriers are in distinctly different lines of commerce ease the severity of this particular section of the antitrust laws? Clearly, the answer to this inquiry is negative; the case law being more than a suggestive guide to dual line cases. In *St. Paul Fire and Marine Ins. Co. v. Barry*[107] the boycott was undertaken by those who sell medical malpractice insurance and was directed at those who were in the business of providing health care services, two fully distinct lines of commerce.[108] "(T)he boycotters and the ultimate target need not be in a competitive relationship with each other."[109]

Perhaps the greatest risk in the boycott area is that the courts view the shipper associations as groups of horizontally aligned competitors who are both "boycotters" and participants in a horizontal agreement not to compete as to pricing of transportation services. In *United States v. Topco Associates*[110] the Court condemned as *per se* unlawful all agreements between horizontally aligned competitors which had service competition restricting provisions relating to factors such as pricing or designated service areas. The *Topco* case represents a high water mark in the rejection of many of the defenses a shippers' association might raise. In *Topco*, the defendants were a group of small grocers each having individually no more than 15% of the marketplace. The defendants sought to facilitate the purchase of wholesale commodities for retail sales, much the same as shippers are purchasers of transportation services. In order to be more competitive with national chains (Safeway, A&P, Kroger, etc.) the Topco purchaser group formed an association which hired a purchasing agent to negotiate in bulk on behalf of the buyers. The Court condemned the practice despite the fact that such collective action might make the marketplace more competitive, on the theory that horizontally aligned competitors simply do not have the right to collectively interact for mutual profit oriented benefits, outside of straight educational programs. Complexity in purchasing, enhancing of the market, maintenance of "mom and pop" grocers (small unit entities) and similar public interest arguments were all viewed as nonpersuasive.[111]

To prevent misunderstanding, it should be noted that a single shipper entity may include or exclude carriers by negotiation based on desirability of terms offered outside of monopolization problems.[112] It is only when there is collective action that serious problems occur.

5. The Controlling Circumstance Exception

Factor five, the "controlling circumstance" phenomenon of *Container Corporation*[113] remains "largely undefined" according to the Supreme Court.[114] Originally, there appeared to be a conflict between the *per se* prohibition on price fixing of *Socony-Vacuum Oil v. United States*[115] and the decision in *Cement Manufacturers Protective Association v. United States*[116] which allowed for the exchange of price information to prevent fraud in the building industry. The fraud had been the result of certain double and triple quantum ordering. In *Container Corporation*, the Court gives lip-service to the phenomenon in *Cement Manufacturers*, but dismisses the defense as inapplicable without explanation. In the *Gypsum* case, the defense was again discussed and the very process was analyzed:

> The exchange of price data and other information among competitors does not invariably have anticompetitive effects; indeed such practices can in certain circumstances increase economic efficiency and render markets

more, rather than less, competitive. For this reason we have held that such exchanges of information do not constitute a *per se* violation of the Sherman Act.[117]

However, later in the same note the court in *Gypsum* gave some very relevant counseling for shipper groups:

> Exchanges of *current price information*, of course, have the greatest potential for generating anticompetitive effects and although not *per se* unlawful have consistently been held to violate the Sherman Act.[118]

This notion of "controlling circumstances" then is not easily contained. There is then some reason to think that a shipper association *data exchange* would be subjected to a rule of reason analysis because of the complexities of the rate process. But frankly, the chances of showing the process reasonable under *any* case is unlikely.

In *National Society of Professional Engineers v. United States*[119] the Court dealt with a negotiation limitation rule which prevented the process of independent one-to-one pricing and competitive bidding, restraints which are not dissimilar to those which occur when an agent of a group of purchasers acts on their behalf after that group sets acceptable price limits.

> In this case we are presented with an agreement among competitors to refuse to discuss prices with potential competitors (individually) . . . While this is not price fixing, no elaborate industry analysis is required to demonstrate the anti-competitive character of such an agreement . . . As the District Court found (in the *National Society of Prof Engineers v. U.S.*, 404 F. Supp. 457, 460 D.C. Cir. 1976) the ban "impedes the ordinary give and take of the marketplace" and substantially deprives the customer of "the ability to utilize and compare prices . . ."[120]

The defendants in that case argued the following "controlling circumstances": "bidding is inherently imprecise, would lead to deceptively low bids, and would (cause) . . . inferior work with consequent risk to public safety and health."[121] The court found these "confirm rather than refute the anticompetitive purpose and effect . . . (further) . . . this court has never accepted such an argument."[122] There is literally nothing in the case law to suggest that the court would change its stance in this area.

6. *Nature of Data Exchanged*

As to factor six, the type of data exchanged, little need be said. Price data that is specific is of the class which finds no safe harbor in antitrust courts.[123] Current price data exchange is particularly apt to create the kind of anticompetitive effects courts are least likely to tolerate.[124] Finally, those situations where purchasers or sellers exercise collective or concerted market power to set prices are so condemned that the seminal case in the price fixing area finds such programs do not require any showing of market effect.[125]

Socony, the seminal case, was a *per se* case. However, even if a rule of reason analysis is applied (as was done in *National Society*) the same result seems inevitable. As the Court said in that case, the defendant has the burden of justifying a patent price oriented restraint and when the "petitioners attempt to do so on the basis of the potential threat that competition poses to the public safety . . . (it) is nothing less than a frontal assault on the basic policy of the Sherman Act."[126] The values at stake, the court found, are quite tangible:

> The Sherman Act reflects a legislative judgment that ultimately competition will not only produce lower prices, but also better goods and services. "The heart of our national economic policy long has been faith in the value of competition." Standard Oil Co. v. F.T.C., 340 U.S. 231, 248, 95 L. Ed. 239, 71 S. Ct. 240. The assumption that competition is the best method of allocating resources in a free market recognizes that all elements of a bargain—quality, service, safety, and durability—and not just the immediate cost, are favorably affected by the free opportunity to select among alternative offers. Even assuming occasional exceptions to the presumed consequences of competition, the statutory policy precluded inquiry into the question whether competition is good or bad.
>
> In sum, the Rule of Reason does not support a defense based on the assumption that competition itself is unreasonable. Such a view of the Rule would create the "sea of doubt" . . . which this Court has firmly avoided . . .[127]

7. <u>As to factor seven, not much can be said until cautious comparative observation can be taken.</u>

VIII. Assuming the antitrust laws are brought to bear on shipper associations or on groups of shippers, what will be the consequences on the shippers?

In <u>National Society of Professional Engineers,</u>[128] the court restated a principle of antitrust law which should come as no surprise: a court upon finding a violation of the antitrust laws may (1) eliminate the prohibited conduct, i.e. disband, sever, or dissolve an improper association; (2) issue an order to prevent the recurrence of such behavior in the future; (3) punish the participants with fines, and in certain cases where "naked restraints" are apparent, incarcerate the participants; (4) seek to change or modify the marketplace by exercising various equitable powers to cause the power in the given market to be more fairly allocated, i.e. behavioral modification of the marketplace.

> Having found the (defendant) guilty of a violation of the Sherman Act, the District Court was empowered to fashion appropriate restraints on the Society's future activities both to avoid a recurrence of the violation and to eliminate its consequences. See, e.g., International Salt Co. v. United States, 332 U.S. 392, 400-401, 92 L. Ed. 20, 68 S. Ct. 12, 75 U.S.P.Q. 184; United States v. Glaxo Group, Ltd. 410 U.S. 52, 64, 35 L. Ed. 2d 104, 93 S. Ct. 861. While the resulting order may curtail the exercise of liberties that the Society might otherwise enjoy, that is a necessary, and, in cases such as this, unavoidable consequence of the violation. Just as an injunction against price fixing abridges the freedom of businessmen to talk to one another about prices, so too the injunction in this case must restrict the society's range of expression on the ethics of competitive bidding. The first Amendment does not "make it . . . impossible ever to enforce laws against agreements in restraint of trade . . ." Giboney v. Empire Storage & Ice Co. 336 U.S. 490, 502, 93 L. Ed. 834, 69 S. Ct. 684. In fashioning a remedy, the District Court may, of course, consider the fact that its injunction may impinge upon rights that would otherwise be constitutionally pro-

tected, but those protections do not prevent it from remedying the antitrust violations. (emphasis added, footnotes omitted).[129]

The courts have upheld plans which not only return all parties to the status quo ante, but indeed restructure the market reviving those who have been affected by the alleged anticompetitive forces. These market "reformations" have been most noticeable in the merger area. In United States v. Ford (Autolite)[130] the court dissolved a corporate integration, and then, to return the market to its original form and insure the maintenance of vigorous competition, the court ordered Ford to (a) maintain a competitor's parts facility, (b) not enter a particular market for five years using its trade name, (c) purchase for an extended period of time a portion of its parts from the impacted party, thus insuring market vitality. In U.S. v. DuPont (General Motors)[131] the remedy included a return to market position, in terms of ownership patterns, that had not existed for forty years.

In the antitrust area, a remedy is limited by the constitutional provision on "property" deprivation of the fifth and fourteenth amendment due process clause which requires that there be a reasonable nexus between the remedy and the wrong.[132] Based on the scope that the case law permits as limited by the nexus requirement, the remedy imposed on a shipper association may be a fine, disassembly, and prohibition on collective conduct. If an association with considerable market power has been price fixing, it is not out of the realm of the possible to anticipate criminal sanctions.[133]

> In November of 1976, however, the Antitrust Division began a significant effort to encourage more appropriate sentences. And subsequent to that date, through April of 1978, there have been 76 individual defendants sentenced, of which 17 have been sentenced to serve actual jail sentences. The percentage of those sentenced in misdemeanor cases actually going to jail rose to 22 percent, a threefold increase over the immediately preceding period. The total time sentenced to be served by those 17 individuals was 1,215 days, an average of just over 71 days each.
>
> The experience with the felony statute is even more dramatic. Twenty-one individual defendants have been sentenced through April of 1978 and 15, almost 75 percent, have been sentenced to jail. Total jail sentences imposed in felony cases have been 96 months—2,880 days—an average of 192 days or 6½ months each.
>
> Thus, today it is safe to draw the following general conclusions, on the basis of the statistics I have just given you: if you are discovered in a price-fixing violation and successfully prosecuted, (1) your corporation will pay a substantial fine and (2) most of the individual defendants prosecuted and convicted will go to jail.[134]

IX. Conclusion

The repeal of the Reed-Bulwinkle Act would commence a period of antitrust activity in the transportation world. Collective action by carriers and shippers, heretofore immune, will likely be the subject of scrutinizing inquiry regarding the exact nature of any joint negotiation for rates or the joint setting of rates. Focussing on the shipper associations or collective shipper activity, it would be illogical and inconsistent with precedent to conclude that there would be little if any modification in the present state of the law. Accordingly, the collective negotiation process will have to be eliminated or radically modified to avoid the price-stabilizing or altering effect of such activities. There is no "half way" point in the process of fusing the free market competitive norm into those processes such as collective rate establishment which are exclusively regulatory in nature.

The antitrust laws are not designed to eliminate the capacity of entities which do not possess monopoly power to be competitive. Their purpose is not to destroy those market forces which generate the normal give and take of a marketplace. Indeed to render an individual entity incapable of meeting a service obligation would be inconsistent with the mandates of the U.S. Supreme Court.[135] However, regulatory operational policies on rate-making and open market latitude, as governed by antitrust policies, are radically different. The gulf between the two is so wide as to suggest that they are irreconcilable. This clash in policy can only mean a change in the functioning of the associations. While elimination of a trade association is not anticipated, the associations must come to grips with their role in the future: dissemination of educational or industrial information, social centers for similarly situated business, and cautious conveyers on non-current cost data.

It will have to be clearly understood that collective negotiation by associations which use their power to achieve collectively that which they could not do individually must stop. To continue this process would invite antitrust litigation, with potentially onerous consequences.

Notes

[1]49 U.S.C.A. §1070 (a)(2) (West. Supp. 1979), Section 5(a), Interstate Commerce Act.

[2]See e.g. United States v. Socony Vacuum Oil, 310 U.S. 150 (1940); Broadcast Music, Inc. v. Columbia Broadcasting Service, ___ U.S. ___, 99 S. Ct. 1551 (1979).

[3]Remarks of President Jimmy Carter: "Announcing Trucking Deregulation," (Press Release, June 21, 1979), and accompanying "Address to Congress on Trucking Deregulation," at 6-7.

[4]Recently the United States Senate Committee on the Judiciary Subcommittee on Antitrust and Monopoly held hearings in the collective ratemaking area. Hearings were held in Chicago, Illinois; Denver, Colorado; Washington, D.C., in Spring, 1978. (Recorded testimony before the U.S. Senate Judiciary, Subcommittee on Antitrust and Monopoly, 95th Congress, 2nd Session). This year, the hearings have continued and there are at least four (4) separate proposals directed toward collective process presently before the U.S. Senate Commerce Committee: S. 710, 96th Congress, 1st Session introduced by Senator Kennedy, generally considered the most direct of the measures; S. 1400 96th Congress, 1st Session; S. 1496 96th Congress, 1st Session; S. 1497 96th Congress, 1st Session.

[5]Most prominent of the agency level proceedings is Ex Parte 297, (Sub-No. 4) Reopening of Section 5(a) Applications to Take Additional Evidence, (1977).

[6]374 U.S. 321 (1963).

[7]Lafayette v. Louisiana Power and Light, 435 U.S. 389, 399 (1978); United States v. Philadelphia National Bank, 374 U.S. 321, 350-351 (1963).

[8]Eastern Railroad Presidents Conference v. Noerr Motor Freight, 365 U.S. 127 (1961).

[9]California Motor Transport v. Trucking Unlimited, 404 U.S. 508 (1972).

[10]U.S. Const. Amend 1. The first amendment arguments in this area have been vigorous, but inconclusive regarding the extent to which the apparent "speech" interest can be curtailed.

[11]317 U.S. 341 (1943).

[12]Lafayette v. Louisiana Power and Light, *supra*, note 7, 435 U.S. at 400.

[13]___ F. Supp. ___ (N.D. Ga. 1979) civil action #76-1909A.

[14]Sullivan, Lawrence, *Handbook of the Law of Antitrust*, (West, 1977) at 746.

[15]49 U.S.C.A. §10706 (West. Supp. 1979).

[16]These criteria are applicable assuming *Parker v. Brown* [317 U.S. 341 (1943)] as modified by *Lafayette v. Louisiana Power and Light Company* [435 U.S. 389 (1978)], in the state action exemption area forms a valid parallel.

[17]See H.R. Rep. 1100, 80th Cong. 1st Session, (1947), p. 12 *et. seq.*, and Minority Report to H.R. 1100, p. 3-4, "Rate Making and the I.C.C."

[18]Statement of A. Daniel O'Neal, Chairman, Interstate Commerce Commission, Before the Subcommittee on Antitrust and Monopoly of the Senate Committee on the Judiciary on Price Competition and the Role of Rate Bureaus in the Motor Carrier Industry, 95 Congress, 2nd Session, April 26, 1978, at 24, 27.

[19]*Id.* at 73.

[20]*Supra*, note 5.

[21]Remarks of Robert C. Gresham, Commissioner, Interstate Commerce Commission, Before the 12th Annual Transportation Law Institute, Steamboat Springs, Colorado, August 9, 1979, at 3-5.

[22]*Supra*, note 8, 365 U.S. at 134.

[23]United States v. Southern Motor Carriers Rate Conference, *supra*, note 13.

[24]*Id.*, slip op. at 22.

[25]*Id.*, slip op. at 22. It should be noted that in the *Southern Motor Carriers Rate Conference* case the district court did not find the immunity persuasive as to pure state action questions for the parties before the court.

[26]49 U.S.A. §10706 (a)(2) (West. Supp. 1979).

[27]*Supra*, note 18.

[28]H.R. Rep. No. 1100, 80th Cong., 1st Session, July 25, 1947, *Minority Report*, at 23-24.

[29]H.R. Rep. No. 1100, 80th Cong., 1st Session, July 25, 1947, *Majority Report*, at 12.

[30]*Id.* at 10 et. seq.

[31]*Id.* at 2.

[32]Southern Motor Carriers Rate Conference, *supra*, note 13, displays an attitude of judicial aggressiveness relating to non-explicit immunity.

[33]H.R. Rep. No. 1100, *supra*, note 28, at 3-4.

[34]49 U.S.C.A. §10706 (West. Supp. 1979).

[35]15 U.S.C.A. §1 *et*. *seq*. (West. Supp. 1979).

[36]15 U.S.C. §1 (as amended, Dec. 21, 1974 and December 12, 1975).

[37]15 U.S.C. §2 (as amended, December 21, 1974).

[38]Summey v. Ford Motor Credit Co., 449 F. Supp. 132 (S.C. 1976).

[39]*See generally* Tower Tire and Auto v. Atlantic Richfield, 392 F. Supp. 1098 (D.C. *Tex 1975)*; Brown Shoe, Inc. v. United States, 370 U.S. 294, 320 (1962).

[40]United States v. Container Corporation of America 393 U.S. 333, 337 (1969).

[41]United States v. Yellow Cab Co., 332 U.S. 218 (1947).

[42]*See e.g.* Loraine Journal Co. v. United States, 342 U.S. 143 (1951); Hospital *Building Company* v. Trustees of Rex Hospital, 425 U.S. 738 (1978).

[43]Kiefer-Stewart Co. v. Joseph E. Seagram and Sons, 340 U.S. 211 (1947).

[44]United States v. Topco Associates, 405 U.S. 596 (1972).

[45]Fashion Originators Guild of America v. F.T.C. 312 U.S. 457 (1951).

[46]Klors, Inc. v. Broadway-Hale Stores, Inc., 359 U.S. 207 (1959).

[47]15 U.S.C.A. §1311-14 (West. Supp. 1979).

[48]*Id*., section (a).

[49]16 C.F.R. §2.7 (a) (1979).

[50]15 U.S.C.A. §45 (a)(1) (West. Supp. 1979).

[51]15 U.S.C.A. §45 (a)(2) (West. Supp. 1979).

[52]*See e.g.* F.T.C. v. Miller 549 F. 2d 452 (7th Cir. 1977).

[53]16 C.F.R. §1.9 (1979).

[54]Sunshine Act Studios v. F.T.C. 481 F. 2d 1171 (1st Cir. 1973); Adolph Coors, Inc. v. F.T.C. 497 F. 2d 1178 (10th Cir. 1974) *cert*. *denied* 419 U.S. 1105.

[55]15 U.S.C.A. §12 (a) (West. Supp. 1979) formally defines the term "antitrust laws" as follows:

> (a) "Antitrust laws," as used herein, includes the Act entitled "An Act to protect trade and commerce against unlawful restraints and monopolies," approved July second, eighteen hundred and ninety; sections seventy-three to seventy-seven, inclusive, of an Act entitled "An Act to reduce taxation, to provide revenue for the Government, and for other purposes," of August twenty-seventh, eighteen hundred and ninety-four; an Act entitled "An Act to amend sections seventy-three and seventy-six entitled 'An Act to reduce taxation, to provide revenue for the Government, and for other purposes,'" approved February twelfth, nineteen hundred and thirteen; and also this Act.

[56]15 U.S.C.A. §14 (West. Supp. 1979).

[57]15 U.S.C.A. §13, 13 (a) (West. Supp. 1979).

[58]United States v. Investors Diversified Services, 102 F. Supp. 645 (D. Minn. 1951).

[59]15 U.S.C.A. §14 (West. Supp. 1979).

[60]Mandeville Island Farms v. American Crystal Sugar, Inc. 334 U.S. 219 (1947); Southern Motor Carriers, _supra_, note 13.

[61]422 U.S. 271, 278 (1975).

[62]425 U.S. 738 (1975).

[63]The hospitals were private institutions, with limited service obligations. The respondent hospital before the Supreme Court was a forty-nine bed unit.

[64]Hospital Building Company v. Trustees of Rex Hospital, 425 U.S. 738, 745-46 (1975).

[65]United States v. South Eastern Underwriters Assn., 322 U.S. 533 (1944); Lafayette v. Louisiana Power and Light, 435 U.S. 389 (1978).

[66]Mandeville Island Farms, _supra_, note 60; Hospital Building Company v. Trustees of Rex Hospital, 425 U.S. 738 (1975).

[67]Sullivan, Lawrence, _Handbook of the Law of Antitrust_, (West, 1977) at 304.

[68]Socony-Vacuum Oil, _supra_, note 1; Container Corporation of America, _supra_, note 40.

[69]Silver v. New York Stock Exchange, 373 U.S. 341 (1963); _Socony_, _supra_, note 2. _Topco_, _supra_, note 44.

[70]15 U.S.C.A. §16 (West. Supp. 1979).

[71]15 U.S.C.A. §15 (C)-(H) (West. Supp. 1978).

[72]___ U.S. ___, 47 U.S.L. W. 4672 (July 12, 1979).

[73]Mandeville Farms, _supra_, note 60, at 236.

[74]Seiden, Elliot, "Life Without Reed-Bulwinkle," remarks delivered to 50th Annual Meeting of I.C.C. Practitioners Ass., June 29, 1979, Hot Springs, Virginia, at p. 10.

[75]_Id._ at 11.

[76]_Id._ at 14.

[77]15 U.S.C.A. §45 (West. Supp. 1979).

[78]_Boise et. al_, Order D. 8958, (February, 1978). The notion of "artificiality" is critical in this field. It is predicated on the supposition that there are "normal" market forces which can be abnormally effected by price fixing, concerted refusals to deal, boycotts or similar anticompetitive practices. These phenomena are "artificial" forces on which the F.T.C. has concentrated.

[79]383 U.S. 333 (1969).

[80]Id. at 336.

[81]310 U.S. 150 (1940).

[82]Id. at 221.

[83]Id. at 221-222.

[84]See e.g. Continental T.V., Inc. v. G.T.E. Sylvania, 433 U.S. 36 (1977).

[85]___ U.S. ___, 99 S. Ct. 1551, 1564 (1979).

[86]Sullivan, Lawrence, Handbook of the Law of Antitrust, (West, 1977), at 286.

[87]Id.

[88]Sullivan, Lawrence, Handbook of the Law of Antitrust, note 67, at 289, citing for reference Jones Knitting Corporation v. Morgan, 361 F. 2d 451 (3rd Cir. 1966).

[89]256 F. 2d 538 (4th Cir. 1958).

[90]15 U.S.C.A. §45 (West. Supp. 1979).

[91]Virginia Excelsior Mills, Inc. v. F.T.C., 256 F. 2d 538 (4th Cir. 1958).

[92]See e.g. United States v. Citizens and Southern National Bank, 422 U.S. 86, 113 (1975).

[93]393 U.S. 338 (1968).

[94]438 U.S. 422 (1977).

[95]268 U.S. 563 (1925).

[96]Lane, "Trade and Professional Associations: Ethics and Standards," 46 Antitrust L.J. 653 (1977).

[97]Container Corporation of America, supra, note 40, 393 U.S. at 331.

[98]United States v. U.S. Gypsum, 438 U.S. 422, 475 (1977), Stevens, J., concurring.

[99]Id. at 441.

[100]Hearings on H.R. 515, Sub-committee No. 2, House Committee on the Judiciary, 80th Cong. 1st Sess., (1945) at 6, Remarks of Senator Kefauver in amending §7 and §11 of the Clayton Act.

[101]Brozen, "The Concentration-Collusion Doctrine," 46 Antitrust L.J. 826 (1977); Johnson, Bruce M., The Attack on Corporate America (McGraw-Hill, 1978).

[102]Container Corporation, supra, note 40, at 38, Fortas, J., concurring; U.S. Gypsum, supra, note 98, at 441, n. 16.

[103]15 U.S.C.A. §3 (West. Supp. 1979).

[104]Kiefer-Stewart Co. v. Seagram and Sons, 340 U.S. 211, 214 (1951); Fashion Originators Guild v. F.T.C., 312 U.S. 457, 465 (1941); Paramount Famous Lasky v. U.S., 282 U.S. 30 (1930).

[105] Bird, "Sherman Act Limitations on Noncommercial Concerted Refusals to Deal," 1970 Duke L.J. 247, 248, cited with favor in St. Paul Fire and Marine Insurance Co. v. Barry, 438 U.S. 531, 545, n. 17 (1977).

[106] Sullivan, Lawrence, _Handbook of the Law of Antitrust_, note 14, at 256-259; Barker, "Refusals to Deal Under the Federal Antitrust Laws," 103 U. Pa. L.R. 847, 875 (1955); Kirkpatrick, "Commercial Boycotts as Per Se Violations of the Sherman Act," 10 Geo. Wash. L.R. 302, 305-6 (1952).

[107] 438 U.S. 531 (1977).

[108] _Accord_, Klor's v. Broadway Hale, 359 U.S. 207 (1959); Times-Picayune v. United States, 345 U.S. 594 (1953).

[109] St. Paul Fire and Marine Insurance Co. v. Barry, 438 U.S. 531 (1977).

[110] 405 U.S. 596 (1972).

[111] United States v. Topco Associates, 405 U.S. 596, 599 _et seq._, (1972).

[112] Times-Picayune, _supra_, note 108, at 625.

[113] _Supra_, note 40, 393 U.S. at 335.

[114] U.S. v. U.S. Gypsum, _supra_, note 98, at 449.

[115] _Supra_, note 2.

[116] 268 U.S. 588 (1925).

[117] U.S. Gypsum, _supra_, note 98, at 441, n. 16, citing U.S. v. Citizens and Southern National Bank, 422 U.S. 83 (1975) and Container Corporation, _supra_, note 40.

[118] U.S. Gypsum, _supra_, note 98, at 441, n. 16, citing American Column and Lumber Co. v. United States, 257 U.S. 377 (1921); United States v. American Linseed Oil Co. 262 U.S. 371 (1923); Container Corporation, _supra_, note 40.

[119] 435 U.S. 679 (1977).

[120] National Society of Professional Engineers v. United States, 435 U.S. 679, 693-4 (1977).

[121] _Id._ at 693.

[122] _Id._ at 194.

[123] _Socony_, _supra_, note 2; _Container Corp._, _supra_, note 40; _Gypsum_, _supra_, note 98; National Society of Professional Engineers, _supra_, note 120; Mandeville Island Farms, _supra_, note 60.

[124] U.S. Gypsum, _supra_, note 98 at 441; Sullivan, _supra_, note 14, at 286.

[125] Socony Vacuum Oil, _supra_, note 2.

[126] National Society, _supra_, note 120 at 695.

[127] _Id._ at 695, 606.

[128] _Id._ at 697.

[129] *Id.* at 697-698.

[130] 405 U.S. 562 (1972).

[131] 313 U.S. 586 (1957).

[132] *See e.g.* In the matter of Consumers Power, 452-ALAB, 12/30/77, U.S.N.R.C. Doc. No. 50-329 (A), 50-330 (A), an administrative antitrust decision.

[133] U.S. Gypsum, *supra*, note 98.

[134] Seiden, Elliot. "Life Without Reed-Bulwinkle," remarks delivered to 50th Annual Meeting of Interstate Commerce Commission Practitioners Association, June 29, 1979, Hot Springs, Virginia.

[135] United States v. Otter Tail Power Co., 410 U.S. 366, 381 (1973).

Discrimination in Transportation and Antitrust Laws*

MARTIN T. FARRIS

[Editor's Note: The fundamental conflict in transportation today focuses upon rates and discrimination practices and upon the provisions of the antitrust laws, of which collective ratemaking is an integral part of the controversy in some quarters. Martin T. Farris provides insight into the relevancy of these conflicting statues in an article entitled "Discrimination in Transportation and Antitrust Laws."]

Probably the major topic in transportation policy for the past several years has been deregulation. Almost every current discussion of transportation ends up discussing the need and proposals for deregulation. Not only is this topic prominent in the specialized press of transportation, but it is increasingly appearing in the general media, in the newsmagazines, and on radio and television.

Of course, a part of this attention is due to the general wave of sentiment sweeping the country, contending that there is too much government interference in our lives. Less regulation, or what people in transportation would call "deregulation," is but a part of the general feeling of too much government and the understandable desire to have less control everywhere in the economy. The actions of the EPA, IRS, OSHA, FERA, and dozens of other alphabetical agencies are lumped together with the ICC, CAB, and FMC (as well as state agencies regulating transportation) in one grand and massive package of "too much regulation."

It is difficult to predict at this point what will be the result of this outcry against what was once called "social controls." However, it is well to look at alternatives and to consider what conditions might be like under changed policies. One might add that in this general movement of discontent with regulation, there has been all too little consideration given to alternatives.

In the literature on transportation deregulation, as well as in the popular debate continuing on this subject, the alternative of application of the antitrust laws is prominent. Over and over again, the point is put forth that antitrust laws

*Reprinted by permission of the ICC Practitioners' Journal.

plus market competition can be relied upon to protect the shipper and the public. Frequent reference is made to the cumbersome, complicated, expensive, and unnecessary regulatory structure via the ICC, CAB, and FMC, and the fact that the existing antitrust structure and the forces of the market place are sufficient for our needs. The "capstone" of this position comes in the statement "transportation should be treated just like any other business."

A quote from a recent background paper for the Transportation Association of America summarizes the point nicely:

> Since regulatory beginnings, there has developed a significant body of law aimed at correcting abuses like those which prompted transportation regulation, but with general applicability to all sectors of the economy. Among these laws are the Sherman Act . . . [all the antitrust statutes are listed] . . . Thus, while the Interstate Commerce Commission was regulating transportation carriers through other laws, the government attempted to establish the 'rules of the game' designed to maintain an effective market system. . . .
>
> There are many who believe that, with these laws in position, competition can substitute for the ICC's regulations, and that where competition fails, these 'rules of the game' will protect the public interest.[1]

Given this oft-heard position, this essay has as its objective the examination of only one part of the regulatory structure of transportation: discrimination. The goal will be to compare and contrast the present regulatory structure concerning discrimination with the application of the antitrust laws to the same topic.

BACKGROUND ON DISCRIMINATION

First, the term "discrimination" has many meanings. Nowadays, the term is widely used relative to sexual discrimination, racial discrimination, age discrimination (and one might add, as a society, we have attempted to legislate in these areas), or general complaints about being "discriminated against" or "discriminated in favor of," etc., etc. Quite obviously the root of discrimination is unequal treatment in some way. Any time a person or group feels it is being treated unequally from others, the charge of discrimination is likely to be heard. As has been evident over and over again, it is very difficult to define what is meant by unequal treatment—and the arguments over the Equal Rights Amendment attest to this fact.

Second, in transportation there is a long history of both statute law and case law which defines what types of discrimination are illegal. Given that most of the law on discrimination goes back to the Act to Regulate Commerce (or I.C. Act) of 1887, in transportation there have been ninety-two years of experience with defining transportation discrimination—and it's still not a settled issue!

Third, the antitrust laws also concern themselves with discrimination. Price discrimination is prohibited in the Clayton Act of 1914 and the amendments to Section 2 of the Clayton Act contained in the Robinson-Patman Act of 1936. There is much less case law on these parts of the antitrust statutes than there is concerning the Interstate Commerce Act. It should also be noted that the Clayton and Robinson-Patman Acts prohibit only <u>price discrimination</u> and only under certain circumstances and conditions—whereas the Interstate Commerce Act as well as the Civil Aeronautics Act and the Shipping Act of 1916, prohibit <u>transportation discrimination</u> broadly and are not limited solely to price discrimination. This difference in approach is not always appreciated or noted.

DEFINITION OF TRANSPORTATION DISCRIMINATION

The provisions concerning transportation discrimination appear in Sections 2, 3, and 4 of Part I of the Interstate Commerce Act and reappear with slight modification in Part II (Motor Carriers), Part III (Water Carriers), and Part IV (Freight Forwarders) of the basic statute. Also in somewhat modified form, the same language appears in the Civil Aeronautics Act, as amended by the Federal Aviation Act of 1958, and in the Shipping Act of 1916 (as amended). The thrust of the control of discrimination can be understood by considering Part I of the Interstate Commerce Act.

Section 2 deals with Personal Discrimination, Section 3 concerns Undue Preference and Prejudice, and Section 4 prohibits a particular type of place discrimination: long haul-short haul discrimination. It is principally Section 4, or long-short haul discrimination, which is missing from the motor, air, maritime, and freight forwarder legislation. However, the same general pattern of Section 2 (personal discrimination) and Section 3 (undue preference or prejudice) applies to all modes of transportation and hence makes up the bedrock issue of the regulation of transportation discrimination.

Turning first to personal discrimination, Section 2 reads:

> If any common carrier subject to the provisions of this Act shall, directly or indirectly, by any special rate rebate, drawback or other device, charge, demand, or collect, or receive from any person or persons a greater or less compensation for any service rendered or to be rendered, in the transportation of passengers or property, subject to the provisions of this Act, than it charges, demands, collects, or receives from any other person or persons for doing for him or them a like and contemporaneous service in the transportation of a like kind of traffic under substantially similar circumstances and conditions, such common carrier shall be deemed guilty of unjust discrimination which is prohibited and declared to be unlawful.[2]

This same prohibition is found in the other parts of the Act dealing with motor carriers, inland water carriers, and freight forwarders. The maritime provisions, although slightly different in language, have the same thrust and meaning.[3]

The intent of Section 2 is that common carriers cannot charge persons different rates for substantially the same service, and common carriers cannot give more or less service to one shipper (or receiver) of freight than another when charging both the same rate. <u>Both rates and services</u> are involved, and this should be emphasized.

Now, it should be noted that there are many forms of personal discrimination, and very early the courts stated: "discrimination and rebates have ever been sought to be hidden under the most subtle disguises."[4] Locklin notes twelve forms of personal discrimination.[5] These are (1) Departure from the published rate, or granting a concession to a particular shipper (it is not discrimination if there is only one shipper or if several shippers receive the same concession), (2) Rebates, (3) Free passes (yet, the statute allows carriage of persons and property for charitable purposes at free or reduced rates, carriage of federal-state-municipal persons or property at reduced charges, and free passes to employees and certain groups of individuals), (4) Underclassification, or knowingly allowing a lower classification of freight to apply, (5) False billing, such as misrepresentation of weight on a shipment or allowing lower export or proportional rates to apply when not entitled to so do, false destinations, etc., (6) Sudden changes in published rates—the old "midnight tariffs"—now stopped since thirty days notice of change is ordinarily required, (7) Excessive payment for supplies (it is claimed that Standard Oil received over $2 million more for oil from the railroads than the fair market price prior to 1907), (8) False claims—excessive claim payments continue to be a form of personal discrimination today, (9) Low rental or leases on property which the carrier owns (there are a whole series of cases on locomotive and car payments, leases or rental of warehouses, etc.), (10) Sale of industrial sites at low prices, (11) Extension of credit (this remains a problem today, and in all of transportation, rules exist on credit extension), and (12) Allowances for services—the whole area of privately owned cars (tank cars, refrigerated cars, special cars) and switching services by industrial-owned carriers. In addition, there is a whole series of problems with rates being discriminatory when they vary by use of the commodity or are based on size of the shipment, such as volume rates, guaranteed rates, and agreed rates.

Reviewing Section 3-type discrimination, or the "undue preference or prejudice" clause, which applies specifically to places and commodities, this Section reads:

> It shall be unlawful for any common carrier subject to the provisions of this act to make, give, or cause any undue or unreasonable preference or advantage to any particular person, company, firm, corporation, association, locality, port, port district, gateway, transit point, region, district, territory, or any particular description of traffic, in any respect whatsoever; or to subject any particular persons, company, firm, corporation, association, locality, port, port district, gateway, transit point, region, district, territory, or any particular description of traffic to any undue and unreasonable prejudice or disadvantage in any respect whatsoever: Provided however, that this paragraph shall not be construed to apply to discrimination, prejudice, or disadvantage to the traffic of any other carrier of whatever description.[6]

The same language is repeated for motor carriers—Section 216 (d)—Water Carriers—Section 305 (c,d)—and Freight Forwarders—Section 404 (b,c). There is a slight variation for air carriers, but the thrust of "undue preference or prejudice" remains. The Federal Aviation Act states:

> No air carrier or foreign air carrier shall make, give or cause any undue or unreasonable preference or advantage to any particular person, port, locality, or description of traffic in air transportation in any respect whatsoever, or subject any particular person, port, locality, or description of traffic in air transportation to any unjust discrimination or any undue or unreasonable prejudice or disadvantage in any respect whatsoever.[7]

In maritime transportation, the language is slightly different, but the essential idea of "undue preference and prejudice" is the same. The statute reads:

> It shall be unlawful for any common carrier by water, or other person subject to this Act, either alone or in conjunction with any other person, directly or indirectly—First, to make or give any undue or

unreasonable preference or advantage to any particular person, locality, or description of traffic in any respect whatsoever, or to subject any particular person, locality, or description of traffic to any undue or unreasonable prejudice or disadvantage in any respect whatsoever.[8]

It should be noted that treatment in rates and services need not be strictly equal, but rather it is only "undue and unreasonable" discrimination that is prohibited. Cities, locations, and shippers often claim they have been prejudiced or others have been preferred. In such cases, a competitive relationship and injury or potential injury must be shown. Also, discrimination implies unequal treatment by the same carrier, and a carrier must have the ability to remove the discrimination or else it is not liable.

APPLICATION OF TRANSPORTATION LAW TO DISCRIMINATION

Turning first to personal discrimination under Section 2 (Elkins Act), violations here are criminal matters and are made misdemeanors. Further, the basic statute makes receipt or acceptance of rebates subject to fine and triple damages.[9] Violations of Section 3 are civil matters and do not involve criminality.

Next, in the courts, the Elkins Act has been applied broadly and with vigor. The substance of the transaction is considered and strict adherence to the published rate is upheld.[10] Further, concessions other than rebates are illegal and every subterfuge, scheme, plan, or device of any person or corporation to give or receive advantages, concessions, discrimination, or rebates is illegal.[11]

While it is not possible to list all the devices and arrangements condemned under Section 2 nor all the cases involved, Guandolo lists twenty-five categories of illegal actions, most with several cases. These are: (1) Discriminatory Practices in Leasing or Selling Property, (2) Paying Less Than the Established Rate Between Two Points, (3) Giving Credit Beyond the Tariff Limits, (4) Rebate on Collateral Services, (5) Insurance on Goods in Transit in Excess of the Tariff, (6) Failure to Charge or Collect Demurrage, (7) Free Franks (franking privileges permitting employees to send personal packages free), (8) Charging a Lesser Rate Over One Through Route Than Over Another, (9) Paying Shipper for a Service the Carrier Is Not Obligated to Perform, (10) Paying or Receiving Rates on Goods Not Entitled to Transit Privileges, (11) Collecting a False Claim from a Carrier, (12) Free Advertising, (13) Becoming a Dealer in a Commodity, (14) Carload Rates on Less Than Carload Lots, (15) Payment of Unduly Large Allowances to a Subsidiary of a Shipper, (16) Granting of Permits for Transportation During an Embargo, (17) Obtaining a Higher Priority During a Time of Car Shortages, (18) Expedited Service or Delivery by a Specified Time (when not in the tariff), (19) Knowingly Undervaluing Property by a Shipper, (20) Ownership or Maintenance of Tracks Inside a Plant for the Sole Benefit of a Shipper, (21) Delay in Route for Benefit of Shipper, (22) Unauthorized For-Hire Transportation, (23) Special Contracts of Carriage, (24) Special Services, (25) Loading and Unloading for Shipper or Receivers Without Charge.

One has to be impressed with the enormity of case law on the subject of Section 2 discrimination, and it seems safe to say that the matter of prohibiting personal discrimination in both rates and services is well settled in transportation law.

Next, considering the "undue preference and prejudice" provisions, this general transportation discrimination clause was originally intended to protect the shippers and receivers, not the carriers. To clarify the matter, the Transportation Act of 1940 added the last sentence of Section 3 that "this paragraph shall not be construed to apply to discrimination, prejudice, or disadvantage to the traffic of any carrier of whatever description." Further, the ICC has allowed lower inland water rates to divert rail movements, noting:

> There seems to be a view prevalent among protestants that we have authority to find a local port to port rate of a water carrier unlawful because it may adversely affect rail lines and the all rail structure. Unsoundness of this view is apparent in its inconsistency with the provisions of Sec. 305(c).[13]

The matter of competition between modes is contained in Section 15a (The Rule of Rate Making) which concerns the level, not the structure, of rates. Here Congress provides:

> In a proceeding involving competition between carriers of different modes of transportation subject to this Act, the Commission, in determining whether a rate is lower than a reasonable minimum rate, shall consider the facts and circumstances attending the movement of the traffic by the carrier or carriers to which the rate is applicable. Rates of a carrier shall not be held up to a particular level to protect the traffic of any other modes of transportation, giving due consideration to the objectives of the national transportation policy declared in this Act.[14]

The point is that competition between carriers or modes of transportation comes under the provision for just and reasonable rates (Section 1). Rate level is involved in those rulings. Undue preference or prejudice (Section 3) involves the structure of rates or differences between rates. Hence, it is aimed at protecting shippers, receivers, localities, etc., etc. It is important to understand the differences between discrimination and reasonableness.

As noted above, the carrier must have the power to remove the alleged discrimination.[15] This involves the matter of joint and through rates and routes[16] and both carriers are equally liable.[17] All competitive points must be treated equally[18] if similarly situated even to the extent that a reduced rail rate to meet water competition at one point must be offered at a competitive point,[19] and lowered rail rates to meet motor competition must be reduced to all competitive points.[20]

Many communities maintain transportation analysts in their Chambers of Commerce who are ever vigilant for potential prejudice or preference against their location. However, a competitive relationship between communities must be shown.[21] The burden of proof is clearly on the complainant when a location or shipper claims prejudice,[22] and, of course, only "undue preference or prejudice" is prohibited.[23] What is "undue" is a matter of fact, not law, and is a matter for the regulatory body to decide.[24] Further, for prejudice to be "undue or unreasonable," injury or potential injury must be shown.[25]

However, the "natural advantage" of a given location has been a sticky point in this matter, and "carriers are not required by law, and could not in justice be required, to equalize natural advantages, such as location, cost of production and the like,"[26] or again: "unjust discrimination by carriers cannot be predicated upon their failure or declination to remove, by preferential rates, services, or privileges, the natural disadvantage of location under which one community rests in competition with another that is more favorably located."[27] Locklin contains an interesting discussion (and cites cases) attempting to answer the questions: "Can equal rates be discriminatory?" and "Can lower rates be prejudiced as compared to higher?"[28] The general rule is that differences in rates must be justified by "transportation conditions" in order to avoid undue preference or prejudice--literally, cost-of-service factors and sometimes value-of-service factors.[29]

Concerning undue preference or prejudice between commodities, many of the same points hold. The burden of proof is upon the shipper (or receiver), the carrier must be able to remove or control the alleged discrimination, the commodities must bear some competitive relationship to each other,[30] and this competition must be real and substantial.[31] Injury must be shown in marketing the commodities.[32] Differences in rates on competing commodities, however, have been allowed because of differences in cost of service,[33] differences in value of the article shipped,[34] and the degree to which commodities are affected by carrier competition.[35] Likewise, differences in rates are allowed between raw materials and finished goods in the same commodity.[36] Once more, what is or is not "undue preference or prejudice" among commodities is a matter of fact for the various commissions to decide and not a matter of law (for a court to decide). Most shippers have traffic departments or traffic consultants who are alert for Section 3 violations against their firms' commodities, and the carrier must be careful that differences in classification and rates reflect only "transportation conditions."

In general, there are four types of transportation competition: carrier competition, producing center competition, consuming center competition, and commodity competition.[37] All four of these are affected by rates and services of various kinds. Discrimination in Carrier Competition more often than not is involved with Section 2 violations, while the latter three types of competition usually involve Section 3 discrimination problems. But the point is that discrimination arising from competition is not simple price discrimination in the conventional sense of one seller decreasing a price to a particular customer to get his business from a competitor. All sorts of variations of service and the manner in which the service is rendered are involved in transportation discrimination. Further, a long and involved background of case law has evolved over time to deal with the many and subtle variations of "undue preference or prejudice" as well as "unequal treatment."

DISCRIMINATION IN ANTITRUST LAWS

Turning now to the antitrust statutes (or "rules of the game which will protect the public interest if competition fails," according to the quote noted above), a bit of background may be in order. Essentially, there are only three antitrust statutes: the Sherman Act of 1890, the Clayton Act of 1914, and the Federal Trade Commission Act of 1914. As with the Act to Regulate Commerce, these basic statutes have been amended a number of times (for present purposes, the Robinson-Patman amendment to the Clayton Act in 1936 is of some importance), and they have been interpreted by case law. The Sherman Act in 1890 essentially codified the common law on restraint of trade and monopolization. Without stopping to analyze this basic statute, suffice it to say that due to lack of definition and interpretation by the courts, considerable concern arose over the efficacy of the Sherman Act in the first decade of this century. The issue of monopolistic abuses came to a head in 1914, and President Wilson recommended that the uncertainty concerning the meaning of the Sherman Act be removed by Congress's prohibiting, item by item, each of the devices by which monopoly might be obtained or competition eliminated. But Congress could not agree upon a comprehensive list of particular practices and finally compromised by prohibiting four specific trade practices and creating an independent commission, the Federal Trade Commission, in a companion piece of legislation, charged with prohibiting "unfair methods of competition." The four specific trade practices were price discrimination, exclusive and tying contracts, intercorporate stockholdings, and interlocking directorates.

The Robinson-Patman amendment (sometimes known as the Anti-Chain Store Act) was passed in 1936 to help independent merchants who found themselves at a disadvantage because large purchasers could force lower prices (quantity discounts) from suppliers because of their great buying power. It made price discrimination caused by buyers illegal (the Clayton Act had dealt only with seller price discrimination), as well as prohibiting specific abuses, such as brokerage commissions, where independent brokers were not used, allowances for services rendered by buyers unless concessions were "on proportionately equal terms," and making it unlawful to "knowingly induce or receive" price discrimination. This was all part of the concern over the Depression with small businesses and the lack of competition.

The exact wording of the part of Section 2 of the Robinson-Patman Act dealing with price discrimination is:

> (a) It shall be unlawful for any person engaged in commerce, in the course of such commerce, either directly or indirectly, to discriminate in price between different purchasers of commodities of like grade and quality, where either or any purchasers involved in such discrimination are in commerce, where such commodities are sold for use, consumption, or resale within the United States or any Territory thereof or the District of Columbia, or any insular possession or other place under the jurisdiction of the United States, and where the effect of such discrimination may be substantially to lessen competition or tend to create a monopoly in any line of commerce or to injure, destroy, or prevent competition with any person who either grants or knowingly receives the benefit of such discrimination, or with customers of either of them: _Provided_, That nothing herein contained shall prevent differentials which make only due allowance for differences in cost of manufacture, sale or delivery resulting from the differing methods or quantities in which such commodities are to such purchasers sold or delivered; _Provided_, however, That the Federal Trade Commission may, after due investigation and hearing to all interested parties, fix and establish quantity limits, and revise the same as it finds necessary, as to particular commodities or classes of commodities, where it finds that available purchasers in greater quantities are so few as to render differentials on account thereof unjustly discriminatory or promotive of monopoly in any line of commerce; and the foregoing shall then not be construed to permit differentials based on differences in quantities greater than those so fixed and established. _And provided further_, That nothing herein contained shall prevent persons engaged in selling goods, wares, or merchandise in commerce from selecting their own customers in bona fide transactions and not in restraint of trade: _And provided further_, That nothing herein contained shall prevent price changes from time to time where in response to changing conditions affecting the market for or marketability of the goods concerned, such as, but not limited to actual or imminent deterioration of perishable goods, obsolescence of seasonal goods, distress sales under court process, or sale in good faith in discontinuance of business in the good concerned.
>
> (b) Upon proof being made, at any hearing on a complaint under this section, that there has been discrimination in price or services or facilities furnished, the burden of rebutting the prima-facie case thus made by showing justification shall be upon the person charged with a violation of this section, and unless justification shall be affirmatively shown, the Commission is authorized to issue an order terminating the discrimination: _Provided, however_, That nothing herein contained shall prevent a seller rebutting the prima-facie case thus made by showing that his lower price or furnishing of services or facilities to any pur-

chaser or purchasers was made in good faith to meet an equally low price of a competitor, or the service or facilities furnished by a competitor.

* * *

(f) It shall be unlawful for any person engaged in commerce, in the course of such commerce, knowingly to induce or receive a discrimination in price which is prohibited in this section.[38]

Now, it should be noted that under antitrust all price discrimination is not illegal—but only that in which (a) the effect of the discrimination "may be *substantially to lessen competition* or tend to create a monopoly in any line of commerce," (b) it does not "make *due allowance for differences in cost* of manufacturer, sale or delivery," and (c) it is not made "in good faith *to meet an equally low price* of a competitor." Further, the Act allows sellers to "select their own customers in bona fide transactions and not in restraint of trade."

Finally, it should be noted that the burden of proof is upon the person or firm charged with discrimination. This is clearly spelled out in the paragraphs concerning the "good faith to meet competition" defense. This is quite the opposite of the case under transportation discrimination where the shipper or locality must shoulder the burden of proof.

APPLICATION OF ANTITRUST CASE LAW TO DISCRIMINATION

A great deal of case law on discrimination under the antitrust statutes has dealt with tying contracts and exclusive dealing, brokerage, and allowances/services. Most of these cases have come under the civil section relative to Federal Trade Commission orders. For instance, Wilcox states: "During the first 20 years after the law [Robinson-Patman] was enacted, nearly half of these orders [by the FTC] were issued under the brokerage section, another fifth under the section dealing with advertising allowances and services."[39] However, the remaining 30 percent of the cases have established some important interpretations.

First, the so-called "test of substantiality" is of some importance since price discrimination (as well as the other noncompetitive devices) is illegal only when the effect "may be to substantially lessen competition or tend to create a monopoly." In attempting to interpret what is "substantial," most of the cases have come under the tying contract provision and have often dealt with the arrangements between petroleum product manufacturers and their retail outlets. In 1949, in the *Standard Oil of California* case, a contract with 6,000 independent dealers and involving 7 percent of the region's gasoline market was deemed "substantial."[40] In 1951, Richfield Oil contracts covering 3 percent of the market were deemed substantial.[41] On the other hand, in 1961, a coal contract to purchase 100 percent of the needs of a Tampa electric generating station for twenty years was not considered "substantial" since it involved only one percent of all coal purchased in the Nashville area.[42] There seems to be no definitive role of what a measure of "substantiality" is—each case standing on its own merits.

Second, the terms "may" in the same phrase and "injury to competition" have caused some problems of definition. Wilcox states that "*may* substantially injure competition" denotes "reasonable probability" and that two meanings have been given to "injure competition." One concerns the vitality of competition in general and is hard to prove in court. The other, using the companion phrase "To injure, destroy, or prevent competition with any person who either grants or knowingly receives the benefit of such discrimination," refers to injury to a particular class of competitors and is used by the FTC since it is easier to prove.[43] "The result has been, in effect, to outlaw all price differences that are large enough to divert trade and thus to prohibit all price cuts save those extended to buyers as a whole."[44]

Local price cutting where a national or regional firm competes with a local firm may be illegal.[45] Functional discounts (according to how the product is used) are legitimate, volume discounts on quantities purchased at a single time are legal,[46] but discounts based on carload lot purchases as compared to less-than-carload purchases are illegal.[47]

Third, the so-called "cost defense" is very difficult to use. The court has accepted differences in freight or delivery costs as a bona fide reason to discriminate, but differences in manufacturing, purchasing or overhead costs have been difficult to prove.

Fourth, the "good faith to meet competition" defense has also been difficult to interpret. To quote Wilcox again (who summarizes the point):

> It cannot be offered . . . in justification of an established discount structure. It cannot be used to justify a price that is lower than that charged by a competitor but only to meet his price. The discriminating seller must have knowledge of the price that he is meeting. And that price, in itself, must not be unlawfully discriminatory, a matter on which a competitor cannot be expected to be informed. The lower price can be used defensively to retain an old customer; it cannot be used aggressively to attract a new one. It can be used to meet a lower price charged by one's own competitors, but not to enable one's customers to meet a lower price charged by their competitors . . . Given its limitations, this defense is rarely offered; it has even more rarely been accepted.[48]

It is not our task here completely to detail the case law on the application of price discrimination under antitrust law. Obviously, each case must be judged on its own merits, and it is difficult to draw out of the series of cases here any general principles. Wilcox summarizes all of Robinson-Patman by stating:

> In principle, the Robinson-Patman Act related differences in price to differences in cost. But in many respects, the law departs from this principle. In some cases, it permits discrimination; in others, it even requires it. Sellers may legally discriminate among customers and among business buyers who do not compete with one another. They may also charge identical prices where costs differ or give discounts that fail to reflect real differences in cost; it is illegal to discriminate in favor of a firm that buys in bulk, but legal to discriminate against it.[49]

It seems safe to say that the case law interpreting price discrimination is neither particularly consistent nor abundantly clear. Antitrust law, as interpreted by the courts, does not always mean what it seems to the casual reader. Perhaps those contending that the Clayton/Robinson-Patman Acts will protect the public interest should wander into the "vast wasteland of antitrust case law" a bit before allowing themselves to be convinced that this alternative is a viable one.

COMPARING AND CONTRASTING

Although it is difficult because two different factors are involved, five comparisons are possible, namely, definition of discrimination, variation in price, preference or prejudice, burden of proof, and general approach.

1. On definition of discrimination, antitrust is in terms of price discrimination and does not concern service factors (except such things as advertising allowances and brokerage services—factors of less importance in transportation). Sellers are even guaranteed the right to select their own customers. Considering this guarantee, plus the limitation to price discrimination, the antitrust definition is narrow and limited, and at that, it applies solely to certain types of price discrimination. Transportation uses a much broader definition of discrimination with all sorts of service factors involved, as well as rate (price) variations and applications. By law, common carriers may not select their own customers. Also, transportation discrimination involves both the Section 2 (Elkins Act) and the Section 3 (undue preference or prejudice) definitions of "discrimination," whereas antitrust looks to price discrimination (both by sellers and buyers) exclusively.

2. Concerning price variations, antitrust law allows considerable latitude and prohibits price discrimination (usually discounting) only where the effect "may substantially lessen competition or tend to create a monopoly," where differences in cost do not justify different treatment, or where concessions are made "in good faith to meet competition." Given these so-called "cost" and "good faith" defenses, plus the matter of substantiality, considerable variations in price are allowed under antitrust. Prices are relatively free to reflect changing conditions and can be changed at any time the seller wishes—but there is no assurance that what is purchased is what is represented. Under antitrust, caveat emptor, at least in theory, is the order of the day, with laws against fraud and misrepresentation available for very gross abuses.

Of course, anyone who has done any "shopping" recently for, say, a used car, can attest to the fact that price variations are prevalent in the general economy. Naturally, free competition in some goods and in some markets is more effective than in others. Economists define all sorts of market structure from pure competition to "workable competition" to "monopolistic competition" to varying degrees of "oligopoly" and finally, to "pure monopoly"—all existing in our economy under the antitrust laws. Given the continued concern with oligopoly and repeated admonitions against "administered prices," "shared monopoly," and "industry concentration," it is difficult to say that the free market and antitrust laws have been successful in forcing price competition broadly on every market in the economy.

Under Section 2 of the Interstate Commerce Act, transportation price variations are closely controlled. Rates must be published and notice given of any change. Published rates must be adhered to strictly and, while carriers may make their own rates or prices, these cannot ordinarily be quickly varied or changed to meet changing situations. In that sense, transportation rates have greater stability, comparisons are more easily made, and the customer is more readily assured of equal treatment under transportation discrimination law than under antitrust law. Price variations both upward and downward are controlled, and all buyers must be treated essentially alike where similar circumstances and conditions prevail.

3. On preference or prejudice, the comparison is difficult because there is not really much antitrust law on this point. The control of "unfair competitive practices" under the FTC has some similarities, but in application it has dealt more with advertising, service allowances, and brokerage (in an attempt to protect the small retailer rather than the consumer). In transportation, there is a long history of what is meant by "undue preference or prejudice" with a Commission (and its staff) making judgments based on hearings. While the FTC has hearings too, the

history of "unfair competitive practices" under antitrust is not nearly as rich and complete as the case law on "undue preference or prejudice." About all that can be said relative to antitrust law as used in a transportation situation is that apparently price concessions would have to be extended to every buyer—and in that sense, antitrust case law is somewhat like transportation case law but much more vague. Courts have had a great deal more to say about "undue preference or prejudice" where regulatory commissions determine the issues of fact and the courts rule on the issues of law in transportation. But the point is there is really no comparable "undue preference or prejudice" doctrine in antitrust.

4. It is easier to contrast the matter of burden of proof under the two sets of law. In transportation law, under Section 2, the carrier must shoulder the burden of proof in criminal proceedings, under Section 3 the shipper or locality must prove undue preference or prejudice in civil proceedings. Under antitrust law, the person accused (the carrier) would have the burden of proof in civil proceedings (relying on the cost defense, good faith defense. the substantiality doctrine, his guaranteed ability to chose his own customers, or that the buyer induced him to discriminate—none of which is easy to prove). Certainly, if antitrust law were to be a substitute for transportation law, the carrier would face a much heavier burden of proof to be able to defend his discriminatory actions. Since there are no "undue" discrimination provisions in antitrust law, it is hard to say what the results on this score might be.

5. As to general approach, transportation law has much more background and material to look to for guidelines than antitrust law. Antitrust law is more court-based and is narrower in approach, whereas transportation law is Commission-based and broader in approach. The broader approach allows much more variation in service and conditions when circumstances justify it. Moreover, antitrust law is vague and not necessarily consistent—but, of course, it has not had to deal with the multitude of problems arising under transportation conditions.

CONCLUDING REMARKS

It is hard to say what exactly would take place if transportation law on discrimination were suddenly abolished and reliance was placed solely on antitrust law. In the short run, carriers could do all sorts of things they cannot do under transportation law. Any rate could be quoted, any service rendered, and changes in both could be made to suit the particular situation at the moment. Certainly there would be no need to publish rates and adhere to them. Certainly there would be no need to serve all shippers alike nor all localities within the rules of "undue preference or prejudice," or the Section 2 prohibitions. Carriers could (indeed they would be guaranteed) the right to choose their own customers. Shippers might be liable for "knowingly inducing" price concessions. The situation would be quite fluid and literally "a new ball game" for both shippers and carriers—and every man for himself.

In the long run, a substantial burden would be placed upon the Federal Trade Commission and the Department of Justice as shippers began to clamor for application and definition of the Clayton/Robinson-Patman anti-discrimination clauses. Carriers would have to defend, and perhaps the "cost defense," "good faith to meet competition" defense, the substantiality concept, the guaranteed right to choose customers, and the "knowingly induce" doctrine would all be more clearly defined. In any case, given time, a new set of "rules of the game" would have to be worked out, and it seems almost certain that since the courts would be involved, this process would take considerable time. It is impossible to predict the outcome—it could end up a situation that pretty much duplicates the existing transportation laws on discrimination all over again. Or, it could result in a whole new set of rules—or even no rules at all.

But the point is there is some substantial question that the antitrust laws are really an alternative to existing transportation laws on discrimination. And, it is not clear that antitrust doctrine, these so-called "rules of the game" for the general economy, will automatically protect the public interest.

Notes

[1]T.A.A. Report (January 23, 1979), p. 2.

[2]U.S. Code, Title 49, Chap. 1(2). This was originally passed as the Elkins Act, 1902.

[3]It shall be unlawful for any shipper, consignor, consignee, forwarder, broker, or other person, or any officer, agent, or employee thereof, knowingly and willingly, directly or indirectly, by means of false billing, false classification, false weighing, false report of weight, or by any other unjust and unfair device or means to obtain or attempt to obtain transportation by water for property at less than the rates or charges which would otherwise be applicable.
U.S. Code, Title 46, Chap. 815.

[4]Vandalia R.R. v. United States, 226 Fed. 713.

[5]D. Philip Locklin, Economics of Transportation, 7th ed., (Irwin, 1972), pp. 469-74.

[6]U.S. Code, Title 49, Chap. 1(3).

[7]U.S. Code, Title 49, Chap. 1374(b).

[8]U.S. Code, Title 46, Chap. 815.

[9]Anyone who "shall knowingly by employee, agent, officer, or otherwise, directly or indirectly, by or through any means or device whatsoever, receive or accept from such common carrier any sum of money or any other valuable consideration as a rebate or offset against the regular charges for transportation of such property, as fixed by the schedule of rates provided for 'in the Interstate Commerce Act,' shall in addition to any penalties provided by this Act forfeit to the United States a sum of money three times the amount of money so received or accepted, and three times the value of any other consideration so received or accepted, to be ascertained by the trial court." U.S. Code, Title 49, Chap. 1(3).

[10]Armour Packing Co. v. United States, 209 U.S. 56, 72; United States v. Standard Oil Co., 148 Fed. 719, 721.

[11]United States v. Union Stock Yard, 226 U.S. 286, 307; New Haven R.R. v. Interstate Commerce Commission, 200 U.S. 361, 391; United States v. Koenig Coal Co., 270 U.S. 512, 519; and, Union Pacific R.R. Co. v. United States, 313 U.S. 450, 461-62.

[12]John Guandolo, Transportation Law, 2nd ed., (Wm. C. Brown, 1973), pp. 560-578.

[13]Cotton from Memphis and Helena to New Orleans, 273 I.C.C. 337.

[14]U.S. Code, Title 49, Chap. 15(a) (3). The final sentence of this section was added by the Transportation Act of 1958.

[15]Central R.R. of New Jersey v. U.S., 257 U.S. 247.

[16]The so-called "Ashland Rules," Ashland Fire Brick Co. v. Southern Ry., 22 I.C.C. 115, upheld by Supreme Court in Texas & Pacific Ry. v. U.S., 289 U.S. 627; and H. Samuels Co. v. Baltimore & Ohio Chicago Terminal R.R., 299 I.C.C. 793.

[17]Illinois Central R.R. v. ICC, 101 F. Supp. 317, 326-327.

[18]Citizens Gas & Coke Utility v. Chicago Northwestern Ry., 314 I.C.C. 271, 274.

[19]Bunker Hill & Sullivan Co. v. Oregon-Washington R.R. and Navigation Co., 132 I.C.C. 266, 271; Spreckles Salvage Tire Co. v. Atchison, Topeka, and Santa Fe Ry. Co., 142 I.C.C. 507.

[20]Iron & Steel to Iowa, Minnesota, Michigan & Wisconsin, 297 I.C.C. 363, Oak Flooring—Pine Bluff, Ark. to Michigan, New York, Ohio & Pennsylvania, 315 I.C.C. 77.

[21]Western Carolina Shipper Association v. Asheville Southern Ry. 174 I.C.C. 353, 358; Fleetliners v. Northern Transportation Co. 54 M.C.C. 575.

[22]Louisville & Nashville R.R. v. U.S., 238 U.S. 1, 11.

[23]United States v. Wabash R.R. 321 U.S. 403, 411; U.S. v. Illinois Central R.R. 263 U.S. 515, 521; Texas & Pacific Ry. v. I.C.C., 162 U.S. 197.

[24]Board of trade of Kansas City v. U.S., 314 U.S. 534, 546; Swayne & Holt Ltd. v. U.S., 300 U.S. 297, 304; and numerous other cases. In Swayne & Holt, the Court stated explicitly: "Whether a discrimination of rates or service of a carrier is undue or unreasonable has always been regarded as peculiarly a question committed to the judgment of the administrative body, based upon application of all the facts and circumstances affecting the traffic."

[25]Federated Metals Corp. v. Pennsylvania R.R., 161 I.C.C. 287, 288; City of Moorhead v. Great Northern Ry., 172 I.C.C. 38, 43; Beneke Corp. v. Columbus & Greenville Ry., 272 I.C.C. 156, 161.

[26]Elk Cement and Lime Co. v. Baltimore and Ohio R.R., 22 I.C.C. 84, 88.

[27]Port Arthur Board of Trade v. Abilene & Southern Ry., 27 I.C.C. 388, 402.

[28]Locklin, op. cit., pp. 518-520. The answer is "yes" in certain circumstances.

[29]York Manufacturing Association v. Pennsylvania R.R., 107 I.C.C. 219, 229; Maritime Association, Boston Chamber of Commerce v. Ann Arbor R.R., 95 I.C.C. 539, 565.

[30]California Walnut Growers Association v. Aberdeen & Rockfish R.R., 50 I.C.C. 558, 568; Boston Wool Trade Association v. Boston & Albany R.R., 78 I.C.C. 178, 183.

[31]Archer-Daniels-Midland Co. v. Great Northern Ry., 171 I.C.C. 192, 195; Illinois Sand Traffic Bureau v. Atchison, Topeka & Santa Fe Ry., 152 I.C.C. 749, 753; Armstrong Cork Co. v. Akron Canton & Youngstown Ry., 136 I.C.C. 9, 14.

[32]Arvonia-Buckingham Slate Co. v. Aberdeen & Rockfish R.R., 174 I.C.C. 767, 769; Aluminum Company of America v. Atchison, Topeka, & Santa Fe Ry., 146 I.C.C. 363, 372; Staley Manufacturing Co. v. Wabash Ry., 167 I.C.C. 12, 13.

[33]Robertson Company v. Alabama Great Southern R.R., 167 I.C.C. 693.

[34]Coke Producers Association of Connellsville v. Baltimore & Ohio R.R., 27 I.C.C. 125, 147; Ogden Packing & Provisions Co. v. Atchison, Topeka, & Santa Fe Ry., 101 I.C.C. 236, 252; Wrigley Jr. Co. v. Aberdeen & Rockfish R.R., 161 I.C.C. 41, 44.

[35]Atlas Cereal Co. v. Atchison, Topeka & Santa Fe Ry., 89 I.C.C. 212, 218; California Growers' and Shippers' Protective League v. Southern Pacific Co., 100 I.C.C. 79, 105; Chicago Live Stock Exchange v. Chicago Great Western Ry., 10 I.C.C. 428.

[36]Aluminum Co. of America v. Atchison, Topeka & Santa Fe, supra n. 32.

[37]Roy J. Sampson and Martin T. Farris, Domestic Transportation: Practice, Theory & Policy, 4th ed. (Houghton Mifflin, 1979), Chap. 14 for a review of these four types.

[38]U.S. Code, Title 15, Chap. 13.

[39]Clair Wilcox, Public Policies Toward Business, 4th ed. (Irwin, 1971), p. 202.

[40]Standard Oil Company of California v. U.S., 337 U.S. 293.

[41]U.S. v. Richfield Oil Corp., 99 F. Supp. 280, sustained 343 U.S. 922.

[42]Tampa Electric Co. v. Nashville Coal Co., 365 U.S. 320.

[43]Wilcox, op. cit, pp. 204-205.

[44]Ibid, p. 205.

[45]Utah Pie Co. v. Continental Baking Co., 386 U.S. 685.

[46]Bruce's Juices v. American Can Co., 330 U.S. 743.

[47]FTC v. Morton Salt Co., 334 U.S. 37.

[48]Wilcox, op. cit., pp. 211-212.

[49]Ibid, p. 212.

The Case for Single-Line Immunity*

GRANT M. DAVIS and CHARLES S. SHERWOOD

[*Editor's Note*: Specific immunity from the antitrust laws was repealed by the 4-R Act in joint consideration of single-line rates by railroads not participating in the traffic being considered. Although the 4-R provisions applied only to railroad collective ratemaking, serious competitive balances between manufacturers and normal trade channels have been affected. A similar provision has been advocated for motor carriers, even though this issue is more complex because of the myriad of rates and routes involved. In an article authored by Grant M. Davis and Charles S. Sherwood, entitled "The Case for Single-Line Immunity," this controversy is examined in depth, based on empirical data. The authors' findings demonstrate that, should a single-line proposal be enacted, not only would tariff publishing costs increase but also existing marketing activities of shippers and carrier would be disrupted.]

Rate bureaus or rate conferences as they exist in the regulated rail and motor segments of the domestic transportation industry have generated considerable pyrotechnics during recent years. Principal critics of bureau operations emanate from academicians, government, shippers, and even carriers themselves. The three most controversial activities of rate bureaus include:

1. Their ability to protest independent action by member carriers;

2. delays inherent in the complex procedure for obtaining rate changes; and

3. immunity to discuss single-line rates.

---

*Reprinted by permission of the *ICC Practitioners' Journal*.

Contemporary endeavors are in force to modify some existing conference procedures to correct these alleged detrimental activities. These allegations, however, ignore the positive procedural dimensions associated with conference activity.

Delays and protests of independent action were recently dealt with by the Interstate Commerce Commission under Ex Parte 297.[1] Citing a potential stifling effect on price competition, the Commission prohibited rate bureaus from opposing independent filings of their member carriers.[2] A time limit of 120 days, moreover, was imposed on bureau proceedings in an attempt to eliminate or diminish excessive delays affiliated with implementing changes. But the third polemical factor, single-line immunity, was not resolved by the ICC investigation. The purpose of this paper is threefold. First, the fundamental nature of single-line immunity will be discussed with a view to explaining its importance. Second, probable effects of repeal of this immunity will be examined in depth in the event that certain administration bills become law. Finally, public policy recommendations regarding the future of single-line immunity will be offered.

NATURE OF SINGLE-LINE IMMUNITY

Before analyzing single-line immunity and the attendant controversy, the concepts of single-line rates, joint-rates, and through routes should ideally be reviewed. A through route has been defined as "an arrangement, expressed or implied, between connecting railroads for the continuous carriage of goods from the originating point on the line of one carrier to destination on the line of another." (St. Louis Southwestern R. Co. v. United States, 245 U.S. 136, 139, N. 2. (1917)). This definition, likewise, applies to other forms of carriage as well.[3] By way of contrast, a local route is essentially a route where the same carrier serves both origin and destination in a single-line haul movement. Rates applying to local routes are defined as single-line or local rates. A through route requires a through rate which may be (1) a combination of the single-line rates established by connecting carriers, or (2) a joint rate which is a single rate applying from the point of origin to destination. In general, joint rates are lower than the sum of the single-line rates. Finally, a rate may have a dual application between a specific origin and destination: a single-line haul by a single carrier and a joint haul by the same single-line carrier jointly with another carrier through interchange at an intermediate point. Therefore, a carrier may have both single-line and joint-line rates between two points, offering a choice of carriers and routes. For example, over 4 million routes are available by rail from Dallas to Detroit.[4]

The practical necessity for maintaining through routes and joint-rates has long been recognized by both the shipping public and governmental agencies. Section 1(4) of the Interstate Commerce Act requires that railroads establish through routes and joint-rates as part of their duty as common carriers. Section 15(3) empowers the Commission to establish through routes and joint-rates for carriers subject to Part I of the Act. Part II of the Act does not require motor carriers of property to establish through routes and joint-rates with other motor carriers. However, the needs of the shipping public have led to voluntary adoption of these structures by motor carriers.[5] Finally, the Transportation Act of 1940[6] requires water carriers to provide through routes and joint-rates with other water carriers.

Early mandates for joint-rates conflicted with the antitrust laws that prohibit cooperative efforts with respect to price setting.[7] Attempts to establish joint-rates through carrier associations were deemed to be in violation of the Sherman Act.[8] This conflict with antitrust statutes continued until 1948 when rate conferences were legalized under the Reed-Bulwinkle Act.[9] This Act provides that carriers may form associations for the purpose of establishing rates, classifications, divisions, and discussion of other matters relating to operations. The agreement creating such associations and the activities carrying out the agreement, upon approval of the ICC, were relieved of antitrust provisions.[10]

Existing procedure under Section 5a permits bureau members to vote on rate changes regardless of whether the rates are joint or single-line. The eventual result of this practice is that carriers may vote on rate proposals for movements in which they do not participate. This, of course, is the center of the current controversy. Opponents feel that individual carriers should be permitted to establish their own rates free of rate bureau consideration when a carrier serves both the origin and destination.[11] In this regard, joint consideration of local rates by carriers who do not participate in a given freight movement has been alleged to delay and hinder individual carrier action.

Several attempts in recent years have been made to remove rate bureau immunity to discuss single-line rates. The "Transportation Regulatory Modernization Act of 1971" contained a provision which would have prohibited carriers from participating in discussions or voting on single-line movements and joint-line movements in which they did not participate. Also, the "Transportation Improvement Act of 1971" contained a provision for eliminating single-line immunity for railroad rate bureaus. Neither bill was enacted, but President Ford has included a similar provision in his most recent call for regulatory reform.[12] Although the change would only involve railroad rate bureaus, history has shown that similar legislation affecting motor carriers cannot be far behind.[13]

POTENTIAL EFFECTS OF REMOVING SINGLE-LINE IMMUNITY

Individuals favoring eliminating single-line immunity appear to be basing their positions regarding repeal on the following tenuous assumptions:

1. Single-line and joint-line rates can be effectively divorced from each other. Implicit in this assumption is that service between two points is either single or joint-line and not both. Also, the presumption is that between any two points there is only one through route. Finally, it assumes that carriers would meet to discuss joint rates without mentioning single-line rates.

2. Rate levels would be reduced as more independent action occurred.

3. Delays in implementing changes would be eliminated as carriers began operating independently of bureaus.

Each of these assumptions will subsequently be dealt with.

Separation of Single-Line and Joint-Line Rates

The maintenance of existing joint-line structures is totally dependent upon the existing level of single-line rates. That is to say, any significant group of carriers includes carriers which compete on both a single-line and joint-line bases. Single-line and joint-line rates between any two points are competitive, with the result that there is no way to prevent one from influencing the other. Carriers who compete on a single-line basis, with a few exceptions, may also participate in joint rates, one with the other, to provide full area service. It follows, therefore, that discussion and collective action respecting joint-line rates would necessarily influence, if not determine, single-line rates.

With the abandonment of single-line immunity, any discussions of these rates would place carriers in jeopardy under the antitrust laws. These carriers would not suddenly venture into a bureau meeting and refrain from discussing their competitive single-line rates (which would be a violation) and at the same time discuss joint-line rates (which would be permitted). Immunity to discuss joint-line rates but not single-line rates would in all probability lead to the elimination of all collective ratemaking procedures in the motor carrier industry and seriously hamper such action in the railroad industry. The following examples of how the two types of rates cannot be effectively separated were provided by bureau executives:

1. For example, every carrier, rendering service between New York and Chicago will participate in through routes between New York and Los Angeles with every carrier rendering service between Chicago and Los Angeles. Let us assume a typical situation: Carriers A, B, C, and D all render single-line service between New York and Los Angeles. All four carriers also maintain joint rates with each other between the same two points. Carriers A and B could collectively fix their rates and carriers C and D could collectively set their joint rates, but none of them could discuss either their joint or single-line rates with each other.

2. Suppose that a new rate on a given commodity from Chicago to all points in the state of Texas is before the rate committee and that Carrier X possesses single-line authority from Chicago to some, but not all, Texas points. In the discussion of this rate proposal, how can Carrier X restrict its discussion only to those points which it can serve only through joint-line service? Obviously, any such restriction is utterly impossible.

3. For reasons of port equalization on import traffic, the same level of transcontinental import commodity rates is observed from all west coast ports. Assume that Seattle interests propose a new commodity rate to Chicago. Under the proposal, how could Carrier X, possessing single-line authority from Los Angeles to Chicago, but not from Seattle to Chicago, lawfully participate in the discussion with the knowledge that its single-line rates from Los Angeles also would be affected?[14]

Potential conflicts are unlimited when considering the complexity of existing rate structures. In the case of the railroads, statutory requirements stipulate that they must establish joint rates. Therefore, carriers would be forced into joint-line discussions which potentially could lead to antitrust prosecution. Monitoring all such discussions would constitute an impossibility, and violations would be commonplace.

Effect on Rate Levels

Essential to the maintenance of the overall rate structure is the averaging of costs in a manner which will enable service to be performed at the lowest possible total cost to the shipping public. Joint-line service for a given distance is obviously more expensive than single-line service. Rates published under the auspices of the various rate bureaus at the present time reflect the average cost of handling the existing mix of single and joint-line traffic. If, however, bureau rates were to have applicability only to joint-line movements, this means that they will apply only to that traffic which is the most expensive to handle. A carrier operating solely joint-line service would be unprofitable.

On the other hand, single-line service would produce more than an average profit. The incentive would be for the carriers to withdraw from the bureau tariffs, thereby eliminating the unprofitable traffic handled under joint rates. Carriers would then handle all traffic only upon their local rates, resulting in a much higher combination of charges on joint-line traffic. In general, traffic now transported under joint rates would move at a combination of local charges which is invariably higher than joint rates.

Even if carrier rate bureaus continued to publish joint rates as required for railroads, a proclivity would develop for each individual carrier to publish its own single-line rates, which is one way to avoid possible antitrust violations. Preparation, publication, and filing of tariffs in compliance with Section 217(a) of the Interstate Commerce Act not only requires skilled technicians, but also is expensive. The following data provided by a motor carrier bureau indicate the potential increase in cost of tariff publication:

1. In 1970 approximately 5,400 carriers participated in one or more of the tariffs published by the ten major general freight bureaus.

2. The ten bureaus published approximately 200,000 tariff pages at a cost of about $111 per page and an average cost of $3,000 per year for each of the 5,400 carriers.

3. Had each carrier published its own tariffs, 540,000 pages would have been required, for an additional expense of over $37 million.

4. Every carrier would need at least one technician with a minimum salary of $10,000, and most carriers would need several.

While the specific estimates may be questioned, there is no doubt that the overall publication cost to the industry would increase. This increase would, of course, be passed on to shippers and the general public with an uneven incidence of the ultimate burden.

Other areas of potential cost increases also exist. One of the major advantages of rate bureaus from the standpoint of shippers is tariff simplification and uniformity. This advantage would be eliminated as individual carriers began publishing their own rates. Shippers, moreover, would have to monitor the rates of many different carriers instead of one bureau publication, and the ultimate result would be a time-consuming and costly examination of rates for the best rate for a given shipment. In addition, with bureaus unable to discuss single-line rates or protest independent action, the burden of monitoring rates for violations of the Interstate Commerce Act would fall primarily on the under-budgeted ICC. In 1972, the 34 most active motor carrier bureaus and the 16 most active railroad bureaus handled a total of 54,746 regular and emergency proposals. Each proposal may contain several changes, and some may affect almost all rates in the tariff. Under its present organization, the Commission would be totally unable to examine such a large number of proposals for reasonableness.

The fact that rates would not automatically decrease should antitrust immunity be removed was reflected in a survey conducted by *Transportation and Distribution Management* during 1974. Shippers were asked to predict the effect on rates of the removal of antitrust immunity. Only one percent of those responding to the survey projected lower rates while eleven percent felt that rates would be *higher*. Significantly, 45 percent said that removing antitrust immunity would result in more competitive ratemaking, but it did not directly follow that this would produce lower rates.

Even if we assume that rate reductions would occur, the nature of these decreases may not be desirable from a socio-economic stance. Competitive pressure producing a downward movement on rates could lead to rampant cut-rate competition and eventual rate wars. This observation would be especially true for the traffic of major volume shippers moving between key metropolitan centers. Uniformity and standardization of pricing services would deteriorate as these conflicts developed. Inadequate revenues caused by downward pressure on rates and increased cost of publication would result in the beginning of unsafe operations and would be followed by a deterioration of reliable service and financial instability. The viability of such a transportation system is at best tenuous.

Elimination of Bureau Delays

The final assumption upon which immunity repeal is predicated is that bureau delays caused by existing procedure would be eliminated. Although it is correct that more independent action would occur, repeal of antitrust immunity would not alter statutory requirements regarding publication, 30-day notice periods, public inspection, reasonableness, or non-discriminatory nature of single-line rates. Also, any interested party would still have the right to protest a proposed change. In reality, repeal of immunity would alter only one factor: a competitor's knowledge of intended publication and justification for change.

With repeal, when a competitor published a new single-line rate, a carrier would be forced to either blindly publish a competitive rate or petition for its suspension. If protested the carrier would have to justify the new rate. Thus, justification would eventually be revealed through the protest procedure rather than through bureau discussion. The result would be a substantial increase in the number of protests and elimination of the present orderly system of ratemaking. Potential delays under this system would exceed those experienced under existing procedure.

Further delays would occur for general adjustments. These adjustments would be restricted to joint rates only, and once such changes were made, independent changes in single-line rates would have to be effected. This would be necessary in order to implement uniform application on both single-line and joint-line shipments. The result would be further delay in establishing general adjustments often urgently needed by carriers or shippers.

CONCLUSIONS AND RECOMMENDATION

During the past "Vietnam" and "Watergate" periods, this country's institutions have been under increased attack. The Interstate Commerce Commission and regulated rate bureaus are merely one small dimension of this widespread attack. Rate bureaus enable the ICC to better administer the Interstate Commerce Act, and they provide the procedural forum for publishing through routes and joint-rates. The purpose of this paper was to demonstrate how removal of antitrust immunity from joint-rate considerations not only will be detrimental to the United States transportation network, but will also be inflationary if enacted.

Before eliminating single-line immunity, legislators should consider the following:

1. Single-line and joint-line rates are so intertwined that they cannot be effectively separated. Any attempt to do so could result in the demise of joint rates in the motor carrier industry and seriously hamper joint rate-making in the railroad industry.

2. Carriers could hardly be expected to meet and discuss specific joint-rates without mentioning single-line rates or other joint-rates.

3. No proof exists that rate levels would in fact fall. On the contrary,

joint rates may increase as they become more of a combination of local rates. In addition, the increased cost of tariff publication and rate monitoring could mitigate possible reduction. Finally, even if single-line rates did fall, the rate cutting nature of such a decrease could be detrimental to service and financial stability.

4. While rate changes would be made independently of bureaus, existing statutory requirements and protest procedures would not permit any significant reduction in time necessary to implement changes. On the contrary, the plethora of protests could overburden an already heavy ICC workload.

5. Support for repeal is not overwhelming. In a study conducted by the authors regarding rate bureau operations, it was found that only approximately 5 percent of the shippers surveyed indicated that single-line immunity was a detrimental activity of rate bureaus. Also, not one rate bureau felt that single-line immunity should be removed. While this latter fact is not surprising, it does reflect to some extent the sentiment of carriers.

The issue of single-line immunity for rate bureaus has centered on an individual carrier's right to establish rates free of rate bureau purview. Under present mandates of Section 5(a) every carrier has this right via independent action. Therefore, it does not appear that removal of this immunity would serve any useful purpose. In fact, the result most likely would be a destruction of rate stability and uniformity.

Notes

[1]Ex Parte 297, Rate Bureau Investigation (June 3, 1975), 349 I.C.C. 811.

[2]Ibid., pp. 841-846.

[3]Although motor carriers publish through routes and joint-rates, Part II of the Interstate Commerce Act does not legally compel these carriers to enter into such arrangements.

[4]Grant M. Davis and Stephen W. Brown, Logistics Management (Lexington, Massachusetts: D. C. Heath and Company, 1974), p. 360.

[5]Supra, note 3.

[6]Public Law 785, 76th Cong., 2d Sess., 1940.

[7]For an in-depth review of early bureau activities, consult Grant M. Davis and Charles S. Sherwood, Rate Bureaus and Antitrust Conflicts in Transportation: Public Policy Issues (New York: Praeger Press, 1975), Chapter 2.

[8]See U.S. v. Trans-Missouri: Freight Association, 171 U.S. 290 (1887), and U.S. v. Joint Traffic Association, 171 U.S. 505 (1898).

[9]Supra, note 7, Public Law 662, 80th Cong., 2d Sess., 1948, enacting Sec. 5a of the Interstate Commerce Act.

[10]See James M. Souby, Jr., "Operations of Railroad Rate Organization Approved Under Section 5a of the Interstate Commerce Act," ICC Prac. J. 977 (1974), for an example of a bureau's functioning under antitrust exemption.

[11]Rate conference executives contend the existing rate structure will be destroyed if such provisions become law.

[12]S. 1876 and H.R. 768, Rail Revitalization Act of 1975.

[13]Presently, legislation is being drafted for motor carrier rate bureaus.

[14]This problem will be even more acute in the motor carrier industry.

Chapter 4

Collective Ratemaking and the U.S. Department of Transportation

Created in 1966,[1] the U.S. Department of Transportation (DOT) was designed to correct historic transportation deficiencies such as lack of program coordination, inadequate intermodal planning, and lack of uniform standards for federal transportation projects predicated on economically sound investment criteria.[2] Considerable opposition to the establishment of the department developed and water transportation promotion was ultimately excluded from the agency's functions.[3]

Presently, the Department of Transportation is the third largest executive agency in the federal government with a budget exceeding $10 billion during the 1980 fiscal year.[4] The department's objectives are:

1. Economic efficiency in transportation
2. Safety
3. Support of other national interests
4. Program coordination

Departmental interest in collective ratemaking is expressed in its objective relating to economic efficiency in transportation. Pursuit of the objective is manifested in the DOT's efforts to deregulate the for-hire intercity trucking industry.[5] Indeed, the DOT invested substantial effort in Ex Parte 297 and has initiated several legislative proposals designed to deregulate the industry. It has lobbied extensively toward its goal by employing activities ranging from maintain-

---

[1]U.S. Congress, Public Law 89-640, 89th Congress, 2nd Sess., 1966.

[2]U.S. National Transportation Policy, 1971.

[3]Grant M. Davis, The Department of Transportation (Lexington, Mass.: D. C. Heath and Company, 1970), Chapters 1-5.

[4]U.S. Administrative Budget.

[5]Grant M. Davis, "The Transportation Acts of 1972 and Evaluation," Arkansas Business and Economic Review, Vol. 5, No. 3 (August 1972), pp. 26-30.

ing a deregulation hot-line in Washington to sponsoring studies of carrier services.[6] One study which revealed shippers were generally pleased with motor carrier services never received general distribution. The DOT position regarding collective ratemaking is similar to that of the Department of Justice[7] in that both want to repeal the present antitrust immunity provisions of Reed-Bulwinkle.

---

[6]Compiled from DOT fact sheets.

[7]Inasmuch as both agencies are a part of the executive branch of government and indeed appear sometimes to co-sponsor similar legislation, their stances with respect to collective ratemaking are similar.

Chapter 5

Collective Ratemaking and the Deregulation Movement

Under the general banner of deregulation, some of the movement's disciples have focused upon the transportation industry, in particular, the trucking industry where they seek to end both entry and rate controls. They believe that competition does not presently exist in the transportation industry and that rates are set to benefit the industry through covert means. They insist that the industry approximates the purely competitive model because of small threshold costs required for market entry, a homogeneous unit of output, and, of course, natural competition in the absence of regulation.[1]

To support their position, advocates of deregulation point to certificate restriction, collective ratemaking, empty backhauls, and energy as principal problems affiliated with motor carrier regulation. They claim that, if market entry barriers achieved through the certification process were eliminated or diminished, together with a concurrent elimination of collective ratemaking, rates would decrease substantially and overall service offerings by the industry would improve considerably.[2] In essence, this summarizes the general position of individuals, groups, and agencies advocating deregulation.

There are numerous flaws with the fundamental position of those advocating deregulation of the intercity freight transportation system. First, available evidence indicates that the industry does not approximate pure competition even though there are over 16,000 motor carriers regulated by the Interstate Commerce Commis-

---

[1]John R. Myer, *et al.*, *The Economics of Competition in the Transportation Industries* (Cambridge, Mass.: Harvard University Press, 1959), pp. 173-174. Also consult Walter Adams and James Hendry, *Trucking Mergers Concentration in Small Business: An Analysis of Interstate Commerce Commission Policy, 1950-56* (Washington, D.C.: U.S. Government Printing Office, 1956). Also, consult Robert S. Spann and Edward W. Eckerson, "The Economics of Railroading and the Beginning of Cartelization and Regulation," *The Bell Journal of Economics and Management Science*, Vol. 1, No. 2 (Autumn 1970), p. 243.

[2]This is most unlikely. See Grant M. Davis and L. J. Rosenberg, "Physical Distribution and the Regulatory Constraints: An Analysis," *Transportation Journal*, Vol. 15, No. 3 (Spring 1976), pp. 87-92.

sion.[3] In terms of industry structure classification, the industry can best be fitted into the differentiated monopolistic competitive model.[4] This classification does not create any particular public policy issues because the ICC has ultimate jurisdictional responsibility over both rates and services. As previously indicated, available evidence indicates conferences materially assist the Commission in its area of responsibility.

A misconception in the regulation versus deregulation controversy involves the unit of production in transportation. The homogeneous unit of production assumption is important to any serious contention that the industry, in the absence of entry and rate control, approximates pure competition. Thus, concern is centered on the basic unit of output in the intercity trucking industry, i.e., the freight ton-mile.[5] While it is certainly true that the reporting aspect of the ton-mile is used in the freight industry, the measurement is anything but homogeneous--the value of a ton-mile varies with the commodity transported and the utility accruing to the individual shipper.[6] The existence of different classifications of freight and different certificates attests to this product offering uniqueness.[7] There is no question but that the ton-mile production unit is employed in measuring transportation output, but this does not imply that any assumptions of homogeneity regarding the measurement are valid.[8] Analogous to the general level of rates, the ton-mile is virtually meaningless in terms of a homogeneous assumption because the service has been differentiated in terms of individual commodities, and this uniqueness is based on commodity and individual shipper preference.[9]

Another misconception involving the regulation-deregulation debate concerns collective ratemaking in transportation pricing. Advocates of deregulation allege that in a free market environment the overall level of freight rates will decline because of the forces of supply and demand in the market. This supposition is again predicated on the purely competitive market assumption, wherein marginal operators will enter and leave the freight market. However, while the entrance of marginal firms into the market can lead to lower rates, their departure can result in higher rates with no corresponding common carrier duties. Any review of the owner-operator dilemma reveals the fragile, undercapitalized nature of this source of transport supply.[10] Pursued to its logical conclusion, this situation could revert the indus-

---

[3] Annual Report, U.S. Interstate Commerce Commission, 1979.

[4] Roy J. Sampson, "Inherent Advantages Under Regulation," American Economic Review, Vol. 62 (May 1972), pp. 55-61.

[5] George W. Wilson, Essays on Some Unsettled Questions in the Economics of Transportation (Bloomington, Ind.: Graduate School of Business, Indiana University, 1962), 182 pages.

[6] Grant M. Davis and Charles S. Sherwood, "Transportation Regulation: Another Dimension," ICC Practitioners' Journal, Vol. 42, No. 2 (January/February 1975), pp. 159-169.

[7] Review any standard text dealing with certificate classification.

[8] Wilson, loc. cit.

[9] Grant M. Davis and L. J. Combs, "Some Observations Regarding Value of Service Pricing in Transportation," Transportation Journal, Vol. 4, No. 3 (Spring 1975), pp. 49-58.

[10] D. Daryl Wyckoff and Davis H. Maistron, "The U.S. Owner-Operator Trucker: A Transportation Policy Based on Personal Bankruptcy," in Proceedings: Transportation Research Forum (Oxford, Ind.: Richard B. Cross Co., 1977), pp. 291-297.

try to conditions worse than those existing in 1935.[11] Not only would rates fluctuate considerably, with an attendant impact on plant location and existing channels of distribution, but historical patterns of commerce would be disrupted.[12] Also, a review of the aggregate rate level reveals that regulated rates have not risen as much in this industry as prices have in others. Current freight rates are, moreover, determined by the forces of supply and demand in the market in terms of price-quality relationships through collective ratemaking. Carriers representing supply and shippers representing demand interact to establish price and service offerings. All parties in this decision-making process have vital and direct input into the pricing process.

As previously indicated, economic efficiency in all modes of transportation represents a paramount goal of the Department of Transportation.[13] In this regard, the agency has asserted that economic regulation in the trucking industry has resulted in substantial resource misallocation due to empty backhauls and certificate restrictions. This is not totally true. Although there are some empty deadhead miles in motor transportation, the amount is considerably smaller among common carriers that belong to bureaus than for other carriers. Most empty mileage is generated by specialized carriers such as automobile haulers who could not physically transport general commodities. The ICC is charged with the administrative responsibility of balancing competition and monopoly in the marketplace. This decision, of course, is influenced by the presence of competing carriers, revenue diversion, and other factors that make certificate restrictions necessary.

Many recent discussions regarding the presence or absence of economies of scale in the intercity trucking industry affirm that the presence of economies of scale is important in the public policy debate involving regulation, of which collective ratemaking plays an important part, because their presence indicates that rate and entry control can result in a larger level of output to society at a lower per unit price.[14] Available evidence recently reported by Garland Chow indicates that economies of scale are present in this industry.

Economic growth represents a major goal of U.S. economic policy. Even though our domestic economy is presently in a state of "stagflation," growth remains a viable national goal as represented by the Employment Act of 1946. The United States consists of numerous interrelated infrastructures that on the whole constitute one domestic economy. One of the principal components of an infrastructure is transportation facilities and services. Stable rates and continuous, discernible services, derived through the medium of rate bureaus and the conference method of ratemaking, enable firms to establish distribution centers based on established rate relationships. Collective ratemaking, through the medium of shipper and carrier input, exerts an important impact upon the location and extent of industrial utilization and distribution in an infrastructure, hence, leading to economic growth through the medium of capital formation.

Collective ratemaking plays an unequivocal role in transportation and contributes to an orderly, expanding transportation network. Not only is economic growth

---

[11]Grant M. Davis, editor, Transportation Regulation: A Pragmatic Assessment (Danville, Ill.: The Interstate Printers & Publishers, Inc., 1975), Chapters 2 and 3.

[12]Ibid.

[13]Grant M. Davis, "The Department of Transportation: A Study of Organizational Futility—A Later View," Public Utility Fortnightly, Vol. 87, No. 11 (May 27, 1971), pp. 29-33.

[14]Statement of Grant M. Davis in Ex Parte 297, Sub. 4.

associated with transportation services and prices, but the pricing efficiency aspects of the industry are designed in such a fashion that reasonable rates are levied through the interaction of both the suppliers and the receivers in the marketplace, i.e., shippers and carriers.

Chapter 6

COLLECTIVE RATEMAKING AND THE SHIPPER

The domestic transportation market can be directly defined as consisting of a definitive number of carriers on the one hand and a plethora of buyers (shippers) on the other hand. Advocates favoring elimination of collective ratemaking basically contend that bureaus and conferences violate the antitrust laws and publish rates higher than could be expected in the so-called free market.[1] Available empirical evidence indicates that collective ratemaking is an acceptable pricing mechanism for the consumers of transportation services.

In a survey conducted at the University of Arkansas Center for Transportation Research in 1975, a questionnaire was mailed to a randomly selected group of traffic executives who were members of the National Council of Physical Distribution. It revealed that not only were a majority of members in favor of retaining the ICC form of regulation, with entry and rate control, but, likewise, the executives were in favor of maintaining the basic structure of collective ratemaking through conferences.[2] Also, the professional group perceived, for the most part, a substantial increase in the level of freight rates in the absence of collective ratemaking. A more recent survey of this group in 1979 revealed this perception of the level of rates had been reinforced considerably. Indeed, a larger number of respondents replied to the most recent survey and indicated that they strongly believed rates would increase substantially within a nonregulated environment.

Relative to collective ratemaking, most of the 1975 respondents favored retaining the present method for publishing rates, an observation reinforced by the 1979 survey.[3] Obviously, from the demand side, the present system of collective ratemaking is adequately meeting consumer needs for transportation output. Another interesting dimension of shipper perceptions of collective ratemaking revealed in the surveys is that cross-subsidization of commodities and communities did not constitute any undue burden on their respective shipping activities.

The same questionnaires, with no modifications, were mailed to a randomly selected sample of certified members of the American Society of Traffic and Transpor-

---

[1]See Grant M. Davis and L. J. Rosenberg, "Physical Distribution and the Regulatory Constraints: An Analysis," Transportation Journal, Vol. 15, No. 3 (Spring 1976), pp. 87-92.

[2]Ibid.

[3]Forthcoming.

tation. This random sample had successfully completed a rigorous testing process designed to measure their relative traffic expertise. Regarding ICC regulations, competition, level of rates, the need for collective ratemaking, service, and other important elements of the regulation-deregulation debate, they responded strongly that there is a need for the commission form of regulation and for collective ratemaking.

A subsequent statistical analysis of perceptions shared between the two groups of transportation professionals was undertaken, with the results being published in a leading academic journal. The results of the statistical tests indicate that, the more familiarity and expertise one gains about transportation and collective ratemaking, the more realistically one is able to assess the debate. That is, those working daily with rate bureaus understand their vital function. From a shipper's perspective, there was clear preference to establish price in this manner in order to purchase transportation from an economically sound common carrier system which provides dependable service, facilitates service to geographical market territories, and provides channels of procurement and distribution.[4]

A follow-up survey conducted during 1979 revealed no basic shifts in shipper group perceptions regarding the need for maintaining collective ratemaking and economic regulation in the industry. Indeed, the percentage of respondents favoring collective ratemaking and economic regulation, with some modifications, actually increased because of a discrete perception of increased freight rates, additional capital investment in distribution centers, uncertainties, and substantially fluctuating channels of procurement and distribution.

---

[4]Grant M. Davis, *et al.*, "An Empirical Assessment of the Traffic Executive's Perceptions Regarding Controversies in Transportation Regulation," *ICC Practitioners' Journal* (November/December, 1976), pp. 60-66.

An Empirical Assessment of the Traffic Executive's Perceptions Regarding Controversies in Transportation Regulation*

GRANT M. DAVIS, L. J. ROSENBERG, and
CHARLES S. SHERWOOD

[Editor's Note: Collective ratemaking, one of the principal issues involved in the regulation-deregulation debate, is obviously a benefit to the vast majority of industrial shippers who purchase transportation in a regulated environment. The certified members of the American Society of Traffic and Transportation, one group of traffic executives, have evidenced their expertise in traffic matters by completing a series of examinations in the field of transportation and physical distribution. A random sample of members of this group were interviewed, and the results are included in an article written by Grant M. Davis, L. J. Rosenberg, and Charles S. Sherwood. In "An Empirical Assessment of the Traffic Executive's Perceptions Regarding Controversies in Transportation Regulation," the respondents were asked if their business firm would benefit if the rate bureau system of establishing rates were: (1) unchanged; (2) slightly modified; (3) greatly modified; or (4) abolished. Nine percent of the respondents favored: (1); 62 percent advocated (2); 26 percent agreed with (3); and only two percent believed in (4).]

During the past several years, the executive branch of the federal government has introduced legislation to the Congress containing provisions designed substantially to modify transportation legislation in the United States.[1] Considerable

*Reprinted by permission of the <u>ICC Practitioners' Journal</u>.

polemics surround these executive branch proposals and an inordinate degree of misinformation ranging from one-sided television special by the American Broadcasting Company,[2] to a highly slanted article in Reader's Digest.[3] Needless to say, during the course of this controversy, none of the framers of the proposed changes appears to have consulted the professional traffic executive who routinely participates in purchasing transport service from regulated carriers.[4]

Indeed, substantial pyrotechnics have been generated as a result of proposed federal legislation regarding transportation regulation. The fundamental issues involved, moreover, in the transportation regulation-deregulation debate are level of freight rates, cross subsidization of shippers, market entry, private carriage, rate bureaus, and others.[5] These issues are comprehensive, and therefore any serious researcher should not anticipate consensus among all professional traffic executives.

The fundamental purpose of this manuscript is to report the results of a questionnaire mailed to 475 traffic executives who have been elected to certified membership in the American Society of Traffic and Transportation. The logic for selecting these executives is simply that they have completed all segments of the Society's certification process and therefore were assumed to be familiar with the comprehensive and complex issues involved in transportation regulation. In no way are the responses by these individual society members reflective of any policy of the American Society of Traffic and Transportation. Indeed, the only reason for selecting certified members was their demonstrated knowledge of transportation which is reflected in their certified status.

THE SAMPLE STRUCTURE

Although there are numerous membership categories in the American Society of Traffic,[6] the certified classification requires successfully completing written examinations in transportation economics, logistics, traffic, transportation law,[7] carrier management,[8] and general business. Also, an original research paper regarding some aspect of transportation is required. A sample group of 475 certified members were selected from the Society's membership roster. Excluded were certified members employed by carriers, government agencies, and universities.[9] The remaining members were selected on a random basis. Two hundred and twenty-one returns, or 47 percent, were received.

Even though the Administration does not outright advocate the abolition of the Interstate Commerce Commission and Civil Aeronautics Board, their existence constitutes an issue to many of the individuals and institutions involved in the current regulation-deregulation debate. We asked our sample of traffic executives if it would be advantageous to their firm if the independent regulatory agencies were: (1) unchanged; (2) slightly modified; (3) greatly changed; or (4) abolished. Only 1.6 percent of the sample respondents answered that it would be advantageous to their respective firms if these agencies were abolished and 21 percent thought a substantial change would help. But 78 percent of the respondents believed that minor modifications could assist their firm. Interestingly, 98 percent did not believe that abolishing the independent agencies would be beneficial to their respective firms.

A second major regulatory controversy in transportation involves rate bureaus. A review of the literature in transportation indicates polemics have surrounded rate bureaus periodically for the past 86 years.[10] Needless to say, the general public does not understand how rate bureaus function, and the recent legislation has restricted many of their activities.[11] In this regard, the respondents were asked if their business firm would benefit if the rate bureau system of establishing rates were: (1) unchanged; (2) slightly modified; (3) greatly modified; or (4) abolished.

Nine percent responded that their firms would benefit if the present system remains unchanged, whereas 62 percent believe they would benefit from a slight modification, and 26 percent contended their respective firms would be assisted if a great change occurred in the present method for establishing rates. Only two percent of the respondents believed the companies they represent would benefit by abolishing rate bureaus.

Another controversial area involved in the regulation debate is the aggregate level of freight rates. One school of thought contends that deregulation would increase competition and result in lower rates. Conversely, another group contends that rates would increase in the absence of Commission and Board price regulation. The level of industrial and aggregate freight rates is important to the industrial purchaser of transportation, so the respondents were asked the following question: If the ICC and other regulatory agencies were abolished, what effect do you think it would have on overall freight rates? Forty-nine percent of the respondents believed that rates would be increased substantially, and 24 percent contended that rates would increase slightly. Twelve percent, on the other hand, believed that no change would occur in rates, but 36 percent contended that rates would be slightly lower. Only 9 percent of the respondents perceived rates to be substantially lower if the regulatory commissions and rate control were abolished.

Proponents of transportation deregulation allege that truck service would improve if market barriers were eliminated. In this regard, the respondents were asked the following question: What effect on the availability of freight service to your firm would deregulation of the trucking industry have? Thirty-five percent of the respondents believed that service would be much worse, whereas 20 percent contended that service would be slightly worse. Also, 14 percent believed there would be no change at all. Conversely, 24 percent of the respondents maintained that service would be slightly better and 4 percent contended that service would be greatly improved.

Another polemical segment of the regulation debate focuses upon the extent of competition in the trucking industry. Advocates favoring deregulation allege that the very existence of the Interstate Commerce Commission reduces or hinders competition in the regulated segment of the intercity trucking industry. Sixteen percent of the respondents asserted that regulatory commissions greatly reduce competition, and 34 percent contended that their presence resulted in a moderate reduction in competition in the industry. Thirty-five percent of the respondents perceived some slight hinderance of competition in trucking, whereas 15 percent believed there is no hinderance.

Continuing with competition, the sample respondents were asked the following question concerning intermodal competition: If the regulatory commissions were abolished, competition between the various modes would: (1) not increase; (2) slightly increase; (3) moderately increase; or (4) substantially increase? Eleven percent of the respondents did not foresee any increase in intermodal competition, and 21 percent contended that some slight increase would develop. Interestingly, 37 percent believed a moderate increase in intermodal competition would occur, and 32 percent asserted that there would be a substantial increase in competition between the various modes for freight transportation.

The Administration's Transportation Modernization Bill contained provisions that would liberalize entry into the motor carrier industry.[12] Many advocates of deregulation favor freer entry into this particular industry because before 1935, trucking approximated the purely competitive model. In this regard, the sample respondents were asked: Will it be advantageous to your company if the existing regulatory barriers preventing unlimited entry in common motor industry are maintained, partially relaxed, greatly relaxed, or eliminated? Thirty percent of the respondents asserted that it would be advantageous to their respective business organizations if the current entry requirements are maintained, and 54 percent stated a partial relaxation should occur. Significantly, only 12 percent of the respondents contended their firms would benefit from greatly relaxed barriers, and 3 percent believed that eliminating entry requirements would be advantageous to their firms.

Another popular argument proffered by advocates of deregulation involves the number of carriers providing service to a given locale. The general scenario of this controversial subject is that service will increase to many points where demand is substantial. Or common carrier responsibilities to serve all points will be effectively negated. One government official alleges that deregulating the motor carrier industry will increase service in rural areas![13] Relative to this controversial subject, the respondents were requested to answer the following inquiry: What impact would the elimination of the transportation regulatory agencies have on the number of common carriers serving their respective firms? Forty-one percent believed a slight increase would occur. But 17 percent stated that there would be a slight decrease in the number of motor carriers providing service, and only 8 percent believed there will be substantially less carriers. Eighteen percent perceived no change in the number of carriers. The sample contained respondents located in both urban and rural areas.

An alternative to common carriage is private fleets. Indeed, proponents of trucking deregulation contend that the number of private fleets would be decreased if market entry barriers were eliminated in motor transportation. With respect to decreases in private carriage, the respondents were asked: What would the impact of eliminating regulatory agencies have on the number of private fleets? Twenty percent replied there would be substantially fewer, and 21 percent believed there would be a few less. On the other hand, 20 percent contended that the number would remain unchanged, and only 19 percent of the respondents perceived there would be more.

Another polemical issue in transportation regulation and deregulation involves cross-subsidization of shippers and communities.[14] Indeed, the general thrust toward deregulation is predicated on a belief that economic efficiency can be attained by eliminating cross-subsidization. Because of the magnitude of this issue, the following question was directed to the respondents: Is your firm subsidizing the cost of providing trucking services to remote areas? Surprisingly, 43 percent of the respondents replied no, and 42 percent believed that some slight cross-subsidization did exist but was not financially detrimental. Only 11 percent of the respondents perceived a substantial degree of cross-subsidization to rural areas by trucking concerns, and 2 percent stated that a great amount exists.

Backhauls, or empty miles, in the trucking industry constitutes yet another controversial issue in transportation regulation. Some studies report 58 percent of all truck mileage is empty,[15] whereas other studies show rates as low as 1 to 2 percent empty mileage.[16] In this regard, the following inquiry was addressed to the sample respondents: On an overall basis, including the effect on common carriers, what would be the impact on your firm if all exempt truckers and private carriers were permitted to pick up payloads on backhauls? Twelve percent of the respondents replied that such an action would greatly help their respective business firms, whereas 22 percent believed there would be a substantial help. Twenty-three percent stated such provisions could be of some slight financial help. Fourteen percent replied that the end effect would be neutral, and 28 percent contended such a course of action would be detrimental. Surprisingly, over 50 percent of the respondents did not perceive any financial advantage accruing to their firms by liberalizing backhauls for private and exempt carriers.

In the area of physical distribution, some claims have been advanced that deregulation of the transportation industry would reduce the need for maintaining an extensive number of distribution centers because more flexibility would be injected into common service offerings. At this point, the respondents were asked:

What effect would the elimination of freight regulatory agencies have on the number of distribution centers operated or utilized by your firm? Five percent of the respondents believed more centers would be required, whereas 36 percent perceived little if any change. Significantly, 56 percent thought the absolute number of distribution centers would remain unchanged, and only 2 percent replied that fewer would be used.

Inventory levels are partially a function of carrier service dependability, as for example, particular companies, such as Ford Motor Company, whose assembly plant parts inventory is virtually zero. In this regard, the respondents were asked: What impact would the demise of the ICC and CAB have on the size of inventory of your firm? Interestingly, only 2 percent replied inventories would be smaller. On the other hand, 67 percent contended that inventory size would not change, and 16 percent stated that they would be slightly larger. Three percent of the respondents believed that inventory size would be much larger.

What sort of profile may be used to describe the respondents other than that they are certified members of the American Society of Traffic and Transportation and are not carrier or educator members? Sixty-three percent were with firms employing more than 2,500 people; 2 percent from firms of 2,001 to 2,500; 6 percent from 1,501 to 2,000; 3 percent from 1,001 to 1,500; 10 percent from 501 to 1,000; and 14 percent from firms of 500 or less. Thirty percent of the respondents were employed by firms with revenues exceeding one billion, 14 percent from 500 million to one billion, 35 percent from 100 to 500 million, 9 percent from 50 to 99 million, 7 percent from 10 to 49 million, and 3 percent earned revenues under 10 million. Seventy-seven percent of the respondents were engaged in manufacturing, 6 percent in wholesaling, 7 percent in retailing, and 7 percent from miscellaneous industries.

CONCLUSIONS

The purpose of this paper is to ascertain how traffic executives who have attained certification status in the American Society of Traffic and Transportation perceive various issues associated with the "regulation-deregulation" controversy. Several pertinent observations may be gleaned from the data collected in the sample survey.

First, these traffic executives do not believe that any substantial advantages would accrue to their firms by abolishing the independent regulatory agencies. Seconly, the majority of the respondents do not perceive any economic benefits to be derived from eliminating the present system of establishing freight rates nor that deregulation would result in any substantial reduction in freight rates. Thirdly, the respondents do not believe that any material increase in truck service would develop under deregulation, and they contend that regulatory commissions do not substantially hinder competition. Fourth, these executives contend market entry should be partially relaxed and they assert that intermodal competition would not increase under deregulation. Fifth, the respondents do not foresee any increase in the number of motor carriers serving their firms under deregulation, and they foresee no decline in proprietary trucking. Sixth, they do not perceive any substantial amount of cross-subsidization in the motor carrier industry and do not believe that eliminating backhaul restrictions would necessarily assist their business firms.

Institutions in our society must be sensitive to changing consumer needs. Changes, however, should be based on real need, not some ideal or assumed need. In this regard, any substantive modification of our present regulatory system should be predicated on shipper and public needs. The industrial consumer of transportation production, for the most part, appears to view the transport issues considerably differently from those individuals desiring extensive modifications of the system.

Notes

[1]The Railroad Revitalization and Regulatory Reform Act of 1976 (Public Law 94-210), which in effect was Senate Bill 2718. Other legislation has been introduced dealing with motor and air carriers.

[2]"The Washington Regulators--How They Cost You Money," American Broadcasting System (February 1, 1975).

[3]Mark Frazier, "Highway Robbery--Via the ICC," Reader's Digest, Vol. 106, No. 633 (January 1975), pp. 72-76.

[4]The National Industrial Traffic League and Southern Traffic League have testified before Congress regarding transportation matters and they do represent shipper interests.

[5]Consult Grant M. Davis, Transportation Regulation: A Pragmatic Assessment (Danville, Ill.: Interstate Publishers, 1976), Chapter 2, which contains an in depth examination of the issues involved in the transportation "regulation-deregulation" controversy.

[6]Other categories include: (1) Educator member; (2) founder member; (3) associate member; and (4) sustaining member.

[7]Members of the ICC Bar are excluded from sitting for this examination.

[8]This is a new examination.

[9]Although these members certainly have views regarding the issues, they were excluded because of the need to identify purchaser of transportation perspections. In this regard, government procurers of transportation were in fact excluded.

[10]See Grant M. Davis and Charles S. Sherwood, Rate Bureaus and Antitrust Conflicts in Transportation: Public Policy Issues (New York: Praeger Publishers, Inc., 1975), Chapter 2, for an extended review of the polemics associated with rate bureaus.

[11]Supra, note 1.

[12]Ibid.

[13]Remarks by Gary Broesmer, U.S. Department of Transportation, before the Transportation Forum: 1975, Little Rock, Arkansas, May 15, 1975.

[14]Cross-subsidization constitutes a major issue in transportation regulation. For reference regarding this issue, consult Davis, Transportation Regulation: A Pragmatic Assessment, loc. cit.

[15]U.S. Department of Transportation, Federal Highway Administration, Highway Statistics: 1973 (Washington: U.S. Government Printing Office, 1973), pp. 78-79.

[16]"Free Entry Is No Answer to Empty Truck Hauls, Study for ICC Concludes," Traffic World, Vol. 1.165, No. 6 (February 9, 1976), pp. 16-17.

Rate Bureau Cost and Benefits: The Carrier Perspective*

GARLAND CHOW and RICHARD F. POIST

[Editor's Note: In a previous article devoted to shipper investment in collective ratemaking, the benefits derived from collective ratemaking were enumerated in detail. However, carrier membership in rate conferences also confers obvious benefits to both the shipping public and the individual carrier members. A recent paper entitled "Rate Bureau Cost and Benefits: The Carrier Perspective," by Garland Chow and Richard F. Poist, delivered before the Transportation Research Forum, reports the results of a survey regarding average cost and bureau control by large carriers. Of the 850 carrier members of the Middle Atlantic Conference Rate Bureau and of the 306 nonmember carriers who were surveyed, a majority of the respondents believe strongly that bureaus are critical to preserving rate stability, to maintaining joint-line rates and service, and, above, all, to preventing rate discrimination.]

INTRODUCTION

Many motor carrier rates are set collectively in the regulated trucking industry. This is accomplished through the regional rate bureau which is an intramodal organization of carriers established to jointly consider rates, classifications, divisions, and other pricing matters in that region.[1] Under ordinary circumstances such collective action would be a violation of the Federal Antitrust laws. However, Congress exempted rate bureaus from the Federal Antitrust laws by passing the Reed-Bullwinkle Act.[2]

---

*Reprinted by permission of the Richard B. Cross Co.

The antitrust exemption for rate bureaus has been a source of controversy from its inception and this controversy has taken heightened importance in this decade of rapid price inflation. The Department of Transportation has repeatedly called for reducing or eliminating the role of the rate bureau in its legislative program for regulatory reform.[3] The ICC concluded one rate bureau investigation in June 1975 and ordered twelve procedural and organizational changes.[4] The ICC started two new proceedings in January 1976, to: (1) reconsider existing section 5a exemptions and, (2) determine if terms and conditions on railroad rate bureaus established by the Railroad Revitalization and Regulatory Reform Act of 1976 should be applied to other modes.[5] The Senate Subcommittee on Antitrust and Monopoly held hearings on Freight Rate Competition in the Motor Carrier Industry and a bill to remove the antitrust exemption is currently before the Senate Commerce Committee.[6] The final report of the National Commission for the Review of Antitrust Laws and Procedures states, "The Reed-Bullwinkle Act should be repealed."[7]

The purpose of this paper is to examine some of the issues raised in connection with the antitrust exemption from the carrier perspective. The carrier perspective can differ from the perspectives of the industry trade organizations and the rate bureaus who have expressed strong opposition to any proposals to weaken the rate bureau structure. It is frequently alleged that large carriers control the rate bureaus, using collective action as a tool to dampen the competitive inclinations of the smaller carriers. Likewise, it is frequently asserted that bureau carriers use the collective power of the rate bureau to restrict and contain independent ratemaking of both bureau and non-bureau members. Finally it is often claimed that the rate bureau's application of average cost pricing prevents efficient carriers from taking advantage of their efficiency and prevents inefficient carriers from charging rates commensurate with their level of costs. This analysis will differentiate between the perceptions of small and large carriers and between the perceptions of carriers with different propensities to act independently of the rate bureau. The information available did not allow a differentiation between efficient and inefficient carriers.

This examination of the carrier perspective on rate bureau issues is of no minor significance since several carriers have made public testimony both in support and in opposition to continued collective ratemaking. Do the viewpoints expressed publicly represent the views of an important segment of trucking or that of a vocal minority? If it is the former, it is clear that modification of collective ratemaking is in order.

METHODOLOGY AND COLLECTIVE RATEMAKING ISSUES

A mail questionnaire was employed to collect data from carriers affected by the actions of a major rate bureau. The questionnaire was designed to solicit responses on the following issues relevant to the current debate over collective ratemaking.

(1) Whether collective ratemaking enhances one or more National Transportation Policy Goals.

Carrier respondents were asked to agree or disagree with statements asserting that the rate bureau and collective ratemaking enhances specific goals.

There are numerous goals identified or implicit in the statement of National Transportation Policy and other parts of the Interstate Commerce Act. With regard to the general issue of collective ratemaking, three goals are especially relevant. It is frequently asserted that the collective ratemaking process:

- protects the shipping public from unjust, unreasonable, and discriminatory rates,
- ensures the shipping public a high degree of rate stability and certainty.
- facilitates the making of joint rates essential to the availability of joint service.

(2) Whether any of the goals that justify the collective ratemaking agreement can be accomplished by some other method than collective action.

Carrier respondents were asked to agree or disagree with statements asserting that specific goals would not be achieved without the existence of rate bureaus and collective ratemaking.

(3) Whether collective ratemaking has harmed interests intended to be protected by the antitrust laws.

Carrier respondents were asked to agree or disagree with statements regarding the significance and nature of competition in trucking. In addition, the carriers were asked questions designed to indicate whether or not bureaus are discouraging rate competition and the extent of that competition.

The questions and issues posed by the questionnaire are based on the premise that the ICC will continue its regulation of entry and rates. The same premises do not exist in all arguments against the existence of rate bureaus. Many arguments that support the abolition of rate bureaus are based on the assumption that the motor freight industry is workably competitive. The underlying premise is that there should neither be rate bureau exemptions nor economic regulation of rates or entry.

Two observations are relevant. First, it is not evident to every academician, transportation policy analyst, and other interested parties that the motor freight industry is workably competitive.[9] Our knowledge of the structure, conduct, and performance of unregulated or regulated trucking is woefully incomplete and we are only just beginning to recognize that the trucking industry may be better viewed as several industries.[10] Basic questions such as whether economies of scale exist in trucking remain controversial despite the plethora of recent empirical evidence.[11] Thus the validity of the expected performance of various deregulation measures is only as good as the underlying assumptions about market structure, and these assumptions are not as certain as they are frequently made out to be.

Second, in analyzing prospective policy changes, what is being changed must be separated from what is not being changed. The purpose of this investigation is to identify consequences resulting from changes in regulation of rate bureaus alone and not changes in overall rate or entry regulation. This was made explicit to the respondents.

Questionnaires were mailed out to 850 carrier members of the Middle Atlantic Conference Rate Bureau (MAC) and a systematic sample of 306 non-bureau carriers who have filed competitive, non-bureau tariffs in the Middle Atlantic territory. A response rate of 35% (N = 309) was realized for the bureau Carrier group and 9% (N = 29) for the non-bureau carrier group. The response rate for the non-bureau carriers was low and any conclusions made from these responses must be tentative.

Bureau carriers were classified in two distinct ways. First, bureau carriers were classified by size. As shown in Table 1 a significant number of bureau carriers in all size classes responded. Class I bureau carriers will be classified as large, and Class II and Class III bureau carriers will be classified as small carriers. The average intercity Class 1 general commodity carrier earned $36,000,000 annually in 1976. This is twelve times more earnings than the largest Class II carrier and 72 times the earnings of the largest Class III carrier.

Secondly, the bureau carriers were classified by whether they filed their own company tariffs independent of the rate bureau. One hundred forty nine (149) carriers indicated that they published their own LTL or TL tariffs and are identified as the 'independent rate' group for this analysis. It is assumed that these carriers publish their own tariffs to be price competitive and represent an industry segment that would object strongly to collective ratemaking if it retards the right to independent ratemaking. The 'non-independent rate' group of carriers is comprised of carriers relying solely on bureau tariff publication. An alternative assumption is that the carriers that do not publish independent rates have been prevented from doing so by the collective ratemaking system. Both the independent and non-independent carrier groups were made up of nearly equal proportions of large and small carriers.

TABLE 1

Size of Respondent Carriers

by I.C.C. Classification

Classification[1]	Bureau Carriers	Non-bureau Carriers	Total	Percent
Class I	125	10	135	40.1
Class II	113	16	129	38.3
Class III	68	2	70	20.8
Unclassified	3	-	3	.8
Total	309	28	336	100.0

[1]Class I — Annual revenue ≥$3,000,000
Class II — Annual revenue between $500,000 and $3,000,000
Class III — Annual revenue less than $500,000

All but two of the bureau carriers identified themselves as general commodity carriers. In contrast 21 of 27 non-bureau carrier respondents identified themselves as special commodity carriers. The non-bureau carriers also tended to be small as shown in Table 1. The non-bureau carriers were considered as one group due to the small number of responses.

CARRIER VIEWS ABOUT THE ROLE OF RATE BUREAUS IN ACHIEVING THE GOALS OF NATIONAL TRANSPORTATION POLICY

Carriers were asked questions relating to the role of rate bureaus in preventing price discrimination, maintaining rate stability, and maintaining joint line rates and service. The summaries shown in Tables 2 to 7 indicate that the large majority of the carriers, regardless of classification, view the rate bureaus as a valuable and necessary instrument used in the achievement of said goals.

The pattern of responses between the large and the small bureau carriers indicates that large carriers agree more strongly that rate bureaus are beneficial. However, the total level of favorable response is nearly identical. For example, 68% of the small bureau carriers strongly agree that rate discrimination would occur without rate bureaus as opposed to over 76% of the large bureau carriers as shown in Table 2. Yet 99.5% of the small carriers agree or strongly agree while only 95.9% of the large carriers both agree or strongly agree. A similar response pattern is observed between bureau carriers who publish their own tariffs and those that do not, with the carriers who publish their own tariffs agreeing less strongly.

While the non-bureau carriers agreed that rate bureaus enhance the said National Transportation goals less strongly than the bureau carriers, the majority of their responses were still favorable.

The Chi Square statistics displayed in Appendix 1 indicate that perception of benefits between large and small carriers were significantly different for the responses summarized in Tables 2 and 4 only. None of the differences in response between the independent carriers and non-independent carriers were statistically different as measured by the Chi Square statistic. Chi Square measures of significant difference in the responses between the bureau and non-bureau carriers were not calculated because of the large difference in sample sizes.

The non-bureau carriers placed the least value to rate bureaus with regard to their role in maintaining joint line service and rates. For example, only 65% of the non-bureau carriers agreed that rate bureaus are essential to the availability of joint rates as shown in Table 7. This may be explained by the dominance of TL operations for the non-bureau carriers which normally is produced as single line service. In fact most of the remaining non-bureau responses were neutral (30.8%) rather than negative suggesting that the non-bureau carrier doesn't have an opinion simply because of the lack of applicability to their operations.

TABLE 2

Rate Discrimination Would Occur Without Rate Bureaus

Respondent Group		Strongly Agree	Agree	Neutral	Disagree	Strongly Disagree
All Bureau Carriers	Percent:	71.2	26.8	1.0	.7	.3
Small Bureau Carriers	Percent:	68.2	31.3	.6	0	0

(Continued)

TABLE 2 (Continued)

Respondent Group		Strongly Agree	Agree	Neutral	Disagree	Strongly Disagree
Large Bureau Carriers	Percent:	76.4	19.5	1.6	1.6	.8
Bureau Carriers Publishing Own Tariff	Percent:	67.8	28.1	2.1	1.4	.7
Bureau Carriers No Individual Tariffs	Percent:	74.4	25.6			
Non-bureau Carriers	Percent:	29.6	55.6	0	11.1	3.7

CARRIER VIEWS ABOUT THE NATURE AND EXTENT OF COMPETITION IN THE TRUCKING INDUSTRIES

Carriers were asked to indicate their level of agreement or disagreement with the following statements about competition and ratemaking.

1. There is significant rate competition for freight traffic.

2. There is significant service competition for freight traffic.

3. Different rates reflecting different levels of service exist for freight traffic.

4. Independent Action through bureau procedure is difficult to get now-a-days.*

5. Rate changes for non-bureau (carrier) tariffs are difficult to get now-a-days.

Separate responses for each statement were requested for LTL and TL traffic.

The large majority of the carriers agree that significant rate competition, service competition and significant rate-service combinations exist in both the LTL and TL freight markets. For example, no less than 88% of any bureau group and 78% of the non-bureau carriers agreed or strongly agreed that significant rate competition exists in the less than truckload freight market. No less than 91% of any carrier group agreed or strongly agreed that significant rate competition exists in the truckload freight market.

The pattern of responses observed between large versus small, independent versus non-independent bureau and bureau versus non-bureau carriers observed earlier

*Not applicable to non-bureau carrier respondents.

TABLE 3

The Rate Bureau's Activities Assist in the Prevention of Rate Discrimination

Respondent Group		Strongly Agree	Agree	Neutral	Disagree	Strongly Disagree
All Bureau Carriers	Percent:	60.4	37.5	1.0	1.0	.7
Small Bureau Carriers	Percent:	56.5	41.2	1.1	.6	.6
Large Bureau Carriers	Percent:	67.5	29.3	.8	1.6	.8
Bureau Carriers Publishing Own Tariff	Percent:	55.1	40.1	2.0	1.4	1.4
Bureau Carriers No Individual Tariffs	Percent:	65.4	34.0		.6	
Non-bureau Carriers	Percent:	25.9	55.6	3.7	11.1	3.7

TABLE 4

Rate Instability and Uncertainty Would Occur Without Rate Bureaus

Respondent Group		Strongly Agree	Agree	Neutral	Disagree	Strongly Disagree
All Bureau Carriers	Percent:	71.4	27.3	.7	.3	.3
Small Bureau Carriers	Percent:	64.8	34.1	.6	.6	
Large Bureau Carriers	Percent:	81.3	17.1	.8		.8
Bureau Carriers Publishing Own Tariff	Percent:	64.4	32.9	1.4	.7	.7

(Continued)

TABLE 4 (Continued)

Respondent Group		Strongly Agree	Agree	Neutral	Disagree	Strongly Disagree
Bureau Carriers No Individual Tariffs	Percent:	77.8	22.2	0	0	0
Non-bureau Carriers	Percent:	37.0	40.7	3.7	18.5	0

is again evident. Small carriers agreed as frequently but less strongly than larger carriers. Bureau carriers who issue their own tariffs responded not too differently from carriers who do not. Again the majority (but a smaller percentage) of the non-bureau responses were in agreement with the bureau carrier responses. It is notable that the non-bureau carrier viewed the present level of competition on the TL markets as more significant than in the LTL markets. For example, over 91% of the response of the non-bureau carriers viewed TL rate competition as significant but only 79% viewed LTL rate competition as significant. Again this may reflect the non-bureau's carrier's greater familiarity with the TL freight market.

The majority of the carriers do not feel there is any difficulty in obtaining independent rates whether it is through bureau procedures or through publication of individual carrier tariffs. With one exception, fewer than 20% of the responses in any carrier grouping agreed or strongly agreed with statements indicating difficulty in obtaining independent rates. Consistent with this previous pattern of responses, the smaller carriers disagree less strongly and less frequently than the larger carriers that independent rates are difficult to obtain. However, the differences are due to the large number of neutral responses made by the smaller carriers. The response closest to being critical of the rate bureau process is the non-bureau carrier response to the "ease of obtaining independent—non-bureau TL rates" where 34.7% of the responses indicated difficulty in obtaining independent TL rates and 66.5% indicated no difficulty.

This paper will not report on the more detailed analysis of the types of services that carriers receive from rate bureaus. It can be assumed that carriers will have to obtain services presently provided by rate bureaus from other firms or from their own efforts. Each carrier was asked to indicate their level of agreement (or disagreement) with a statement that carrier costs will go up without rate bureaus. The results indicate that the majority of the bureau carriers feel that the costs of these services will rise.

SUMMARY AND IMPLICATIONS

There is significant controversy as to whether motor carrier rate bureaus should retain their antitrust immunity. Whether the activities performed by rate bureaus benefit the shipping public depends on whether such activities enhance the achievement of National Transportation Policy goals and to what degree this is offset by reduced competition. This paper analyzed survey responses which represent the carrier perspective of the latter costs and the former benefits of rate bureaus.

TABLE 5

Rate Bureaus Help Prevent Rate Stability and Uncertainty

Respondent Group		Strongly Agree	Agree	Neutral	Disagree	Strongly Disagree
All Bureau Carriers	Percent:	61.6	36.4	1.0	.3	.7
Small Bureau Carriers	Percent:	57.0	41.3	1.1	0	.6
Large Bureau Carriers	Percent:	69.1	28.5	.8	.8	.8
Bureau Carriers Publishing Own Tariff	Percent:	57.1	39.5	1.4	.7	1.4
Bureau Carriers No Individual Tariffs	Percent:	65.8	33.5	.6	0	0
Non-bureau Carriers	Percent:	33.3	40.7	11.1	11.1	3.7

The survey was made in the context of the continuation of present ICC regulation of rates and entry.

The responses indicate that the majority of the carriers perceive the rate bureau as critical to preserving rate stability, maintaining joint line rates and services, and preventing rate discrimination. These are all widely recognized goals of National Transportation Policy. Theoretically, any collusive structure, i.e., the rate bureau cartel, will lead to noncompetitive performance and conduct in the form of decreased rate and/or service competition. However, a majority of the carriers agree that significant rate and service competition exists in both the LTL and TL freight markets. Based on these responses, it can be concluded that the majority of the responding carriers feel that rate bureaus do provide essential benefits without seriously reducing competition.

The frequency and degree of independent action and bureau protests has been documented elsewhere and the impact on competition is subject to considerable debate. It is notable that the majority of carrier respondents agree that significant rate competition exists and agree that independent rates are not difficult to obtain.

The responses verified the notion that the intensity of competition differs slightly between the LTL and TL markets. The results indicate that the carriers perceive slightly less rate competition, somewhat fewer rate/service combinations, and somewhat greater difficulty in getting independently filed rates for LTL traffic than for TL traffic. However, it is not clear that the existence of rate bureaus are the cause of this difference since it is well recognized that tendencies toward industry concentration are much more evident in the LTL segment than the TL segment of traveling.

The responses suggest that small carriers have different attitudes and perceptions than large carriers though these differences are a matter of degree rather than conflict. The majority of both the small and large carriers agree that rate bureaus perform necessary functions but generally a larger percent of large carriers agree, more strongly. The majority of both large and small carriers also agree that their costs of operating their business will go up in the absence of rate bureaus and the availability of their services similar pattern of responses was found to exist between bureau and non-bureau carrier respondents.

TABLE 6

Joint Line Agreements Would Be Cancelled and the Benefits of Joint Line Service Lost Without Rate Bureaus

Respondent Group		Strongly Agree	Agree	Neutral	Disagree	Strongly Disagree
All Bureau Carriers	Percent:	58.7	34.0	5.3	2.0	0
Small Bureau Carriers	Percent:	57.8	35.5	5.8	1.7	0
Large Bureau Carriers	Percent:	61.6	31.2	4.8	2.4	0
Bureau Carriers Publishing Own Tariff	Percent:	56.3	34.7	6.9	2.1	0
Bureau Carriers No Individual Tariffs	Percent:	60.9	33.3	3.8	1.9	0
Non-bureau Carriers	Percent:	22.2	33.3	37.0	7.4	0

The evidence does not suggest that large carriers control the rate bureaus for their benefit and at the expense of their smaller competitors. The efficient development, consideration and publication of rates through the rate bureau process seems to be beneficial to large and small carriers alike. Similarly no significant difference of opinions exists between bureau carriers who publish their own tariffs and those who do not. Finally the views of the non-bureau carriers who responded did not differ significantly from the bureau carrier responses. In conclusion, the majority of carriers in all of the differentiated segments of the trucking industry perceive the rate bureau as an important tool for achieving National Transportation Policy goals and reducing carrier costs without seriously reducing the level and quality of competition.

TABLE 7

Respondent Group		Strongly Agree	Agree	Neutral	Disagree	Strongly Disagree
All Bureau Carriers	Percent:	60.1	34.9	4.0	1.0	0
Small Bureau Carriers	Percent:	56.7	37.4	5.3	.6	
Large Bureau Carriers	Percent:	65.3	30.6	2.4	1.6	
Bureau Carriers Publishing Own Tariff	Percent:	55.9	37.8	4.2	2.1	0
Bureau Carriers No Individual Tariffs	Percent:	63.9	32.3	3.9		
Non-bureau Carriers	Percent:	23.1	42.3	30.8	3.8	0

APPENDIX 1

STATISTICAL SIGNIFICANCE OF RESPONSE DIFFERENCES BETWEEN CARRIER CLASSIFICATIONS

The Chi-square test statistics (χ^2) helps us determine whether there is a systematic relationship between two variables. The χ^2 was computed for the relationship between the response to or question and the classification of carrier. The probability of obtaining the computed χ^2 for each relationship is shown below.

Significance Level of χ^2 Statistic For

Table	Large versus Small Bureau Carrier Responses	Independent and Non-independent Bureau Carrier Respondents
2	.0485	.1341
3	.2620	.0990
4	.0126	.0570
5	.1539	.2582
6	.8143	.6424
7	.2601	.1955

Footnotes

[1]A detailed description of rate bureau activities may be found in Grant M. Davis and Charles S. Sherwood Rate Bureaus and Antitrust Conflicts in Transportation, Public Policy Issues (New York: Praeger Publishers, 1975), pp. 52-60; Your Rate Association and You, Partners for Progress (Akron, Ohio: Eastern Central Motor Carriers Association); Charles Taff Commercial Motor Transportation 5th ed. (Cambridge, Md.: Cornell Maritime Press, 1975), pp. 374-83.

[2]49 U.S.C. 59. The legislative history of the act is traced concisely in James C. Johnson and James P. Rakowski, "The Reed-Bulwinkle Act (1948): A Thirty Year Perspective" Proceedings of the Nineteenth Annual Meeting of the Transportation Research Forum (Oxford, Ind.: Richard B. Cross Co., 1978): pp. 20-25.

[3]Transportation Regulatory Modernization Act (H.R. 11826 and S. 2842) submitted November 5, 1971 and Motor Carrier Reform Act (U.S. Department of Transportation, Dec. 1976).

[4]Ex Parte No. 297, "Rate Bureau Investigation." 349 I.C.C. 861 (1975). The most controversial of these changes appears to be the prohibition against rate bureaus protesting independent actions by its members. This change was challenged in court and upheld on June 1978.

[5]Ex Parte No. 297 (Sub No. 3), "Modified Terms and Conditions for Approval of Collective Ratemaking Agreements Under Section 5a of the Interstate Commerce Act" and Ex Parte No. 297 (Sub No. 4), "Reopening of Section 5a Application Proceedings to Take Additional Evidence." At the time of the writing of this paper, the I.C.C. served notice that they will apply to motor carriers the 4-R restrictions on collective ratemaking agreements. See Transport Topics, p. 1, March 5, 1979.

[6]"Kennedy Trucking Probe Shifts Stress to Effect of Limited Entry on Industry" Traffic World, Aug. 14, 1978, pp. 37-38; "Kennedy Introduces Bill Which Immediately Goes to Cannon's Committee" Transport Topics, March 26, 1979, p. 1.

[7]Final Report of the National Commission for the Review of Antitrust Laws and Procedures Chapter 10, p. 1 (Wash., D.C., 1979).

[8]Statements of Jack Beitler, W. J. Beitler Co., William J. Spina, Rite-Way Express, Richard E. Van Winkle, Arbet Truck Lines and Liniel G. Gregory, Jr., Russell Transfer before the Subcommittee on Antitrust and Monopoly, Committee on the Judiciary, U.S. Senate, October 27, 1977, on Freight Rate Competition in the Motor Carrier Industry.

[9]John C. Spychalski "Criticisms of Regulated Freight Transport: Do Economists' Perceptions Conform with Institutional Realities?" Transportation Journal, Vol. 14, No. 3 (Spring 1975) pp. 5-17.

[10]For a critique of the literature on the economics of trucking see Garland Chow The Economics of the Motor Freight Industries (Bloomington, Ind.: Division of Research, School of Business, Indiana University, 1978), pp. 42-100.

[11]See Garland Chow "The Status of Economies of Scale in Regulated Trucking" Proceedings of the 19th Annual Meeting of the Transportation Research Forum (Oxford, Ind.: Richard B. Cross Co., 1978), pp. 365-72.

The Reed-Bulwinkle Act (1948):
A Thirty Year Prospective*

JAMES C. JOHNSON and JAMES P. RAKOWSKI

[Editor's Note: Even though the Reed-Bulwinkle Act amended the Interstate Commerce Act, polemics have periodically erupted between the Antitrust Division of the U.S. Department of Justice and collective ratemaking. Not only do James C. Johnson and James P. Rakowski provide the reader with an essential historical perspective, but they also reveal that fears of monopoly abuse are unfounded in a paper entitled "The Reed-Bulwinkle Act (1948): A Thirty Year Perspective," presented before the Transportation Research Forum.]

INTRODUCTION

The Reed-Bulwinkle Act (1948) created Section 5a of the Interstate Commerce Act. It ended a long period of ambiguity concerning the exact legal status of carrier rate making organizations. The bill legalized rate bureaus by exempting them from the anti-trust laws as long as the agreements setting up the rules and procedures of the associations were approved by the Interstate Commerce Commission. Also, the right of individual carriers to make their own independent decisions regardless of the feeling of the bureau was guaranteed. The Reed-Bulwinkle Act is now thirty years old and many parties are questioning its usefulness and desirability under current conditions.

The Reed-Bulwinkle Act is today a highly emotional issue. Defenders of the present system are unequivocal in their advocacy:

- The American Trucking Association has declared, "Collective rate making is a transportation virtue, not a vice."[1]
- Jesse J. Friedman, an economic consultant, has charged, "It requires extraordinary, if not blind, faith in the therapeutic virtues of unrestricted com-

*Reprinted by permission of the Richard B. Cross Co.

petition as a universal medicine to give it serious consideration as a substitute for collective rate-making in motor freight service."[2]

Opponents of the Reed-Bulwinkle Act have been equally vociferous:

- John H. Shenefield, an antitrust lawyer for the Justice Department, declared, "It is the ICC—the government—that protects the cartel rates of bureau members from the competition of lower rates. We are the cartel managers, doing for the industry what other businessmen are indicted for."[3]

- Joe Sims, a Department of Justice lawyer, sarcastically quoted an ICC practitioner who noted, "Additionally, we have found the collective rate-making process produces a healthy, upward influence on prices which allows many small carriers to get rate adjustments they need to stay in business."[4]

This paper will trace the legislative history of the act, examine President Truman's veto, look at developments in the years after the 1948 Act was passed, examine current controversies, and the authors will present their opinion regarding this controversial subject.

LEGISLATIVE HISTORY

The impetus for the Reed-Bulwinkle Act was a 1942 investigation by the U.S. Department of Justice into railroad ratemaking practices. The act was not favorably reported out of congressional hearings and committees initially. It was voted on and rejected by the 79th Congress. A modified version of the bill was passed by the 80th Congress in 1948—it was vetoed by President Truman—and Congress easily overrode the veto. The debate in Congress was vigorous and lengthy. The circumstances surrounding the introduction and passage of the bill will now be examined.

Two suits were in the courts. In *United States v. Association of American Railroads*[5] the government claimed:

> The defendants merged the preexisting national and regional railroad rate bureaus and trade associations into an integrated hierarchy of bureaus and associations constituting a cartelized private government of the railroad industry which has continued to this day. The power of this private government derives from its collective control over railroad affairs and its authority is maintained by the economic discipline of its adherents.[6]

This case, in essence, claimed that the bureaus had monopoly control of the industry and used this power to keep various regions of the country in a subservient position to the eastern industrial and financial interests. This was accomplished by a complex system of discriminatory freight rates which severely hindered industrial development in many parts of the country. A similar suit, *Georgia v. Pennsylvania Railroad Co.*,[7] claimed that the railroad organizations purposely discriminated against the Southern region of the United States.

The Department of Justice claimed that the proposed bill was a railroad attempt to have Congress either head off or nullify whatever adverse rulings might conceivably result from the court actions. Railroad interests saw the legal proceedings as unnecessary intrusions by the Justice Department and judicial system into a complex and technical transportation matter with which they had no expertise. In one sense the entire debate over the legislation was a governmental jurisdictional dispute.

Who would supervise the methods and means of transportation ratemaking? Would it be the Department of Justice through its anti-trust division or would it be the Interstate Commerce Commission through its normal regulatory functions?

More specifically the dispute centered on which congressional commandment was to govern: enforcing competition through the anti-trust laws or carrying out the specific transportation mandates contained in the Declaration of National Transportation Policy, which is the preamble to and the guiding philosophy of the Interstate Commerce Act. The problem was summarized in a Senate report on the proposed bill:

> A question of public policy for Congress is therefore presented and it is the plain duty of Congress to take the necessary remedial steps for the purpose of harmonizing and reconciling the policy of the anti-trust laws, as applicable to common carriers, with the national transportation policy in such a way as to protect the public interest.[8]

Proponents of the legislation built their arguments on two primary issues. One was the practical argument that joint rates were required by law. As Senator Reed stated on the floor of Congress, "By law we require joint rates; and the only way to make them is to permit the carriers to confer with each other."[9] In a similar vein the venerable Joseph Eastman added his support to the bill:

> No railroad can live unto itself. It must work closely with its neighbors, interchange cars and participate in a multitude of through routes and joint rates. What we actually have is a single transportation system made up of a large number of parts separately owned by individual companies.[10]

The second argument was that the shipping public was in almost unanimous support of the bill. Congressmen were bombarded with correspondence from hundreds of shippers associations, chambers of commerce, and even numerous government agencies—all of whom were strongly in favor of the legislation. Colonel J. M. Johnson, Director of the Office of Defense Transportation, noted in Congressional hearings that, "The unanimity of those interested in and with knowledge of transportation in favor of this legislation is perhaps unprecedented."[11] Parties in opposition to the bill claimed that this almost universal support was merely the result of an unprecedented grass roots propaganda campaign by the Association of American Railroads and related organizations.

Major opposition to the bill was clear and straightforward. There was a fear that exempting a critical industry from the antitrust laws would be the opening wedge in a new burst of monopolistic activity. Senator O'Mahoney stated that, "It may be possible to repeal the antitrust laws by little bits and pieces."[12] Senator Russel claimed that the proposed legislation would, "Be a precedent for Congress to take up other industries which might claim that the antitrust laws handicaps them . . ."[13]

Perhaps the strongest statements along this line of reasoning came from Senator Johnston of South Carolina who renamed the legislation "A Bill to Create a Giant Transportation Cartel-Monopoly." He claimed the bill would,

1. Effectively repeal the antitrust laws as applied to public transportation.

2. Legalize the continuation and expansion of control over every phase of a carrier's operations by the Association of American Railroads and the traditional railroad bankers.[14]

These types of statements run throughout the congressional debate. Certain Southern and Western senators claimed that not only were the railroads a monopoly because of control by the rate associations, but that the railroads were in turn controlled by a few large New York financial organizations. These banks then used the railroads as a tool to insure that the Eastern Manufacturing complex would not receive any significant competition from other regions of the country. In essence, it was claimed that rail rates were used to keep other parts of the United States in a semi-colonial status subservient to Eastern interests.

The question of rate structure was another point for consideration. Senator Russell stated:

> The carriers have built up a complicated rate structure, aided and abetted by the Interstate Commerce Commission, which has never gone to the heart of the question and simplified the rate structure so that the people who were paying the freight could understand what they were paying and why they were paying it and determine whether or not it was a just charge against them . . . Not only will the bill end forever any hope of securing simplification of the very complicated rate structure, but the enactment of the bill will be a death blow to the hopes of the Southern and Western States to be permitted to share in the industrial development of the Nation.[15]

No one would argue that the rate structure was not complex and complicated. However, Senator Hawkes who was a former governor of Florida did testify that the I.C.C. had been very helpful when the State of Florida had contested supposedly discriminatory rates before the Commission. The state had received relief in several cases and the Senator spoke most highly of the interest and abilities of the I.C.C.

While only a few Congressmen were totally opposed to the general concept of the Bulwinkle bill, a number expressed concern over the exact wording of certain sections. The apprehension centered on two issues. First, what types of activities would be exempted from antitrust scrutiny. The original wording of the bill was very general and could have been interpreted to mean anything vaguely connected with transportation. The final bill more closely defined the activities to be those connected with rates, fares, and charges. Second, there was major concern over what would happen to carriers who disagreed with whatever determination might be made by the rate bureaus. Under the existing rate bureau agreements the associations could stop any carrier from taking individual action on rates. The proposed legislation definitely guaranteed the right of independent action to any carrier who did not care to go along with any or all rate bureau practices.

Throughout the congressional debate there seemed to be some confusion as to the freedom the railroads would have if exempted from the antitrust laws. The bill would exempt the rate bureaus from the antitrust laws if the agreements setting up the rules and procedures of the bureaus were approved by the I.C.C. That is to say, the bill would legalize the Associations; it would not legalize everything the rate bureaus might do. Individual rates and other matters would still have to be approved by the Commission. Many of the objectors to the bill seemed to be hazy on this critical point.

The bill passed with a very wide margin. With respect to the two major issues noted above the legislation read:

> Any carrier party to an agreement between or among two or more carriers relating to rates, fares, classifications, divisions, allowances, or charges . . . or rules and regulations pertaining thereto, or procedures

for the joint consideration, initiation or establishment thereof, may, under such rules and regulations as the Commission may prescribe, apply to the Commission for approval of the agreement . . .[16]

Concerning the freedom of individual carriers to act independently the bill reads:

The Commission shall not approve under this section any agreement which establishes a procedure for the determination of any matter through joint consideration unless it finds that under the agreement there is accorded to each party the free and unrestrained right to take independent action either before or after any determination arrived at through such procedure.[17]

PRESIDENT TRUMAN'S VETO

The Reed-Bulwinkle Act was vetoed by President Truman on June 10, 1948. Noting that he had listened at length to the debate on the bill he wrote:

It would permit an important segment of the economy to obtain immunity from the antitrust laws, and would do so without providing adequate safeguards to protect the public interest . . . Acting through these rate bureaus, groups of carriers could exercise a powerful deterrent influence upon the filing by an individual carrier of proposed rates which might benefit the public . . . Power to control transportation rates is power to influence the competitive success or failure of other businesses . . .

By sanctioning rate control by groups of carriers, this legislation would represent a departure from the present transportation policy of regulated competition.[18]

Congressional debate after the veto centered on the previously discussed questions of monopolization, threats to the free enterprise system, and rail discrimination against the South and West. The veto was easily overridden and the bill became law on June 17, 1948.

EXPERIENCE UNDER THE REED-BULWINKLE ACT

Problems and controversies concerning implementation of the Reed-Bulwinkle Act were of a minor and technical nature, generally revolving around the specific interpretation of the wording of various subsections. One of the first issues the commission had to face was that of the goals and scope of agreements that might be allowed under the legislation. In the Western Traffic Association case the Commission noted that agreements approved under the new law would have to further the goals of the Declaration of National Transportation Policy, "Those parts of the policy, however, most directly pertinent here call for the promotion of 'adequate, economical and efficient service' . . . 'sound economic conditions in transportation' . . . 'reasonable charges' . . ."[19] The scope of the agreements could cover only the items specifically mentioned in paragraph (2) of the bill, as noted above.

Methods and procedures for rate determination activities had to be specifically stated in the proposed agreements, as did the membership and organization of the rate bureaus. The Commission stated in the Movers' and Warehousemen's case, "An agreement under which joint procedures are to be followed should specify the procedures."[20] Probably the most sensitive issues revolved around guaranteeing the right of independent action to each and every carrier. The I.C.C. has been adamant that any carrier have complete freedom to make decisions independently whether before, during or after the association determination. In a related matter the Commission has made known its distaste for any kind of regimentation being forced on a carrier by a rate bureau. One agreement was not approved by the Commission because the bureau insisted on an exclusive agent for the purpose of publishing tariffs.[21] This was deemed to be an infringement on the right of independent action.

The Commission has ruled[22] that the rate associations must be open to membership to any carrier that meets the same qualifications as existing members. Conversely, members cannot be expelled except for failure to meet financial obligations, such as dues payments.[23]

RECENT CHANGES IN THE REED-BULWINKLE ACT

The Reed-Bulwinkle Act has had two significant changes—one by the ICC and the other by Congress—since 1975. Each will be examined. The ICC conducted an extensive investigation into the operations of rate bureaus in 1975. It was known [as] Ex Parte 297—Rate Bureau Investigation. Its report was issued in June, 1975.[24] The report was basically tolerant and supportive of rate bureau activities. One significant modification regarding rate bureau activities was mandated by Ex Parte 297. It stated that if a rate bureau desires to maintain its exemption from the antitrust laws, then henceforth it must cease—as a rate bureau—from protesting to the Commission when a member decides to take independent action. (Individual rate bureau members can still protest independent action if they believe the proposed rate violates the Interstate Commerce Act.) The ICC in January, 1976, issued a report which reconsidered their initial requirements in Ex Parte 297.[25] The Commission strongly reiterated its findings and noted that when rate bureaus—as an organization—could protest independent actions the effect was to "inhibit competition." The ICC also noted that in the six months that Ex Parte 297 was in effect, there had been a "substantial increase in the publication of independent action proposals and a decrease in the number of protests filed."[26]

As would be expected, certain carriers were displeased with the inability of rate bureaus to protest independent action. Five trucking company members of the Middle Atlantic Conference—a rate bureau—asked the Fourth Circuit Court of Appeals to set-aside this provision of Ex Parte 297. Justice Clark, upholding the ICC declared:

> To permit a rate bureau to protest the proposals of a member individually, so chills the individual proposal that it stands little chance of adoption, while providing the opportunity for misuse of the bureaus as policing agencies against individual action.
>
> There is nothing irrational about the new rule. . . . In fact, the new rule is in the true tradition of our free enterprise system which has been the keystone of our economic accomplishment for nearly a century.
>
> Certainly, the purpose of the Commission was to stimulate competition by removing the inhibitions against the filing of independent actions, a

move not only in the spirit of section 5a . . . but in furtherance of the national transportation policy which is the essence of this case.[27]

The second significant change in the Reed-Bulwinkle Act was contained in the Railroad Revitalization and Regulatory Reform Act of 1976—commonly known as the 4 R Act. It went into effect on February 5, 1976, about six months after Ex Parte 297. Congress ordered that railroad collective rate making procedures—via rate bureaus—must become more competitive and free from bureau constraints. Transportation attorneys Pearce and Clearwaters have noted, "It is expected that ratemaking procedures will change so that single-line rates and rates for particular joint line movements that is, the bulk of railroad pricing—will be done in a competitive fashion"[28] As noted above, the 4 R Act restricts railroad rate bureaus activities in two situations. First, a railroad proposal to establish or change an existing rate or allowance—which will be exclusively transported on that carrier's track—cannot be protested at the rate bureau by other railroads. Secondly, when through-routes and joint-rates are involved, only carriers which can "practically participate" in the traffic involved are allowed to vote on the rate bureau's acceptance or rejection of the proposed change. G. J. Rooney notes "practically participates" appears to have the following interpretation: a carrier would be allowed, "voting eligibility on interline proposals if such carrier participates in any commodity rate from an origin involved in the proposal to a destination involved in the proposal."[29]

PROPOSED CHANGES

Two proposals are currently being considered to further amend—or repeal—the Reed Bulwinkle Act. First, President Carter has been quoted as saying he is in favor of repealing the antitrust exemption contained in the Reed-Bulwinkle Act.[30] This emasculation of the 1948 Act would be the equivalent of repealing it. Senator Edward Kennedy is of the same opinion as Carter. At a recent Senate hearing he noted that, "Our concern is whether there should be cartels." Chairman of the ICC, Daniel O'Neal, noted at the Senate hearings, that rate bureaus do not have a complete hold on motor carrier pricing. In 1972 independent actions accounted for three out of every ten bureau rate filings. At that point, Kennedy interrupted O'Neal and stated, "If the system were free, there would have been ten out of ten independent actions."[31]

The second proposed change is less drastic than the first. In January, 1978, the ICC stated that it was considering applying the 4 R Act requirements on railroad rate bureaus activities to all other surface transport modes. Thus motor carriers, water carriers, and freight forwarders would have the same restrictions that railroad rate bureaus have regarding single line and through-routes and joint-rates.[32] In March, 1978, Congressman James Howard, Chairman of the House Subcommittee on Surface Transportation, wrote a letter to ICC Chairman O'Neal stating that the extension of the railroad rate bureau restrictions to the other surface carriers is, ". . . of such importance and to be of such a nature, that they should be considered and resolved by the Congress."[33]

CONCLUSION

The authors believe that both Ex Parte 297 and the 4 R Act changes in rate bureau activities have been constructive and supportive of the U.S. National Transportation Policy. However, further efforts to expunge the Reed-Bulwinkle Act would not appear to be in the public interest. We base this conclusion on two points. First, further changes in the Reed-Bulwinkle Act—as discussed above—would primarily affect the motor common carrier industry. It should be remembered that this segment of the trucking industry is far from dominant. In 1976, the Transport Association of America estimated that ICC regulated truckers—both common and contract—performed 14.9 percent of all intercity freight tonnage. By comparison, non-ICC regulated trucking—private and exempt—accounted for 21.5 percent. Note that by this measure, non-regulated trucking transports 44 percent more intercity tonnage than regulated truckers. The 1972 Census of Transportation notes that the number of trucks with three, four, or five axles (which are exclusively freight hauling vehicles) is approximately 1,157,000. Of this number, 54 percent are used for private carriage and 46 percent are employed by for-hire carriers. The effect of the above is that motor common carriers, unlike railroads, must compete against a powerful competitor—private carriage. In addition, contract carriers can adjust their rates without government authorization and this segment of trucking appears to be healthy and experiencing a slow but steady growth.[34] The effect of these two robust competitors is that motor common carriers cannot "rip-off" the public, because shippers generally have the option of switching to private or contract carriage. In addition, freight-forwarders and shippers' associations are additional options to dissatisfied shippers.

Secondly, when it comes to taking independent action, motor common carriers do not possess the monolithic position against them that their opponents assume. Professor Charles S. Sherwood studied the incidence of independent action in motor rate bureaus, and found that 28.6 percent of rates filed with the bureaus were independent actions.[35] Of these independent actions, very few were protested to the ICC by motor common carriers. In 1973, of 7,468 independent actions, only 199 were protested by bureaus, or 2.66 percent of the total.[36]

In summary, the Reed-Bulwinkle Act has worked smoothly since its passage. It appears that the fears of monopoly heard so often in the Congressional debates were unfounded. Rate bureaus actually have less control on the industry than they did prior to the 1948 legislation. Commission rulings have limited the scope of rate bureau activities and the right of independent action has been staunchly safeguarded.

Footnotes

[1]"The Truth About Rate Bureaus," (Washington, D.C.: American Trucking Association, 1976), p. 4.

[2]Jesse J. Friedman, *Collective Ratemaking In Trucking: The Public Interest Rationale* (Washington, D.C.: October, 1977), p. 33.

[3]Testimony of John H. Shenefield, Assistant Attorney General, Department of Justice, before the Subcommittee on Antitrust and Monopoly, U.S. Senate, mimeographed (October 27, 1977), p. 8.

[4]Speech by Joe Sims, Assistant Attorney General, Justice Department, to the Motor Carrier Lawyers Association, mimeographed (January 13, 1978), p. 5.

[5]*Congressional Record*, 80th Congress, 2nd Session, p. 6661.

[6]*United States v. Association of American Railroads*, *4* F.R.D. 510 (D. Neb. 1945).

[7]324 U.S. 439.

[8]*Senate Report No. 44*, 80th Congress, 1st Session, "Amending the Interstate Com-

merce Act With Respect to Certain Agreements Between Carriers," p. 3.

[9]Congressional Record, supra, p. 6642.

[10]Senate Report No. 44, supra, p. 3.

[11]Report No. 1100, House of Representatives, 80th Congress, 1st Session, "Amending the Interstate Commerce Act, With Respect to Certain Agreements Between Carriers," p. 2.

[12]Congressional Record, supra, p. 6644.

[13]Ibid., p. 6650.

[14]Ibid., p. 6654.

[15]Ibid., p. 6647.

[16]Section 5a, paragraph 2.

[17]Section 5a, paragraph 6.

[18]Senate Document No. 169, 80th Congress, 2nd Session, Message from the President of the United States returning Without Approval the Bill (S. 110) entitled, "An Act to Amend the Interstate Commerce Act With Respect to Certain Agreements Between Carriers."

[19]Western Traffic Association—Agreement, 276 I.C.C. 183, 211.

[20]Independent Movers' and Warehousemen's Association—Agreement, 286 I.C.C. 651, 654.

[21]Columbia River Tariff Bureau—Agreement, 284 I.C.C. 436.

[22]Waterways Freight Bureau—Agreement, 277 I.C.C. 593, 597.

[23]National Bus Traffic Association, Inc.—Agreement, 278 I.C.C. 147, 154.

[24]349 I.C.C. 811.

[25]Report and Order of the Commission on Reconsideration of Ex Parte 297, 351 I.C.C. 437.

[26]Ibid. at 460.

[27]Traffic World (August 22, 1977), p. 19.

[28]C. Jack Pearce and Keith I. Clearwaters, "Rate Bureaus and the Railroad Revitalization and Reform Act," ICC Practitioners' Journal (May-June, 1976), p. 485.

[29]G. J. Rooney, "The RRRR Act—Some Implications For Railroad Rate Bureaus," Transportation Journal (Winter, 1977), p. 28.

[30]Traffic World (October 17, 1977), p. 25.

[31]Transport Topics (November 7, 1977), p. 54.

[32]Transport Topics (January 16, 1977), pp. 1 and 22.

[33]Transport Topics (March 6, 1978), p. 31.

[34]Charles A. Taff, "Grants of Motor Contract Carrier Operating Authority—1970-75," Transportation Journal (Winter, 1976), pp. 92-103.

[35]Charles S. Sherwood, "The Operational Reality of Independent Rate Making: Some Empirical Findings," Transportation Journal (Winter, 1975), pp. 5-12.

[36]Traffic World (August 22, 1977), p. 21.

Transportation Regulation: Another Dimension*

GRANT M. DAVIS and CHARLES S. SHERWOOD

[Editor's Note: Collective ratemaking represents a key element to any common carrier system committed to avoiding undue preference, prejudice, and discrimination. The principal benefits from collective ratemaking may be measured either directly or indirectly. Direct benefits to society include joint rates and through routes and prices established by the forces of supply and demand. Also, information is disseminated to shippers and carriers and is subject to administrative review. On the other hand, indirect benefits, such as assistance to the ICC, stable rates, industry distribution efforts, and, above all, economic development of infrastructures, are frequently difficult to measure definitely. An article by Grant M. Davis and Charles S. Sherwood entitled "Transportation Regulation: Another Dimension" examines these indirect consumption benefits and collective ratemaking.]

When approaching the subject of transportation regulation, contemporary critics are vociferous, although few in number. They contend that the regulation of various segments of the domestic transportation industry has resulted in substantial resource misallocation and a suboptimization of the U.S. transportation effort, together with lesser calamities.[1] Congress and practitioners, on the other hand, certainly are not confronted with any paucity of regulatory practice problems, but are hesitant to suddenly discard the present institutional system of regulation.[2]

Resource allocation in the public sector frequently is accomplished through use of the pricing mechanism when no indirect consumption benefits are present. Many transportation projects such as highways, airways, and navigable waterways do contain substantial indirect consumption benefits and hence price cannot be used as

---

*Reprinted by permission of the ICC Practitioners' Journal.

the principal allocator. In transportation's private sector, resources are allocated by the market mechanism, i.e., price. However, substantial indirect consumption benefits accrue to many regulated carriers using publicly provided transportation facilities. In this case, a strong argument can be advanced that an analogous situation exists between output levels achieved by privately owned transport carriers and the concept of marginal social benefits/marginal social costs. If this is correct, another justification for regulating substantial segments of the transportation industry can be theoretically justified.

The primary purpose of this study is to explore the interrelationship between MSB/MSC and domestic regulated transportation. To achieve this goal, the following related and supportive areas will be examined: (1) the concept of regulated monopoly; (2) functions of economic regulation; (3) deficiencies associated with transport regulation; and (4) the concept of marginal social benefits/marginal social costs as related to transport firms.

CONCEPT OF REGULATED MONOPOLY

Although trade regulation and the concept of common carriage date back to antiquity, transportation regulation in this country was originally developed to cope with discriminatory practices of the railroad industry. The salient economic dimensions of this particular industry, of course, are inordinate fixed cost and economies of scale.[3] Regarding monopoly and competition, Professor Clare Wilcox writes: "In a few industries, notably those producing transport and public utility services, government has accepted monopoly as unavoidable, and has substituted administrative regulation for competition as a method of control."[4] This form of control basically involves market entry and abandonments, securities and accounts,[5] service quality, and structure and levels of rates.

Thus, the fundamental concept of regulated monopoly focuses upon rate and entry control. Critics of monopoly correctly point out that firms in that particular industry structure maximize profits by restricting output. Economists use pure competition as a standard by which other industry structures can be compared; because there is no long-run economic profit, larger output levels are achieved, and there is no economic waste.[6] By controlling market entry and exit, together with rate levels, regulators should endeavor to regulate in such a fashion that firms falling within their jurisdictional purview should produce a level of output where average total costs intersect with average revenue.[7] If this is achieved, society will receive a larger level of transportation production without any attendant economic waste.[8]

While the regulated monopoly abstraction is theoretically sound, several factors prevent it from functioning properly. First, how much transportation production should be produced annually? Second, will the individual transport carrier produce to some hypothetical cost/demand intersection? Third, what is an adequate amount of competition? _Ad infinitum_. Nevertheless, the fundamental concept is valid.

GOALS OF ECONOMIC REGULATION OF TRANSPORTATION

Even though entry and rate control represent the quintessence of transportation regulation, the codified statutory goals are: (1) reasonable rates; (2) reasonable service; (3) no undue discrimination; and (4) no undue preference. Freight rates have increased substantially during the past ten years, yet the rate of increase has for the most part been beneath the wholesale price index. In this regard, Table I depicts transportation revenue vs. general price trends. As indicated, the ton-mile index for three of the four modes examined was materially less than the wholesale price index. A somewhat different situation exists in passenger transportation. Table II shows average revenue per passenger-mile vs. consumer prices for the period 1947-1972. These data fail to provide an accurate view of transport pricing because the private automobile generated 87 percent of total intercity passenger-miles for the past decade,[9] and ninety percent of the regulated intercity passenger market-miles was generated by regulated airlines. The revenue index for domestic scheduled airlines has been considerably lower than the index of consumer prices, since 1951.

Providing reasonable and adequate service to the extent specified in their operating certificates and permits represents an important goal of economic regulation. Numerous complaints have been levied against carriers regarding service, but the combination of due process and the adversary system frequently delays introducing new service. Available evidence indicates that when a service void develops, such as the small shipment problem,[11] new services such as those provided by United Parcel Service inevitably appear. Private carriage, on the other hand, also develops.[12] Nevertheless, regulated carriers have increased their relative share of intercity freight market during recent years.[13]

TABLE I

Transportation Revenue vs. General Price Trends

(In Cents)

Average Revenue Per Ton-Mile vs. Wholesale Prices[@]

Year	Rail (Class 1)		Truck (Class 1)		Air (Domestic) (Scheduled)		Oil Pipe Line		Wholesale Prices Index	
	Revenue	Index	Revenue	Index	Revenue	Index	Revenue	Index	1967=100	Index
1947	1.08	100	4.85	100	24.18	100	.292	100	76.5	100
1948	1.25	116	5.15	106	20.10	83	.299	102	82.8	108
1949	1.34	124	5.24	108	19.67	81	.310	106	78.7	103
1950	1.33	123	5.01	103	18.10	75	.315	108	81.8	107
1951	1.34	124	5.17	107	19.01	79	.320	110	91.1	119
1952	1.43	132	5.62	116	19.78	82	.328	112	88.6	116
1953	1.48	137	5.73	118	20.66	85	.322	110	87.4	114
1954	1.42	121	5.83	120	21.85	90	.319	109	87.6	115
1955	1.37	127	5.80	120	21.15	87	.322	110	87.8	115
1956	1.38	128	5.97	123	20.66	85	.317	109	90.7	119

(Continued)

TABLE I (Continued)

Year	Rail (Class 1)		Truck (Class 1)		Air (Domestic) (Scheduled)		Oil Pipe Line		Wholesale Prices Index	
	Revenue	Index	Revenue	Index	Revenue	Index	Revenue	Index	1967=100	Index
1957	1.45	134	6.14	127	21.39	88	.313	107	93.3	122
1958	1.46	135	6.19	128	22.62	94	.318	109	94.6	124
1959	1.45	134	6.28	129	22.76	94	.314	108	94.8	124
1960	1.40	130	6.31	130	22.80	94	.315	108	94.9	124
1961	1.37	127	6.30	130	22.08	91	.315	108	94.5	124
1962	1.35	125	6.41	132	21.31	88	.320	110	94.8	124
1963	1.31	121	6.38	132	21.72	90	.318	109	94.5	124
1964	1.28	119	6.66	137	20.97	87	.304	104	94.7	124
1965	1.27	118	6.46	133	20.46	85	.279	96	96.6	126
1966	1.26	117	6.34	131	20.21	84	.269	92	99.8	130
1967	1.27	118	6.65	137	19.90	82	.259	90	100.0	131
1968	1.31	121	6.93	143	19.97	83	.257	88	102.5	134
1969	1.35	125	7.08	146	21.03[#]	87	.266	91	106.5	139
1970	1.43	132	7.46	154	21.91	91	.271	93	110.4	144
1971	1.59	147	7.85	162	22.58	93	.285	98	113.9	149
1972(p)	1.62	150	8.00	165	22.76	94	.295	101	119.1	156

[@]See "Source Data" page for 1969-1974 average revenue per ton-mile for ICC-regulated barge lines.

[#]1969 revised to include Alaska and Hawaii as will all future years.

(p)TAA Preliminary Estimate.

Source: Compiled from Transportation: Facts and Trends, Tenth Edition, October, 1973. A publication of the Transportation Association of America.

Regulatory provisions contained in Title 49 of the U.S. Code do not specifically prohibit discrimination, i.e., only undue or excessive discriminatory practices by carriers.[14] Judicial procedures and avenues for appeal exist for eliminating undue discrimination inflicted upon any shipper or community. Closely related to undue discrimination is the goal of avoiding any undue preference to shippers. Again, institutional safeguards exist to protect transport consumers.[15]

TABLE II

Transportation Revenue vs. General Price Trends

(In Cents)

Average Revenue Per Passenger-Mile vs. Consumer Prices

	Rail (Class 1)		Bus (Class 1)		Air (Domestic Scheduled)				Consumer Prices Index	
					Coach	1st Class	Total			
Year	Revenue*	Index	Revenue	Index	Revenue	Revenue	Revenue	Index	1967=100	Index
1947	2.24	100	1.71	100	—	5.05	5.05	100	66.9	100
1948	2.51	112	1.75	102	4.01	5.76	5.76	114	72.1	108
1949	2.64	118	1.85	108	3.96	5.85	5.78	114	71.4	107
1950	2.74	122	1.89	111	4.11	5.79	5.56	110	72.1	108
1951	2.75	123	1.95	114	4.44	5.77	5.61	111	77.8	116
1952	2.79	125	2.03	119	4.17	5.89	5.57	110	79.5	119
1953	2.78	124	2.06	120	4.13	5.91	5.46	108	80.1	120
1954	2.73	122	2.08	122	4.33	5.92	5.41	107	80.5	120
1955	2.70	121	2.06	120	4.32	5.90	5.36	106	80.2	120
1956	2.78	124	2.13	125	4.29	5.91	5.33	106	81.4	122
1957	2.95	132	2.29	134	4.25	5.95	5.31	105	84.3	126
1958	2.99	133	2.43	142	4.52	6.38	5.64	112	86.6	129
1959	3.00	134	2.59	151	4.63	6.78	5.88	116	87.3	130
1960	3.03	135	2.71	158	5.01	7.06	6.09	121	88.7	133
1961	3.08	138	2.69	157	5.42	7.34	6.28	124	89.6	134
1962	3.10	138	2.72	159	5.76	7.57	6.45	138	90.6	135
1963	3.18	142	2.78	163	5.62	7.17	6.17	122	91.7	137
1964	3.16	141	2.80	164	5.58	7.26	6.12	121	92.9	139
1965	3.14	140	2.88	168	5.52	7.33	6.06	120	94.5	141
1966	3.13	140	2.89	169	5.28	7.24	5.83	115	97.2	145
1967	3.13	140	2.98	174	5.13	7.24	5.64	112	100.0	149
1968	3.33	149	3.18	186	5.11	7.33	5.61	111	104.2	156

(Continued)

TABLE II (Continued)

Year	Rail (Class 1) Revenue*	Index	Bus (Class 1) Revenue	Index	Air (Domestic Scheduled) Coach Revenue	1st Class Revenue	Total Revenue	Index	Consumer Prices Index 1967=100	Index
1969	3.63	161	3.39	198	5.27#	7.78#	5.79#	115	109.8	164
1970	4.02	179	3.60	211	5.46	8.31	6.00	119	116.3	174
1971	4.64**	207	3.83	224	5.81	8.58	6.32	125	121.3	181
1972(p)	5.31	237	3.90	228	5.86	8.85	6.42	127	125.3	187

**Includes AMTRAK and Auto-Train, as will future years.

#1969 revised to include Alaska and Hawaii as will all future years.

*Excludes Commutation.

(p)TAA Preliminary Estimate.

Source: Compiled from Transportation: Facts and Trends, Tenth Edition, October, 1973. A publication of the Transportation Association of America.

The National Transportation Policy preamble to the Interstate Commerce Act[16] sets forth regulatory goals and objectives for the ICC in administering the Act.[17] Essentially this policy statement directs the Commission to regulate in such a fashion that the inherent advantages of each carrier be maintained, and that a strong common carrier system be developed that meets the needs of commerce, national defense, and the Postal Service. Similar policy statements pertain to the administration of the Federal Aviation Act[18] and the U.S. Shipping Acts.[19]

DEFICIENCIES OF ECONOMIC REGULATION

Professor Clare Wilcox succinctly identifies the principal deficiencies associated with transportation regulation as being threefold in nature: (1) employing regulation as a substitute for competition; (2) regulation-minded regulators; and (3) regulatory agencies that possess power but lack responsibility.[20] While these represent inherent defects, more or less, Professor Ronald H. Coase observes:

> . . . Lawyers focus on the fact that public officials and tribunals are going to be fallible at best and incompetent or abusive at worst. This is not the way in which economists habitually think about governmental bodies. We tend to think of them as benevolent associations waiting to take over when the Invisible Hand points in the wrong direction.[21]

Professor Wilcox's statement describing regulatory defects is general. In the case of transportation regulation, the primary deficiencies are: (1) monopoly power; (2) insensitivity to changing consumer needs; and (3) resource misallocation. Regarding monopoly power, for the most part, monopoly abuses have not constituted a burden on the shipping public. That is to say, competition does exist in transportation. As previously illustrated in Tables I and II, moreover, the regulated carriers' revenue index per ton-mile, with one exception, was substantially less than the wholesale price index for two decades. Also, an index of airline revenue passenger-miles was considerably lower than an index of consumer prices. Price exploitation, a central tendency among strong monopolies, does not appear to be present in the regulated transportation industries.[22]

With respect to the complaint regarding insensitivity to changing consumer needs, there is no question but that "regulatory lag" deters many companies from purchasing transportation efficiency. The regulatory agency's case load, when combined with the adversary system and due process, usually results in a delay. Conversely, a recent study conducted by the authors revealed that industrial shippers believed that in the area of independent action, carriers and rate bureaus were responsive and sensitive to their changing needs.[23]

What is the cost of regulation in terms of resource misallocation? Professor Merton Peck estimates that third degree price discrimination costs the domestic economy almost $3 billion annually.[24] Also, Professor Thomas G. Moore contends that value-of-service pricing and regulation results in economic waste of as low as $3 billion to a high of $12 billion each year.[25] Significantly, complaints concerning a resource misallocation emphasize the indirect cost facet of transportation regulation.

Regarding resource allocation, Table III represents regulated Intercity Freight Ton-Miles, Index of Industrial Production, and GNP for the interval 1955–1972. As shown, a regression equation for the following variables was computed:

$$Y = X_1 + X_2 \ldots X_N$$

where Y = Intercity regulated ton-mile
X_1 = Index of industrial production
X_2 = Index of GNP

The resulting regression equation is:

$$Y = 504.48952 + .79041771X_1 + 6.0659060X_2$$

A multiple r^2 of 0.96 was computed with a F-statistic of 210.5195 and the probability of obtaining a F this large or larger by chance when the hypothesis of no correlation is true is .000006. Data from Table III produced the following forecasts:

TABLE III

Year	Regulated Inter-City Ton-Miles (in billions)	Index of Industrial Production (1947=100)	GNP 1972 Dollars	Index (1947=100)
1955	1535	151	620	141
1956	1611	156	632	144
1957	1584	159	641	146
1958	1456	149	633	144
1959	1550	167	674	154
1960	1570	169	691	157
1961	1563	172	704	160
1962	1622	185	750	171
1963	1697	197	780	178
1964	1780	210	823	187
1965	1865	228	875	199
1966	1972	251	932	212
1967	1997	256	956	218
1968	2065	272	1001	228
1969	2120	285	1028	234
1970	2212	274	1023	233
1971	2230	274	1050	239
1972	2319	295	1118	255

Source: Transportation Facts and Trends, 1973, Transportation Association of America, Washington, D.C.

Using the following variables a regression and correlation analysis was run:

Y = Intercity regulated ton-miles.
X_1 = Index of industrial production
X_2 = Index of GNP

The resulting regression equation is:

$$Y = 504.48952 + .79041771X_1 + 6.0659060X_2$$

The Multiple R^2 is 0.96559942.

The F-Statistic is 210.5195 with 2 and 15 D.F. and the probability of obtaining F this large or larger by chance when the hypothesis of no correlation is true is 0.00000006.

	Regulated Intercity Ton-Miles (billions)	Industrial Production[26] Index (1955=0)	GNP Index[27] (1955=0)
1978	2558.37	353.05	292.59
1984	2864.18	410.64	335.50

Even though the increase in transportation production does not appear to be keeping abreast of increases in Industrial Production and GNP (as shown in Table III), this is misleading. Between 1955 and 1972 the Index of Industrial Production expanded 95 percent, and GNP rose 81 percent. Regulated Intercity Freight Ton-Miles, however, increased only 52 percent. But, these data are in trillions, not millions or billions, so in real terms, the increase has been consistent with overall economic activity. The forecast expansion to occur between 1972 and 1984 is an impressive 24 percent.

CAN THE CONCEPT OF MARGINAL SOCIAL BENEFITS/ MARGINAL SOCIAL COSTS BE APPLIED TO TRANSPORTATION REGULATION?

Defenders of domestic transportation regulation quickly identify stable rates, dependable services, shipper participation,[28] and reductions of uncertainty as some of the more significant attributes of regulation. In short, transportation regulation is supported by all but a few industrial users even though many problems exist relative to its administration.

Inasmuch as resource misallocation constitutes a major complaint by transport regulatory critics, a brief review of how resources are allocated in the private and public sectors of the U.S. economy is in order. In the private sector, the pricing mechanism functions as the primary allocator. In the public sector, however, resources are allocated by the ballot, the pricing mechanism in some instances, and by government institutions when investments or programs possess indirect consumption benefits.

Figure 1 consists of two panels. Panel A represents marginal social benefits for a good in question, and Panel B illustrates the hypothetical cost structure of the U.S. transportation industry subject to regulation. As indicated in Figure 1, MSB is the movement down the demand curve from P_1 to P_3. Each point along the demand line represents society's marginal evaluation of a given good. In Panel B of Figure 1, the downward slope of the average revenue line could conceivably represent aggregate transport demand. Each of the corresponding points from Panel A to B, could be interpreted as the industrial user's or society's marginal evaluation of transportation services offered.

Marginal social costs, on the other hand, are society's marginal sacrifice required to obtain each incremental unit of production. In this regard, Figure 2 depicts how government ascertains an optimum level of output when indirect consumption benefits are present. MSB is subject to diminishing marginal utility and slopes downward and to the right, while MSC experiences increasing costs and slopes upward. The intersection of MSB/MSC represents an optimal production point, or MSB/MSC >1 constitutes a desirable project, and MSB/MSC 1 is undesirable. The sacrifice of optimal resource allocation in order to attain a common carrier system that is stable, that precludes undue preference and discrimination, and that charges reasonable rates could theoretically represent society's marginal sacrifice required to obtain incremental units of transportation output.

One fundamental question associated with using MSB/MSC theoretically in part to justify domestic transportation regulation concerns the essential presence of indirect consumption benefits. In this regard, four observations appear in order. First, transportation demand is basically a derived demand dependent upon aggregate business activities and, as such, is involved in the use of publicly provided facilities in many instances. Second, indirect consumption benefits are present in all modes of transportation even though railroads and pipelines provide their own rights-of-way. Third, are the industrial user and consumers of transportation, the primary beneficiaries of services rendered? No, geographical infrastructures also benefit from transportation offerings. Fourth, and last, the indirect consumption benefits affiliated with the production of a unit of transport are virtually impossible to calculate.

CONCLUSIONS AND RECOMMENDATIONS

Transportation regulation has been criticized because of misallocation of resources, lack of competition, and insensitivity regarding changing consumer needs. During the course of this study, the basic concept of regulated monopoly was examined together with the functions and goals of economic regulation. Because of the indirect consumption benefits associated with the domestic regulated transportation industry, an argument has been offered that transportation regulation can theoretically be partially justified on the basis of the marginal social benefits/marginal social costs concept because of the presence of indirect consumption benefits.

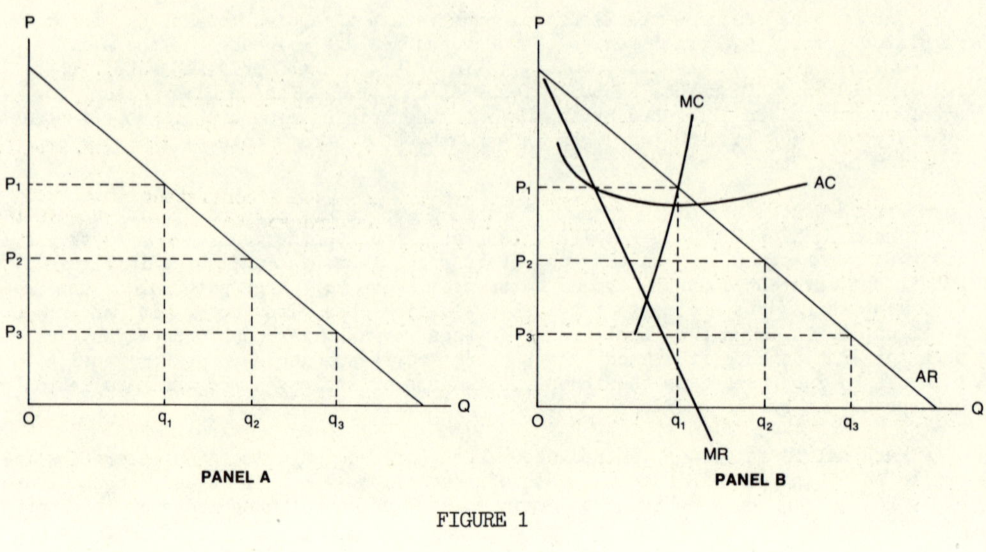

FIGURE 1

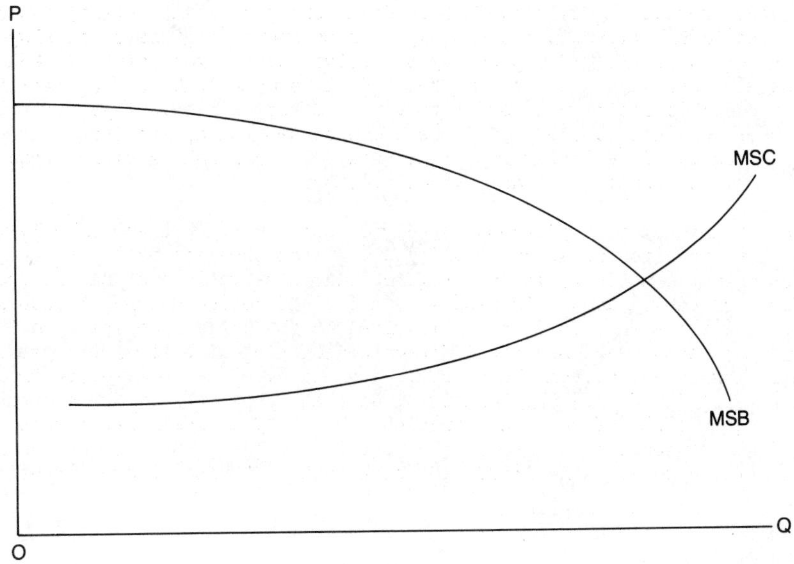

FIGURE 2

Transportation regulation is essentially controversial to many economists who favor deregulation of the industry or at least partial deregulation. Marginal social costs/marginal social benefits does provide some theoretical justification for regulating the industry in addition to the traditional arguments of balancing competition, avoiding monopolies, controlling prices, providing reasonable services, *ad infinitum*. Critics of the domestic transportation industry essentially want to change the industry, particularly that part dealing with trucking, but as Professor Stigler so eloquently stated, they should use political processes—not economic analyses.[29]

Notes

[1]George Hilton, "The Basic Behavior of Regulatory Agencies," American Economic Review, Vol. LXII, No. 2 (May 1973), pp. 47-54. Also, consult John C. Spychalski, "An Evaluation of Messrs. Hilton's and Sampson's Proposed Cures for Regulatory Defects," Transportation Journal, Vol. 12, No. 1 (Fall 1972), pp. 23-31.

[2]The U.S. Department of Transportation has displayed a consistent proclivity toward deregulation by introducing such bills as the Transportation Improvement Act, (H.R. 12891). For an evaluation of DOT's economic policy, see Grant M. Davis, The Department of Transportation (Lexington, Mass.: D. C. Heath & Co., 1970), Chap. 5.

[3]Roy J. Sampson and Martin T. Farris, Domestic Transportation (2nd Ed.: Boston: Houghton Mifflin Co., 1970), pp. 52-53.

[4]Clare Wilcox, Public Policies Toward Business (4th Ed.: Homewood, Ill.: Richard D. Irwin, Inc., 1971), p. 15.

[5]The Civil Aeronautics Board does not possess statutory authority to regulate airline securities.

[6]R. Murray Havens, John S. Henderson, and Dale L. Cramer, Economics (New York: The Macmillan Co., 1966), Chapter 15.

[7]A small dividend to attract capital is considered a cost in micro-economic theory, so a carrier producing to the intersection of average revenue would be profitable in most instances, ceteris paribus.

[8]Supra, Note 6. Also Donald S. Watson, "Price Theory and Its Uses" (3rd Ed.: Boston: Houghton Mifflin Co., 1972), Chapter 14.

[9]U.S. Bureau of the Census, Statistical Abstract of the United States: 1973 (94th Ed.: Washington: U.S. Government Printing Office, 1973), p. 538.

[10]For example, see Charles F. Phillips, Jr., "Interveners in the Telephone Investigation," Public Utilities Fortnightly, Vol. 78 (Dec. 22, 1966), p. 26.

[11]Barrie Vreeland, "An Imaginative Possible Solution to the Small Shipment Problem," Transportation Journal, Vol. 11, No. 2 (Winter 1971), pp. 34-44.

[12]Ann F. Friedlaender, The Dilemma of Freight Transportation (Washington: The Brookings Institution, 1969), contains an excellent section regarding the growth and development of private carriage.

[13]Supra, Note 9.

[14]For an excellent treatment of discrimination in transportation, see John Guandolo, Transportation Law (2nd Ed.: William C. Brown Publishers: Dubuque, Iowa, 1965), Chapters 35-37.

[15]The Civil Aeronautics Board, for instance, publishes a guide entitled, "Air Travelers' Rights," as part of its consumer education program.

[16]Title 49 U.S.C. preceding Sec. 1.

[17]Consult Grant M. Davis and Jack J. Holder, Jr., "Does the United States Have a Cohesive National Transportation Policy?--An Analysis," ICC Practitioners' Journal, Vol. XXXXI, No. 3 (March-April 1974), pp. 332-349, for an evaluation of several national transportation policies.

[18]72 Stat. 760 (1938), 49 U.S.C. 1374(a).

[19]46 U.S.C. Sec. 1101 (1964).

[20]Wilcox, op. cit., pp. 476-478.

[21]Ronald H. Coase, "What Can Regulators Regulate? Comment," in The Crisis of the Regulatory Commissions, Paul W. MacAvoy, editor (New York: W. W. Norton & Co., 1970), p. 55.

[22]Many economists would strongly insist that regulation has resulted in higher transport prices. An ex post examination of Tables I and II does not support this view. On the other hand, regulatory critics argue that prices could be lower if regulation did not exist.

[23]Grant M. Davis and Charles S. Sherwood, "Rate Bureaus and Antitrust Conflicts: Public Policy Issues" (New York: Praeger Press, Inc., 1974), Chapter 4.

[24]Merton J. Peck, "Competitive Policy for Transportation," in The Crisis of the Regulatory Commissions, Paul W. MacAvoy, editor (New York: W. W. Norton & Co., 1970), p. 73.

[25] Thomas Gale Moore. "The Feasibility of De-regulating Surface Freight Transportation" (Washington: The Brooking Institution, 1974), forthcoming.

[26] $Y = 132.30994 + 9.5975232X$
t statistic is 16.5936 (significant at .001)
F statistic is 275.3464 (significant at .001)

[27] $Y = 128.099420 + 7.1517028X$
t statistic is 22.7048 (significant at .001)
F statistic is 515.5059 (significant at .001)

[28] In the regulated transportation industries, the customer plays a direct role in establishing prices. For an example, see Grant M. Davis and Stephen W. Brown, Logistics Management (Lexington, Mass.: D. C. Heath & Co., 1974), Chapters 11 and 12.

[29] George J. Stigler, "The Theory of Economic Regulation," The Bell Journal of Economics and Management Science, Vol. 2, No. 1 (Spring 1970), p. 18.

Adapting to New Regulatory Regimes*

L. L. WATERS

[Editor's Note: Collective ratemaking assists the ICC in its daily administration process regarding rates. In the absence of the conference method of ratemaking, complex shipping and cost problems would confront individual shippers. In an article entitled "Adapting to New Regulatory Regimes," L. L. Waters gives an ominous assessment of collective ratemaking and explores the problems facing both users and carriers of regulated carrier services.]

The title presumes a significant change toward deregulation. Twenty minutes or seven pages cannot possibly deal with the form of things to come. So many complications are associated with costs, rates, numbers of competitors, desires of shippers, and so forth, that the results of varying degrees of deregulation or complete deregulation cannot be anticipated. What can be done is to comment upon certain of the pending measures in relation to our institutional arrangements so that certain developments can be expected. The assumption is made that some legislation relating to the railroads will emerge from the current Congress. Prospects exist for legislation affecting airlines, but very little is expected in the motor carrier field. The discussion assumes that some of the proposed changes will be passed over a period of time, if not currently.

Changes expected in the railroad field deal largely with money. The House and the Senate differed by two billion on the financial package to be made available. Your attention is called to the paradox of the widespread desire to return to competition in transportation with all or many of the alleged shackles of regulation removed while at the same time authorizing major subsidies which would obviously distort the competitive model. The rationale is in part that the industry was short changed in the past and that the money is to make amends. Advances to CONRAIL obviously are scarcely debatable. The system has to be put back on its feet. There is much to be said for an outright grant instead of a $3 billion loan of dubious quality which will entail more distress than benefits. The proposed $3 billion loan in the Senate bill to AMTRAK at no interest surely must have more political features to commend it than economic. Finally, various low interest loans to railroads and

*Reprinted by permission of the Transportation Journal.

guarantees of private loans should be considered in relation to the move toward deregulation.

Pressure has existed for some time to permit the railroads to raise rates by any amount as long as they did not have "market dominance" over a transportation route. On the low side, rates could be cut so long as costs were covered without ever defining costs twice in the same way. The administration and others have proposed that railroads be allowed to raise or lower rates by 7 and then 15 percent per year without the right of the Commission to suspend them. This seems like the "snake in the pipe" arrangement for the stabilization of international rates of exchange. Variations of this magnitude are interesting in relation to the status of rate bureaus and ICC control. A review of a hundred or more cases under the Sherman and Clayton Acts reveal that price discrimination in various forms of the magnitude proposed under the unsuspendable freedom are very common. In the grocery industry where margins are extremely narrow, many cases can be found in which the alleged abuses are nominal in comparison with the degree of freedom sought for carriers.

Freedom to change rates with minimal or no commission review should logically call for repeal of the Reed-Bulwinkle Act and subjection of carriers of all modes to antitrust laws. The transport industry cannot have its cake and eat it, too.

Application of the antitrust laws introduces new complications. First, there is no way that joint rates on through routes could be provided. When companies that may be competitive in parts of their territory get together on "end to end rates," there are consequences back in the area of competition. The point is sometimes made that the country has the parallel of the Webb-Pomerene Act which enables competing American companies to join with each other in international pricing. The trouble with this line of argument is that when rivals get together to unite on international pricing, they inevitably are determining volume of foreign sales and ultimately costs of those sales which are a part of domestic costs. There may be adverse as well as beneficial effects on domestic prices growing out of the Webb-Pomerene Act.

A second problem of complete rate freedom, or a snake in a pipe whose length is less than the diameter of the pipe, lies in the very nature of intramodal competition. If the rail industry has unused capacity or great capacity which could be provided with the elimination of present bottlenecks, then certain pressures might drive them toward rate cuts. On the other hand, we would have perfect examples of oligopolistic competition in which collusion rates would be maintained or advanced. The conditions simply do not exist for competition to work.

A third factor is certain institutional rigidities which do not respond as they are supposed. The whole economy is plagued with these barriers to structural adjustment, which account currently for inflation and high unemployment at the same time. Ameliorative efforts in classical economic terms have been singularly ineffective for largely structural reasons. The case could be argued that transport underregulation has perhaps behaved better than most sectors of our economy.

FREEDOM OF ENTRY AND RATES

The entry problem in relation to rates poses no great problem for rail. Threshold costs are incredibly high and it is unlikely that new railroads will be built. On the other hand, freedom of entry to markets can be related to merger policy. The federal government may wish to block mergers in the interests of competition, yet the number of carriers is so low that intramodal competition does not exist in adequate amounts for shipper protection and, paradoxically, there may be too much supply for railroad financial protection.

The case of the motor carriers is somewhat different. Motor carriers really represent many industries and should never be analyzed as a single one. There are many kinds of specialized carriers with varying threshold costs and varying services. Steel haulers are not to be compared with those engaged in the movement of agricultural products or local distribution carriers of general commodities. The nationwide common carriers of general commodities represent another of the many kinds of subindustries within the general industry. The scale economies in one are not transferrable to the scale economies of another. Nationwide carriers are sometimes preferred by nationwide distributors because the latter wish companies which could serve most of their sales points. This, incidentally, may provide internal scale economies within the traffic or distribution department. As one large shipper expressed it, "I want a carrier big enough to have his computer talk to my computer." Just as there are many industries or sub-industries among motor carriers, there would be varying consequences of new entrants. There would probably not be challenges to some of the major carriers in their spheres. Entrants would emerge in those sub-industries which operate on a smaller scale. Barriers to shifts from one sub-industry to another would leave some sub-industries relatively unaffected. A probable result is that well-managed enterprises which get good results under the present ground rules would assess the new order and adapt to it.

There are many half-way houses on the relationship between rates and entry. Under the California system, minimum or almost standard rates are set by the Commission but entry is relatively easy. Indeed, the intrastate rate regulation may be more pervasive and effective than interstate controls. The British have used maximum rate regulation and not required publication of specific charges by rail, although most of the information gets out. A variant of this could be considered for the U.S.

The problem of complete rate freedom in the motor carrier field is even more vexing in relation to application of antitrust laws and elimination of rate bureaus. The cooperation needed for through rates on joint routes seems completely at variance with the ground rules that are applicable to industrial and distribution establishments under our antitrust laws. An enormous burden would fall back on the traffic departments of companies which might well result in great difficulties in distribution. We have at present under regulation an extremely complex rate structure. Some carriers and users have learned to apply computers reasonably successfully to the calculation and determination of charges. Independent action on the part of each carrier should promote an enormous increase in traffic departments of shipping companies as well as carriers. Employment in this sphere might well equal the employment of lawyers in pursuing antitrust cases.

Details of the current bill changing airline regulation will not be reviewed. The proposals will probably not pass in their present form, if ever. The alterations would enable considerable invasion of territory. The minimum freight and passenger carrying capacity of planes would be increased which would be exempt from regulation. Back of much of the legislation is the feeling that the freedom accorded on an intrastate basis in California was good for the rest of the nation. The heavily traveled L. A.-San Francisco run, though, is somewhat comparable to the situation of the Erie Canal. Not too many city pairs are to be found which afford comparable opportunities. As in the case of other modes, the industrial leaders are on the one side and the economists are on the other. Much could be said for a variable fare structure for presently existing domestic carriers. The case can be made for international travel. The charger lines have cut heavily into the regularly scheduled airlines internationally and forced the latter to resort to subsidiaries or various other arrangements to cope with competition. Within the domestic market the industry has simply suffered along with users.

Few changes are in the offing with regard to pipeline entry and rates. Concern is expressed by promoters of coal pipelines that they will secure rights of eminent domain. The proposed break-up of major oil companies might raise problems of the new ownership of existing pipelines for crude and its derivatives.

Bargelines are relatively unaffected; since the change in the mixing rule, the degree of rate freedom has been fairly complete. Water carriers have their annual apprehension over user charges. The principal concern of this industry deals with the great freedom which might be accorded railroads. This should not be a matter of as great a concern as is ordinarily voiced. If the railroads acquired all of the business of the water carriers, the shift would add only two percent to the gross revenues of the rail lines and would probably result in a reduction in net income. The argument might be advanced that "water compelled" low rates could be raised by the railroads, but the relief afforded by this to the land carriers might be minimal in view of the possibility of re-entrance of carriers on the waterway system. The preceding remarks are not intended to minimize the consequences of rate cuts by the railroads on current investments in bargelines. The harmful effects might ensue whether the rate cuts were enlightened or unenlightened.

WITHDRAWAL OF SERVICES AND FACILITIES

Some progress has already been made for the rails in coping with the problem of abandonment. This has really been as much a problem with state commissions as it has been with the ICC. The precedent in the northeast for requiring local subsidies along with the temporary federal aid has much to commend it. This is similar to the requirements for continued service of AMTRAK in certain situations. A parallel exists with the policy of the CAB of "use it or lose it." The railroads are greatly in need of freedom to adapt their systems to the changing requirements of their territories. A pruned network offers far more hope of quality service to the nation than the present system.

Motor carriers have never had quite as much of a problem of relating supply to demand for transport. Their higher variable costs make the adjustments easier. Moreover, the large fleet of private, contract, exempt, and independent haulers have provided a pool to assist in meeting peaks. During recessions the burdens of cutbacks have been widely diffused. Regular route common carriers of general commodities have had difficulty in living up to their obligations. Enlightened ones who knew the relationship of costs and revenues have moved an enormous amount of freight without trying to cultivate an expansion of it. Less enlightened carriers have wondered why their operating ratios were so high. Little imagination is needed for an analyst to outline the types of traffic and areas from which many carriers would wish to withdraw their service or alter their rates to arrive at new equilibria.

LABOR

A review of all the proposed legislation of recent years reveals an interesting omission. Labor problems are seldom mentioned or discussed. Between 50 and 60 percent of the operating costs of most carriers are wages and fringes. Common carriers are unionized with high levels of pay and fringe benefits in relation to less organized sectors of transport represented by contract, private and exempt haulers. To the extent that freedom of entry would result in companies which were nonunion or represented less aggressive unions than those now having contracts, differences in costs would ensue. These in turn would have rate consequences and conflicts would ensue. For a variety of reasons which you can think of faster than a speaker can relate them we scrupulously avoid the labor relations—especially in the motor carrier, rail, and air fields.

SUMMARY

This country has a functioning albeit imperfect system. We do not know how to determine the costs of most of our carriers in the many markets which they serve. We seemingly do not like value-of-service pricing and being unable to ascertain costs; the resulting components of the rate structure can be challenged for the next decades and centuries as they have in the past. We cannot establish Smithian economics in operation for the railroads, airlines, pipelines, and water carriers. An analysis of the motor carrier industry reveals that it is a series of sub-industries with a mixture of competitive and monopolistic circumstances. The logic of deregulation of rates and freedom of entry would entail repeal of the Reed-Bulwinkle Act and elimination of rate bureaus. The carriers would be subjected to new legislation comparable to our present antitrust laws which apply to other sectors of the economy. We do not, unfortunately, know how to arrive at the joint rates on through routes which are essential to our industry. The general public would require protection in the ensuing period. Consultative committees of the British type would have to emerge and employment in the new enforcement section of the Attorney General's office should exceed that of the ICC and the CAB. The proposed amplitude of rate freedom with continued regulation might also call for a role by the Attorney General's office. The range for rate adjustment seems to be well beyond that which is reprehensible in price discrimination cases in those portions for our economy now subject to the Sherman and Clayton Acts.

The best we can hope for perhaps is a benevolent and enlightened despot taking ameliorative actions from time to time as the needs of our economy change. There is a rule of thumb in technology that if more than 10 percent of a system is new, the result will be a failure. Perhaps this is true in restructuring our transport systems, as far as control policies are concerned. All those shippers and carriers who are doing well at the present time are reasonably happy while the others are somewhat mutinous. On the sideline are various academicians and concerned citizens with little direct investment who would like to see major changes. These outsiders have some insight and they do use the service as well as pay taxes. On the other hand, those with vested interests feel that the movement from reform comes from a visitor to the gaming table who would like to participate in the gambling but use somebody else's money. One wonders whether there is much logic to moving to competition in the world of transport when so little prevails in other sectors of the economy. Institutionalists who note the difficulties of adjustment may wonder why we would expect classical economics to work in transport in the last quarter of the twentieth century. The admonition is worth repeating, that overemphasis be avoided on rate savings from deregulation. Some rates would advance. All rates in our modern economy are only one element in a complex of distribution costs. Logistical adjustments have yet to be analyzed on a macro basis.

Finally, this discussion has dealt largely with economic matters. Less control is probably in store in this sphere while an avalanche of new controls of diverse environmental character descends upon the industry. These may be of far more importance to costs and rates than what has been discussed. A final cynical note might be added that the resolution of many of the issues thus far raised may turn out to be as much or more a political matter as economic.

The Shipper's Investment in
the Conference Method of Ratemaking

GRANT M. DAVIS

[Editor's Note: The shipping public, according to most research, prefers to function through collective ratemaking. Indeed, society has an interest in continuing with the conference method of ratemaking because of through routes and joint rates. In the following article entitled "The Shipper's Investment in the Conference Method of Ratemaking," Grant M. Davis discloses that the individual shipper is concerned about and interested in: (1) knowing the rate level; (2) having stable rates; (3) securing administrative procedures and resources which are known to all; (4) concentrating on his own business specialization; (5) influencing the establishment of transportation prices. The chaotic alternatives would be costly not only to the carriers but also to the individual shippers.]

The current deregulation in the railroad and aviation industries probably leaves much to be desired by the shipping public and by the general public as well. There seems to be no question but that these legislative movements will prove ultimately to be detrimental to the American public. Also, current proposals to deregulate the intercity trucking industry by both legislative and regulatory decree are disturbing.

All of us are aware of the parties involved in this great debate—parties which range from organizations such as the U.S. Department of Transportation, the Antitrust Division of the Justice Department, the Interstate Commerce Commission, the Brookings Institution, and the American Institute for Free Enterprise to Senator Kennedy, and last but not least, to us.

One would think that the Interstate Commerce Commission would possess a tremendous amount of expertise in dealing with bureau activities in its role of establishing prices in the regulated segment of our industry. Unfortunately, any casual reading of Ex Parte 297 and of some of the strange proposals embodied in its sub proceedings does not support this general observation.

Like all great public policy issues, there tends to be a rather large diversity of opinion, depending upon which government entity happens to be involved. Briefly, let's look at some of these issues and see where the various parties stand. First, is the United States government, which, while being a rather broad classification, is the area for the impetus for changing Section 5a collective ratemaking roles. When Congress was reluctant to change these laws substantially, the ICC undertook to change the laws on its own. This is rather surprising because the Commission does realize, or should realize, the important role that rate bureaus play in the Commission's administration of the Interstate Commerce Act. Of all the agencies directly involved in transportation regulation, this august body should be aware of the relative facts involved.

We must also consider the Antitrust Division of the Justice Department, whose record for the past seventy-some odd years reveals that it has never been able to understand collective ratemaking. It has blamed this concept for every malady ranging from fallen arches to our current cold war posture regarding the presence of Soviet troops in Afghanistan.

Of course, we have always had the Ralph Naders among us, those individuals who seem to think that collective ratemaking is nothing more than a cartel. Most economists share the view that collective ratemaking is a cartel, but most of them also understand how rate bureaus work and how they function, most also understand that there are beneficial cartels and detrimental ones. Ratemaking provides society with a beneficial service in the form of rate stability which enables planning and reducing the risk of procedural redress. Unfortunately, however, the Antitrust Division has designated collective ratemaking to be a detrimental cartel, one which is devoted primarily to taking advantage of the public.

The ICC appears to vacillate with respect to Ex Parte 297. Actually, the condition precedent for exemption, the right to exercise independent action, has been effectively ignored by both the Commission and the Department of Justice. This is in contrast to most of the surveys conducted by the Center for Transportation Research at the University of Arkansas, which indicate that shippers are relatively satisfied with the known existing procedures for establishing rates in the industry and that they desire to maintain this particular mechanism.

Section 5a, as we all know, deals with joint rates and through routes. The Commission has eliminated single-line immunity for the railroad industry. This is myopic at best—a recent study conducted by Charles S. Sherwood and Grant M. Davis reveals that eliminating single-line immunity for rates would increase publishing costs approximately $60 million. Thus, in the area of motor transportation, because of the voluminous number of combinations of rates and routes that are present in this industry, one cannot even venture an estimate as to how high these publishing costs would go. Nevertheless, any increased costs would go into the rate base, which means that the industrial shipper would pay, which in turn, means that the consumer would end up paying.

In this regulation-deregulation debate there are many issues. At the Center for Transportation Research at the University of Arkansas, we send out a survey every five years to industrial shippers and physical distribution managers to determine what they consider the major issues in transportation to be. Two of these issue involve collective ratemaking. Almost 80 percent of the respondents in all the surveys have favored retaining collective ratemaking. Although some have disagreed with various aspects of the system, all in all, they prefer to maintain it. Furthermore, while most of them do recognize that cross-subsidization of commodities and communities occurs, they do not see this as a problem of any substantial magnitude. (Most of the economists at Brookings and on the Council of Economic Advisors attack value of service pricing and cross-subsidization as the worst thing to have happened since the Civil War!)

Rate stability and known avenues of redress, together with independent action, represent the beneficial contributions of rate bureaus. In the absence of rate bureaus, what would happen in industries, in particular, the automotive industry, which depend upon rate relationships for establishing manufacturing operations? The transportation industry is a dynamic growth industry, and failure to protect its institutions would retard the dynamic aspects of all industry.

Of the numerous witnesses who testified on behalf of Eastern Central's application under Section 5a, the Antitrust Division scrutinized two individuals, Jessie Friedman and Grant M. Davis. Senator Kennedy, who is vehemently opposed to collective ratemaking, has seized upon it as a political issue—not as an economic issue. Political issues are many times more difficult to defeat and/or defend than economic issues. Thus, the various ramifications of collective ratemaking will accelerate, not diminish.

This leads one to ask: Are we correct in our defense? What makes our opinion of collective ratemaking and the rate bureau process so sacrosanct? Why are we the only ones to get involved in defending this particular method of setting price? Economic analysis indicates there are rights of appeal, there are known mechanisms for stating one's opinion, there are certain procedures to be followed by practitioners before the bar, in short, all we have to do is examine transportation rates and contrast them with the consumer price index and the general price index, and we will realize just what a bargain transportation really is.

In the event that we are not correct, what are the alternatives with which the shipper is faced? First, there would be enforcement of the antitrust laws through the courts (we all know the judiciary's batting record with respect to enforcing the antitrust laws!). Not only would there be disastrous delays, but due process would result in expensive litigation and costs to the shipper. Second, rates would fluctuate, and known geographical markets would vacillate almost daily. So, in this respect, the alternative enforcement of the antitrust laws through the judiciary would be a cumbersome, awkward, Neanderthal approach to a day-to-day activity of setting price in the economy.

Another area that should be examined is our concept of monopoly and economies of scale. Because of stable rates and the industry's contribution to the economic and social development of a given industry structure, which is an economic term for "an area," we know that other people benefit besides those who primarily pay the freight bill. Without known avenues of redress and procedure, this contribution to the infrastructure could be seriously diminished, and the industry might not be able to take advantage of its economies of scale.

Let's face it—we are a part of transportation regulation—probably the most hated part. How do we sway public opinion? Do we contact our Congressmen? Can we appeal to plain common sense? Again, when a seller must have joint rates that are cheaper than combination rates, he cannot make prices in a vacuum as long as a shipper has as much input as the seller and the transportation company. Although the physiocrates concept of natural law does not work in all instances, when it does, it would be permitted to function under known institutional procedures.

Gathered here to discuss rate bureaus and the impact of reopening 297, we must ask what the shipper's stake is in all of this great debate. There are essentially six things that shippers should be concerned with in trying to resolve 297. First, is the rate level which, being a nebulous, meaningless concept at best, does present certain parameters with respect to delivering freight and picking up raw materials. Under ratemaking and collective ratemaking procedures, the rate level would be subjected to review. There is no way the Commission can do this on a day-to-day, carrier-by-carrier basis.

Second, the shipper has a stake in this debate because of stable rates. In many instances market territories are determined by rate relationships. If we have a fluctuating rate on commodities and a general rate level, no one will be able to determine precisely a geographical market territory. The known procedures of rate bureaus not only provide stable rates with a known mechanism for working within a conference but also focus upon stable rates as long as they meet certain conditions such as being compensatory and nonpredatory.

The shipper's third stake in this debate concerns administrative procedures and recourse. Empirical data indicate that the shipper has as much input on setting transportation prices as does the carrier. Also, the individual shipper can appeal to the ICC and to the courts. Should we substitute this known avenue of procedure and administrative law for the unchartered waters of the Antitrust Division of the Justice Department?

Another stake that the shipper has in this debate is his primary activity—the distribution and manufacture of goods. In the event the collective method of ratemaking was dissolved, a substantial amount of his resources and of his time would have to be contributed to non-manufacturing and distribution activities.

The development and maintenance of an efficient transportation network is also at stake. A shipper wants viable shipping alternatives, and failure to have an institutional method of ratemaking would certainly diminish these alternatives.

Lastly, the shipper has a stake in the pricing process. Perhaps in no other industry utilizing direct institutional methodology does the industrial shipper have as much impact on setting a price as he does in the transportation industry. We know about the committees within the rate bureaus; we know the publishing procedures; we know our appellate rights. To substitute this with the unknown aspects of our judicial system seems to be inviting chaos.

The collective method of ratemaking is economically and socially beneficial to the transportation industry, the consuming public, and the country as a whole for one simple reason—it provides a known institutional method for setting stable, compensatory, efficient prices.

We have the most efficient transportation network in the world, because of the collective ratemaking institution. If we can refocus the debate from _destruction_ to _construction_, we can improve the institution. However, the immediate threat is destruction, and that will benefit no one.

Chapter 7

SUMMARY AND CONCLUSIONS

The purpose of rate bureaus in transportation is often misunderstood by members of Congress, the Interstate Commerce Commission, and certain academic leaders who are not very familiar with the functions of these institutions. These agencies are designed primarily to publish rates in compliance with federal law and to provide orderly functions in the area of price and service in the transportation industry.

Unfortunately, rate bureaus have been portrayed by many individuals as being cartels. Technically they are, but there is a widespread misconception regarding the connotation of the word "cartel." There are beneficial cartels, as well as detrimental ones. Rate bureaus in the motor carrier industry perform a valuable societal function that contributes to the overall implementation and success of our domestic transportation system.

The reasons why public policy requires the continuation of the bureau technique for establishing and publishing prices have been analyzed. Rate bureaus do not defy the antitrust laws of this country, but rather, they accomplish similar objectives more effectively than would antitrust regulation.

Rate bureaus, as previously indicated, are organized along geographical lines, with more bureaus present in the motor carrier industry than in the rail industry. These bureaus are non-profit organizations owned by carriers, and their single purpose, of course, is to publish collectively determined rates. In the motor carrier industry this task is more complicated because of the large number of carriers involved and because many carriers publish their own rates when confronted with specialized service offerings. Nevertheless, the fundamental purpose of rate bureaus in the motor carrier industry is to disseminate rate information to the general public as well as to their members. The ICC's options over published rates include setting a maximum rate, a minimum rate, a range of rates, and, of course, an exact rate. Under Section 5a, each carrier member of a bureau has the absolute right to exercise free and independent action for activities other than those approved by the bureau. In fact, the bureau is merely an agency for the carrier and functions exactly in that way.

In the past the question has always focused upon the existence and utilization of independent action by carrier members of the bureaus. Recent research indicates that this particular activity has not been abused, and it strongly suggests that bureaus play an important role in assisting firms in new location activities because of existing rate structures which are free of undue preference, prejudice, and discrimination in terms of both commodities and sites.

There is no question but that the existence of rate bureaus provides a very valuable public service. What are the advantages of rate bureaus to the American public? These include stable rates; established procedures for redress of any undue discrimination, preference, and prejudice; methods for increasing and protecting competition; ascertainable rates to aid in determining the location of distribution facilities; inflation-resistant rates when compared to the consumer price index and wholesale price index; and also assistance to the Commission in its daily implementation of its responsibilities.

Considerable controversy, of course, surrounds the rate bureaus because they are not understood with respect to their important role in society. These agencies are merely extensions of the carriers in that they provide the forum within which prices and services are determined, with participation by both the sellers of the service and the buyers of the service. There are serious antitrust implications for both users and sellers of these services in the event that the bureau technique for establishing rates is seriously modified, curtailed, or eliminated. Society has a definitive stake in the outcome of this debate and would be well advised to examine the issues carefully, with the intent of resolving those issues in the furtherance of its best interest.